100 GREATEST™ CANADIAN COINS and TOKENS

Harvey B. Richer

Forewords by Kenneth Bressett and Emily S. Damstra

100 GREATEST CANADIAN COINS and TOKENS

1794 Chandalar Drive • Suite D • Pelham, AL 35124

100 GREATEST is a registered trademark of Whitman Publishing, LLC.

Correspondence concerning this book may be directed to Whitman Publishing,
Attn: 100 Greatest Canadian, at the address above.

ISBN: 0794849830
Printed in China

Disclaimer: No warranty or representation of any kind is made concerning the accuracy or completeness of the information presented, or its usefulness in numismatic purchases or sales. The opinions of others may vary. The author may buy, sell, and sometimes hold certain of the items discussed in this book.

Caveat: The price estimates given are subject to variation and differences of opinion. Especially rare coins trade infrequently, and an estimate or past auction price may have little relevance to future transactions. Before making decisions to buy or sell, consult the latest information. Grading of coins is subject to wide interpretation, and opinions can differ. Past performance of any item in the market is not necessarily an indication of future performance, as the future is unknown.

Contents

Foreword by Kenneth Bressett v
Foreword by Emily S. Damstra vi
Publisher's Preface vii
Introduction viii
Auction Companies, Catalogs, Grading Services, and Compilations x
Chapter 1: The Early Money of Canada 1
Early North America Wampum Belts (No. 18) 1
The Coinage of New France: Louis XIV 1670 5 and 15 Sols; Double (No. 16) 2
Playing Card Money (No. 7) 4
Copper Company of Upper Canada 1794 Half-Penny Token (No. 49) 6
Prince Edward Island Holey Dollars and Dumps, and Canada's 1804 Silver Dollar (No. 5) 8
Magdalen Island 1815 One-Penny Token (No. 19) 9
Anchor Money 1820–1822 Half Dollar (No. 60) 11
Canada Half-Penny Token: Ships Colonies & Commerce (No. 41) 12
Montreal Militia Token, circa 1830 (No. 30) 13
Nova Scotia "1382" Counterfeit Thistle Half-Penny Token (No. 31) 14
Ship / St. John's Half-Penny Token (No. 22) 16
Bank of Montreal 1837–1845 Tokens (No. 15) 17
"Pro Bono Publico" 1837 Half-Penny Token, Lower Canada (No. 20) 19
Hudson's Bay Company Tokens (No. 8) 20
Weir & Larminie 1862 Encased Postage Stamp (No. 46) 22
Canadian Indian Chiefs 1871–1877 Peace Medals (No. 12) 23
Chapter 2: Pre-Confederation and Related Coinage of Canada and the Provinces 26
First Coinage of the Province of Canada, 1858 (No. 10) 26
Province of Canada 1858 Pattern Cent (No. 27) 29
Province of Canada 1858 Pattern 20 Cents (No. 67) 30
Province of Canada 1859 Brass Cent (No. 23) 31
Province of Canada 1859 Pattern Cent (No. 54) 32
Nova Scotia 1861 Circulati on Strike and Pattern Cent (No. 53) 33
New Brunswick 1861 Half Cent (No. 56) 35
New Brunswick 1862 Pattern 10 Cents (No. 58) 36
British Columbia 1862 Gold $10 and $20 (No. 2) 37
Prince Edward Island 1871 Cent (No. 25) 39
Canada 1871 Trial/Pattern 20 Cents (No. 29) 40
New Brunswick 1870–1875 Trial/Pattern 5, 10, and 20 Cents (No. 64) 41
Chapter 3: The Coinage of Newfoundland 43
1864 Pattern Coins (No. 35) 43
1865 Gold Pattern $2 (No. 11) 45
1871-H 10 Cents (No. 95) 47
1872-H 20 Cents (No. 98) 48
1873-H 5 Cents (No. 71) 49
1874 Specimen 50 Cents (No. 83) 50
1880 Gold Specimen $2 (No. 39) 51
1882-H Specimen Set (No. 85) 53
1885 Gold Specimen $2 (No. 66) 55
1917-C 25 Cents (No. 93) 56
Government of Newfoundland January 1932 $25 Bond (No. 99) 57
1938 Cent (No. 91) 58
1946-C 5 Cents (No. 70) 60
Chapter 4: Canadian Coins from the Victorian Era 61
1870 No LCW 50 Cents (No. 17) 61
1875 No H 5 Cents (No. 36) 62
1875-H 10 Cents (No. 59) 63
1875-H Specimen 25 Cents (No. 62) 64
1876-H Pattern Cent (No. 44) 65
1876 No H Cent (No. 82) 66
1884 Specimen Cent (No. 74) 68
1884 10 Cents (No. 65) 69
1885 5 Cents (No. 96) 70
1887 25 Cents (No. 92) 71
1889 10 Cents (No. 42) 72
1890-H 50 Cents (No. 14) 73
1891 Cent (No. 77) 74
1892 50 Cents (No. 84) 75
1893 10 Cents, Flat Top and Round Top 3 (No. 21) 76
Chapter 5: Canadian Coins from the Reigns of King Edward VII and King George V 78
1905 50 Cents (No. 68) 78
1906 25 Cents, Large and Small Crown on Reverse (No. 55) 80
1890-H and 1907-H Cent (No. 100) 81
1911 Pattern $1 (No. 1) 83
1913 10 Cents, Small and Broad Leaves (No. 47) 85
1914 50 Cents (No. 94) 86
1915 25 Cents (No. 86) 87
1920 Large and Small Cent (No. 43) 88
1921 5 Cents (No. 13) 89
1921 50 Cents (No. 4) 90
1923 Cent (No. 89) 91
1926 5 Cents, Near 6 and Far 6 (No. 75) 92
1932 50 Cents (No. 81) 93
1935 $1 (No. 32) 94
$1, J.O.P. Counterstamp (No. 28) 96
1936 Dot Coins (No. 3) 98
Chapter 6: Development of Canadian Gold Coins 100
1908 Gold Sovereign (No. 26) 100
1909 Gold Pattern $2.5 and $10 (No. 52) 101
1910 Gold Uniface Pattern $5 (No. 50) 103
1911 Gold Pattern $5 and $10 (No. 33) 104
1912 Gold $5 and $10 (No. 45) 106
1916-C Sovereign (No. 6) 107
1928 Bronze Pattern $5 and $10 (No. 57) 108
Chapter 7: Canadian Coins of Consummate Beauty and Conditional Rarities (No. 72) 110
Canadian Coins of Consummate Beauty in the British Museum 110
Conditional Rarities 112
Chapter 8: Canadian Coins from the Reign of King George VI 116
1937 New Coinage Designs (No. 24) 116
1938 50 Cents (No. 80) 119
1939 $1 (No. 61) 120
1942–1945 Tombac and Steel 5 Cents (No. 38) 121

1944 Specimen Set (No. 90) 122
1947 Maple Leaf Silver Dollar (No. 73) 125
1947 50 Cents, Maple Leaf, Curved Right 7 (No. 37) ... 126
1948 $1 (No. 9).......... 127
1949 $1 (No. 63).......... 128
1950–1952 and 1955 $1, Arnprior (No. 78) 129
1951 5 Cents, High Relief (No. 88).......... 130
Chapter 9: Canadian Coins from the Reign of Queen Elizabeth II 132
1953 $1, Without and With Shoulder Strap (No. 87) ... 132
1966 $1, Small Beads (No. 76).......... 134
1967 Commemorative Coin Set (No. 40) 135
1967 $1, Diving Goose and Double Struck (No. 48) 137
1969 10 Cents, Large Schooner, Large Date (No. 34)... 138
1973 25 Cents, Large Bust (No. 69) 139
2000-P 25 and 50 Cents (No. 79) 141
2003 $1 Gold (No. 97).......... 142
2007 $1 Million Gold Coin (No. 51).......... 144
Appendix: Auction Records for Canadian Coins and Tokens 145
Bibliography 146
Credits and Acknowledgments.......... 148
Image Credits 148
About the Author 149
Index 150

100 GREATEST CANADIAN COINS AND TOKENS, IN RANK ORDER

1. 1911 Pattern $1 83
2. British Columbia 1862 Gold $10 and $20 37
3. 1936 Dot Coins 98
4. 1921 50 Cents 90
5. Prince Edward Island Holey Dollars and Dumps 8
6. 1916-C Sovereign 107
7. Playing Card Money 4
8. Hudson's Bay Company Tokens 20
9. 1948 $1.......... 127
10. First Coinage of the Province of Canada 26
11. Newfoundland 1865 Gold Pattern $2.......... 45
12. Canadian Indian Chiefs 1871–1877 Peace Medals.......... 23
13. 1921 5 Cents 89
14. 1890-H 50 Cents 73
15. Bank of Montreal 1837–1845 Tokens.......... 17
16. Coinage of New France: Louis XIV 1670 5 and 15 Sols; Double.......... 2
17. 1870 No LCW 50 Cents.......... 61
18. Early North America Wampum Belts.......... 1
19. Magdalen Island 1815 One-Penny Token 9
20. "Pro Bono Publico" 1837 Half-Penny Token, Lower Canada.......... 19
21. 1893 10 Cents, Flat Top and Round Top 3 76
22. Ship / St. John's Half-Penny Token 16
23. Province of Canada 1859 Brass Cent 31
24. 1937 New Coinage Designs 116
25. Prince Edward Island 1871 Cent 39
26. 1908 Gold Sovereign.......... 100
27. Province of Canada 1858 Pattern Cent 29
28. $1, J.O.P. Counterstamp 96
29. 1871 Trial/Pattern 20 Cents 40
30. Montreal Militia Token, circa 1830.......... 13
31. Nova Scotia "1382" Counterfeit Thistle Half-Penny Token.......... 14
32. 1935 $1.......... 94
33. 1911 Gold Pattern $5 and $10 104
34. 1969 10 Cents, Large Schooner, Large Date.......... 138
35. Newfoundland 1864 Pattern Coins.......... 43
36. 1875 No H 5 Cents.......... 62
37. 1947 50 Cents, Maple Leaf, Curved Right 7 126
38. 1942–1945 Tombac and Steel 5 Cents 121
39. Newfoundland 1880 Gold Specimen $2.......... 51
40. 1967 Commemorative Coin Set 135
41. Half-Penny Token: Ships Colonies & Commerce.......... 12
42. 1889 10 Cents 72
43. 1920 Large and Small Cent.......... 88
44. 1876-H Pattern Cent.......... 65
45. 1912 Gold $5 and $10.......... 106
46. Weir & Larminie 1862 Encased Postage Stamp 22
47. 1913 10 Cents, Small and Broad Leaves.......... 85
48. 1967 $1, Diving Goose and Double Struck 137
49. Copper Company of Upper Canada 1794 Half-Penny Token.......... 6
50. 1910 Gold Uniface Pattern $5 103
51. 2007 $1 Million Gold Coin.......... 144
52. 1909 Gold Pattern $2.5 and $10.......... 101
53. Nova Scotia 1861 Circulation Strike and Pattern Cent 33
54. Province of Canada 1859 Pattern Cent 32
55. 1906 25 Cents, Large and Small Crown on Reverse 80
56. New Brunswick 1861 Half Cent.......... 35
57. 1928 Bronze Pattern $5 and $10.......... 108
58. New Brunswick 1862 Pattern 10 Cents 36
59. 1875-H 10 Cents 63
60. Anchor Money 1820–1822 Half Dollar 11
61. 1939 $1.......... 120
62. 1875-H Specimen 25 Cents.......... 64
63. 1949 $1.......... 128
64. New Brunswick 1870–1875 Trial/Pattern 5, 10, and 20 Cents.......... 41
65. 1884 10 Cents 69
66. Newfoundland 1885 Gold Specimen $2.......... 55
67. Province of Canada 1858 Pattern 20-Cent.......... 30
68. 1905 50 Cents 78
69. 1973 25 Cents, Large Bust 139
70. Newfoundland 1946-C 5 Cents 60
71. Newfoundland 1873-H 5 Cents 49
72. Canadian Coins of Consummate Beauty and Conditional Rarities 110
73. 1947 Maple Leaf Dollar.......... 125
74. 1884 Specimen Cent 68
75. 1926 5 Cents, Near 6 and Far 6 92
76. 1966 $1, Small Beads.......... 134
77. 1891 Cent.......... 74
78. 1950–1952 and 1955 $1, Arnprior 129
79. 2000-P 25 and 50 Cents 141

80. 1938 50 Cents 119
81. 1932 50 Cents 93
82. 1876 No H Cent 66
83. Newfoundland 1874 Specimen 50 Cents 50
84. 1892 50 Cents 75
85. Newfoundland 1882-H Specimen Set 53
86. 1915 25 Cents 87
87. 1953 $1, Without and With Shoulder Strap 132
88. 1951 5 Cents, High Relief. 130
89. 1923 Cent. 91
90. 1944 Specimen Set. 122
91. Newfoundland 1938 Cent. 58
92. 1887 25 Cents 71
93. Newfoundland 1917-C 25 Cents 56
94. 1914 50 Cents 86
95. Newfoundland 1871-H 10 Cents 47
96. 1885 5 Cents 70
97. 2003 Gold $1 142
98. Newfoundland 1872-H 20 Cents 48
99. Government of Newfoundland January 1932 $25 Bond 57
100. 1890-H and 1907-H Cent. 81

FOREWORD BY KENNETH BRESSETT

In this delightful repast by author/teacher Harvey Richer we come face-to-face with a plethora of choices as to which exactly are the greatest of all Canadian coins and tokens. The results of his investigation have not been determined solely by chance or by personal opinion, but through the careful consideration of recommendations provided by a substantial cadre of seasoned numismatists. A treasure trove of background information has also been presented herein to solidify the factors that were considered when determining the winners.

Professor Richer has not only laid this intriguing meal before us, but has added to it a concise history of Canadian numismatic items ranging from primitive trade beads to some of the Royal Canadian Mint's latest innovations, designs, concepts, and assorted novelties. And he has left his readers with the option of selecting which of these would be their personal recommendation for inclusion among the hundred greatest, or perhaps even at the top of the list. Given so many qualifying attributes, selecting a winner presents a conundrum.

Undaunted by the challenge, and guided by the detailed descriptions and historical background Richer's careful research provides, I recalled my personal interest in Canadian coins and history, as well as collecting opportunities presented in the past. Growing up in New England, with immediate family and relatives living close to the Canadian border, gave me ample opportunity to become very familiar with the cultures and coinages of both the United States and our neighbors to the north. It was not at all uncommon for us to use Canadian and U.S. coins interchangeably, in small quantities.

I vividly remember frequent trips across the border with my parents for visits or shopping, and as a youngster I was able to set aside enough of the small cents and five-cent coins to complete a date set of each from circulation. Some of the higher-denomination coins were available, but too expensive for my pre-teen budget. One particularly thrilling prize that I did not pass up was a Very Fine specimen of the 1936 Dot quarter. My all-time favorite, however, came later when the 1944 and 1945 Victory coins became available. They were inspirational, attractive, and patriotic at a time when we needed it most. As well as having a novel and exciting design, they contained a secret message in Morse code! What youngster would not hold such a coin dear regardless of its value or rarity? That's the kind of coin that surpasses all other qualities

A World War II–era five-cent coin with the denomination as a "V" for Victory. "These are among my favorite Canadian coins," says Kenneth Bressett. "They are not the most famous, or rare, or valuable, but I still find it exciting to recall those war-weary days when these very pieces told of the efforts and sacrifices that were typical of everyone's involvement in the fray."

of greatness, and it is still my favorite. With my early exposure to all such coins, my enthusiasm for them has never waned. And, with a solid background and interest in Canadian coins and history from about age 5, I continued to delve deeply into all aspects of numismatics. By 1950 I was aware of the formation of the Canadian Numismatic Association and was eager to join as one of the first members from the United States. (Today I am the only such member still active in the Association's 72nd year.) Later, in 1960, my first assignment as numismatic editor for Whitman Publishing was to work with Jim Charlton on his *Standard Catalogue of Canadian Coins*

Tokens and Paper Money, where I assisted him in adding pictures, mintages, and updates for many years. For me those treasured experiences were the beginning of a lifetime interest in numismatics that has now been reinforced through reading Professor Richer's latest book. I invite you to continue on and be ready to enjoy a most delightful involvement in learning all about Canada's most celebrated coins.

Kenneth Bressett has been involved in the numismatic hobby since the 1940s. He has written many articles and is author or editor of more than a dozen related books on such diverse areas as ancient coins, paper money, English, and United States coins. He has served for many years as the editor, senior editor, and now editor emeritus of A Guide Book of United States Coins. He is a founder of the Rittenhouse Society, a past appointee to the U.S. Assay Commission, a past member of the Citizens Commemorative Coin Advisory Committee, and former president of the American Numismatic Association. Bressett is the recipient of numerous awards, including induction into the Numismatic Hall of Fame, and he is the namesake of the ANA's Kenneth E. Bressett Young Numismatist Literary Award.

FOREWORD BY EMILY S. DAMSTRA

A few years ago I had the opportunity to visit the Bank of Canada Museum in Ottawa. Several items piqued my interest, one of which was the gift shop's $9.50 collection of wildlife coins from around the world. I'm pretty sure the package, boldly titled REAL COINS, was intended for a much younger audience, but I was curious and bought it on a whim. As a natural-science illustrator, I can't help but notice and contemplate the ways that nature is depicted in popular culture, including on coins, and as a coin designer I like to consider how coin designs reflect the values of a nation. For those reasons, I wondered if this package of animal coins might give me some food for thought.

1967 Confederation Centennial silver dollar.

The "20 Genuine Mint Uncirculated" coins from 15 countries included a fairly impressive diversity of animals. The olm (aquatic salamander) on the 1992 10-stotinov coin from Slovenia might be my favorite in the set because of the way it seems to glide across an empty background field, and because this obscure cave-dwelling "baby dragon" is part of that nation's identity for mythological rather than commercial reasons. The same can be said for some others in the set. These got me thinking about Canada's current circulating coins and what it means that the beaver, caribou, loon, and polar bear are part of our numismatic heritage.

2013 $20 silver coin designed by Emily S. Damstra.

In this wonderful book, Dr. Harvey Richer deepened my knowledge about some of these beloved Canadian animal coins and broadened my knowledge about many other Canadian coins and tokens. In some of the early examples he discusses, we see nature depicted as a secondary element surrounding text (for example, the maple leaves and seeds on the Province of Canada 1858 pattern cent reverse) or chosen for its value as a resource (such as the seal and the filleted cod on the Magdalen Island 1815 penny token). Sometimes the subject depicted is from the settlers' original homeland rather than native to what is now Canada (such as 1823 and 1832 Nova Scotia half-penny and penny thistle tokens).

2015 $50 silver coin designed by Emily S. Damstra.

It's gratifying to see that in more recent coins—such as the iconic Newfoundland one-cent pitcher plant coin, Emanuel Hahn's enduring caribou quarter, and Alex Colville's brilliant 1967 commemorative series—Canada's native species are depicted as primary devices and chosen for their own intrinsic and symbolic values. This shift suggests to me that the way we Canadians value nature and view it as part of our heritage has changed over time, and for the better. These coins are part of my own small collection and would take top billing if I were to create my own list of Canada's 100 Greatest Coins and Tokens. We can't help but compare our own favorites to Harvey Richer's carefully conceived list.

Nature wasn't the only thing that drew me through these pages; I also love any good story that's well told. This book is full of them. I felt a little astonished when reading about some of the ingenious ways that people facilitated commerce in the absence or shortage of an official currency, as Richer so enthusiastically details. Bits of playing cards as currency? Check. Clandestinely minted tokens? Ah, those Nova Scotians! Coins made from the buttons on soldiers' uniforms? That's in here, too, and readers are left to speculate as to how those soldiers subsequently fastened their coats. A book is more fun if it raises as many questions as it answers.

There are also great stories about Canadian coins, such as how an unsatisfactory design contributed to Canada's lack of a $2.50 gold coin, and why the nickels produced in 1942 had 12 sides. I was surprised to learn that events on the other side of the world affected the details of a Canadian coin's design and its rarity (see chapter 8). Fortunately for us readers, Richer is not shy about peppering his tales with fascinating bits of background information. In these pages, we learn how long a cord of wood might last as the primary source of heating in the middle of the eighteenth century in New France (chapter 1), and where on this planet are the three largest meteoric impact craters (chapter 8).

As every coin collector understands, a great way to explore a nation's history is through its numismatic legacy, and Harvey Richer's thoughtfully guided tour of the 100 greatest Canadian coins and tokens is a marvelous journey.

Emily S. Damstra is a natural-science illustrator, nature artist, and coin and medal designer. Through her work, she explores many aspects of nature, science, and culture, from Paleozoic seas to modern life. Her illustrations appear in numerous publications, on interpretive signs in museums and natural areas, and occasionally in our pocket change. As of this writing, she's created more than 40 designs for the Royal Canadian Mint and 17 coin and medal designs for the United States Mint. Outside of work, she is often found in the yard, engaged in a perpetual campaign to oust the invasive species from her native-plant garden.

PUBLISHER'S PREFACE

Dr. Harvey Richer's *100 Greatest Canadian Coins and Tokens* takes its place among nearly 75 years of related Whitman books and hobby supplies.

The company began an extensive lineup of Canadian coin folders in 1950. Up in Toronto, James E. Charlton was self-publishing his *Catalogue of Canadian Coins, Tokens & Fractional Currency*. In 1959 R.S. Yeoman, father of Whitman's popular *Guide Book of United States Coins*, approached Charlton to publish his book and distribute it in the United States. Yeoman tripled the page count and expanded the content, and sales reached 100,000 copies per year in the 1960s. Whitman also published a *Standard Grading Guide to Canadian Decimal Coins* and distributed a "Canadian Coin Hobby Starter Kit" and a checklist and record book for collectors.

In the 1970s Robert C. Willey and James A. Haxby pioneered the modern study of Canadian coins in a new Whitman book, *Coins of Canada*. Willey (1927–1993), of Saskatchewan, was well established as a numismatic researcher and writer. Haxby was known for his authoritative papers on die-making and his scholarship in Canada's decimal coinage. Their book was groundbreaking. Whitman published it into the early 1980s.

I met James Haxby in 2007. We planned a brand-new, 464-page *Guide Book of Canadian Coins and Tokens*—a full-color illustrated history, price guide, and reference book published in 2012. Whitman also updated its Canadian coin folders, for large cents through modern dollars and Toonies.

In 2017 Boulder Publications released Harvey Richer's excellent *Gold Coins of Newfoundland, 1865–1888*, subtitled *How Newfoundland Came to Possess a Spectacular Mintage of Gold Coins*. I met Dr. Richer that year at the American Numismatic Association show in Denver, and we discussed the potential of a new volume in Whitman's library of "100 Greatest" books. We immersed ourselves in the best way to present a subject as far-reaching as "the best of Canadian coins." Dr. Richer developed the manuscript, including consultation with the Canadian Numismatic Research Society, and in 2021 we began its final editorial work.

Part of what made *Gold Coins of Newfoundland* such a remarkable book was Dr. Richer's talent as a writer and a teacher, as well as his approach to numismatics. He began with the formation of the solar system, moved into continental drift and a theory of geographical connection between Britain and Canada, and then a summary of 9,000 years of

Newfoundland history! With this fascinating background Dr. Richer led up to the minting of Newfoundland's gold coins. "One aspect I was particularly interested in," he told me, "was the effect such a magnificent issue of coinage had on the Newfoundland population 150 years ago. Recall that this was a very poor society largely driven by fishing and seal hunting. What was the impact of the coinage on commerce, on how the Newfoundlanders viewed themselves?"

Dr. Richer brings that same intellectual curiosity—asking questions, laying the groundwork, and always looking for the human element—to *100 Greatest Canadian Coins and Tokens*. His writing is embellished with personal asides (the connections that make numismatics an art as well as a science). And he's not afraid to push boundaries in his exploration of what defines a "coin" or "token." Among the 100 Greatest you'll find playing cards, wampum belts, and encased postage. While clearly not *coins*, are these forms of *token* money? Such questions always enliven the conversations around Whitman's "100 Greatest" books—not to mention how to define "greatness," and what constitutes the greatest of the great.

Accompanying his narrative are outstanding pictures of the coins and tokens themselves. The photographs shared by Heritage Auctions make up the majority of the coin images—not surprising, given Heritage's status as the largest collectibles auctioneer and third-largest auction house in the world. Many of the Canadian rarities find their homes through the Dallas-based firm's sales. PCGS and Stack's Bowers Galleries also contributed photographs, as did numerous museums, archives, and libraries. The result is a gorgeous numismatic panorama, a virtual coin cabinet that can be opened and enjoyed any time.

As a professor of astronomy, Harvey Richer has used the Hubble Space Telescope and major terrestrial telescopes to gaze into the heavens. The numismatic community is fortunate to have his attention turned to the richly interesting field of Canadian coins and tokens. And at Whitman Publishing we're proud to add him to our roster of Yeoman, Charlton, Willey, and Haxby in the exploration of Canadian numismatics.

Dennis Tucker
Publisher, Whitman Publishing

Introduction

How does one choose the greatest coins and tokens of any country? A survey of experts will unquestionably turn up a huge diversity of results. Nevertheless, this was one route I took to establish Canada's top 100 coins and tokens. There is a society of active numismatic historians and writers in Canada, the Canadian Numismatic Research Society (CNRS), of which I am a member. Other affiliates who are likely well known to the general collecting community include Paul Berry, past curator of the National Currency Collection of the Bank of Canada; Brian Cornwell, founder of the ICCS grading service, which grades and encapsulates mainly Canadian coins; and James Haxby, author of the bestselling Whitman *Guide Book of Canadian Coins and Tokens*. This group is not composed of active coin dealers (although there are a few in the society), but their collecting and writing tastes generally run to more eclectic subjects, such as tokens and medals.

Early in the research for this book, David Bergeron, the president of this society and current curator of the National Currency Collection of the Bank of Canada, polled the members of the society at my suggestion, asking them to name up to five of their favorite coins and tokens related to Canada. A number of very useful suggestions were proffered by the group, and about half a dozen that I had not originally chosen were included in the final list. In the end, however, the choices were largely mine.

Those well versed in Canadian numismatics may find some of the entries in this anthology a bit odd, such as wampum belts, a U.S. encased postage stamp, a Government of Newfoundland $25 bond, a very common 1938 Newfoundland 1-cent coin, counterstamped Canadian dollars, and a number of high-mintage Canadian commemorative silver dollars. It may be fair to say some of these are not even coins or tokens, and as such do not belong in this anthology. But each of these selections has a wonderful story to tell related to the development of Canadian coinage, and that is what most interested me in writing this book. Of course, all the high-priced, famous Canadian coins are here, too: the 1911 silver dollar, once called the world's most expensive coin; the gold $10 and $20 pieces from British Columbia; the 1890-H (the "H" mintmark indicating that it was struck at the Heaton Mint in Birmingham, England) 50-cent coin; the 1893 Round Top 3 10 cents; the 1936 Dot coins; and the unique 2003 gold $1 coin, among others.

Instead of ordering the coins or tokens by some criteria of greatness (for example, recent auction prices or total number of examples known), I have chosen to produce a more or less chronological ranking. In this way, the reader is able to make historical connections between the various entries and follow, in a more continuous and comprehensive manner, the development of Canadian coinage from the earliest examples of wampum—used in trade among the Indigenous population and later with Europeans—all the way to Canadian coinage after Confederation, when Canada had its own mint and was a member of the British Commonwealth of Nations. All the physical details, auction, pricing, and rarity information is included for each entry, but the narrative is a historical one. For further reference, I provide a table (page 145) that lists the highest prices achieved at auction for Canadian coinage, and another (pages iv–v) that provides a ranking, ordered by "greatness," based on input from a group of experts' personal criteria of rarity and desirability.

While the title of this anthology is *100 Greatest Canadian Coins and Tokens*, the book contains many more than 100 individual coins and tokens. This is because several coins and tokens have been treated in a single essay both for clarity and to reduce duplication. For example, each of the three 1936 Dot coins clearly deserves its own unique entry, but this would be unduly repetitive. Additionally, only a few examples of major varieties were included (for example, Flat Top and Round Top 1893 10 cents), and less dramatic varieties generally did not find their way into the final compilation.

For anyone desiring a reference book on Canadian coins, my recommendation is *A Guide Book of Canadian Coins and Tokens* by James A. Haxby. This reference has virtually everything both a casual and a serious collector could desire in terms of history, coinage design, mintages, and pricing. A similarly useful guide is *A Charlton Standard Catalogue, Canadian Coins* by W.K. Cross. I consulted both works extensively in preparing *100 Greatest Canadian Coins and Tokens*.

A Brief History of Canada's Coinage

If we consider money to be the means through which trade is accomplished between individuals, then the early Canadians were extremely ingenious in providing it. Long before the arrival of Europeans, the Indigenous population of North America carried out trade using whatever commodities were available: animal pelts, corn, fish, beads. With the arrival of Europeans, there was a desire to make this process more formal, and since currency of any sort was generally unavailable, wampum (generally belts of shells) became the most popular medium of exchange in early-seventeenth-century Canada. Animal skins (particularly beaver) later displaced the belts, as did crude copper tokens imported from France and later England. But there was never enough specie of this sort for extensive commerce, so local solutions were devised. In French Canada in the late 1600s, one of the most ingenious of these was "playing-card money": cut-up playing cards used as a medium of exchange. This proved to be extremely popular and was employed in one form or another for almost a hundred years.

By 1763 Britain controlled a huge territory in North America, stretching from what is now the Maritime provinces to the eastern edge of the prairies. This enormous region was not well provided with coinage for carrying out trade. A veritable United Nations of coinage circulated: British, French, Spanish, Portuguese, and Dutch. Making change from one variety to another was a nightmare, and the valuation of goods in the various media was highly dependent on who was buying and who was selling. This gave rise to a plethora of private merchant tokens, generally in copper or brass. But success here led to abuse, with the metallic value of these largely one- and half-penny tokens declining with time. This eventually led Britain to establish a monetary system in the Province of Canada, which had been formed in 1841 with the merger of the colonies of Upper Canada and Lower Canada (Ontario and Quebec). The British sovereign, the U.S. gold $10 coin (the eagle), and the U.S. and Spanish silver dollars were made legal tender in the Province of Canada.

In 1858 the Province of Canada finally acquired her own coinage, minted in London by the British Royal Mint. This issue consisted of a 1-cent coin in copper and 5-, 10-, and 20-cent emissions in silver. In the 1860s, both Nova Scotia (with only copper coins produced for it in England) and New Brunswick (both copper and silver coins) had their own distinctive coinage. In 1867 the Dominion of Canada was established when the Province of Canada (the future provinces of Quebec and Ontario) joined with New Brunswick and Nova Scotia in Confederation. Beginning in 1870, coinage was regularly struck for Canada. The 20-cent piece was dropped and replaced by a 25-cent coin and a 50-cent coin introduced in the same year. Manitoba joined Confederation in 1870, British Columbia in 1871, and Prince Edward Island in 1873. Of the latter three, only Prince Edward Island had an official coinage before joining Confederation. British Columbia produced a clandestine gold coinage in 1862, but it was rejected by Britain.

From a coinage perspective, Canada came of age in 1908 when its own mint was established in Ottawa. In the same year it struck its first gold coin, a 1908-dated sovereign with the identical design as the British sovereign. The Canadian coin was distinguished from the British and other Commonwealth sovereigns by the presence of a small "C" mintmark on the reverse. The first true Canadian gold coins, containing distinctive Canadian symbols, appeared in 1912 and were minted only until 1914. The onset of the First World War limited their production and distribution, and a distinctive Canadian circulating gold coinage was never again produced. Sovereigns, however, continued to be minted until 1919.

In 1935 the first silver dollars were struck, serving a dual purpose as Canada's first circulating silver crown-sized coin and also its first commemorative coin, celebrating the Silver Jubilee of King George V. The reverse featured the beloved "voyageur" design, which was used until 1987, when the reverse was completely redesigned and a loon became its dominant image.

Ranking the 100 Greatest Coins and Tokens of Canada

No one person should decide on the ranking of anything, let alone something as controversial as the 100 greatest coins or tokens of any country. Collectors have their own favorite areas regarding what appeals to them, be they from a historical perspective or because of scarcity or availability, while dealers often pursue those coins that they believe can be resold at a profit. These would introduce very different biases into the selection of the greatest coins and tokens, so I decided to let a knowledgeable cross-section of the community do this hard work for me.

I contacted a number of dealers and collectors whom I knew and asked them to contribute to the ranking process. The members of the Canadian Numismatic Research Society, a group of Canadians interested in the history and promotion of Canadian numismatics, were also asked to rank the entries in the book. I sent all these individuals a list of the 100 entries ordered more or less chronologically, as they currently appear in the book. The rules were few and simple:

1. No new additions allowed at this ranking stage. During the summer of 2021, I had solicited input from the CNRS. A number of very interesting suggestions were put forward, and six of these made it into the final compilation.
2. At least 20 entries had to be ranked but, of course, more were preferred.
3. The top 100 Canadian coins and tokens were chosen from a list where a number 1 vote was worth 100 points, a number 2 vote 99 points, and so on. The weighted scores were then tabulated to produce the order of the entries on pages iv–v.

Not surprisingly, the 1911 pattern silver dollar was ranked the number 1 Canadian coin or token—identical to its ranking in *100 Greatest Modern World Coins*. In fact, it would have been a surprise if the 1911 pattern dollar had not achieved this exalted position, as at one point it also carried the moniker of the "World's Most Expensive Coin." The number 2 coins are the British Columbia gold coins of 1862, of which only eight are known of both denominations together. Entries 3 and 4 are the 1936 Dot set and the 1921 50-cent coin. Tokens and fiat money of various sorts fared very well, holding down nine spots among the top 20 entries.

I am indebted to the following individuals for providing their ranking choices and sharing their knowledge and experience with the collecting community: Darryl Atchison, David Bergeron, Sandy Campbell, Clément Chapados-Girard, John Deyell, Michael Findlay, Robert Forbes, Michael Joffre, Greg Jones, Robert Kokotailo, Svetolik Kovacevic, Warren Long, Oliver M., George Manz, Andrew McKaig, Barry Renwick, David Rubin, Dale Schaffer, Jared Stapleton, and Rob Turner.

AUCTION COMPANIES, CATALOGS, GRADING SERVICES, AND COMPILATIONS

Throughout this book, references are made to various auction companies, catalogs, grading services, and compilations of Canadian coins used most frequently in this anthology. Scan the QR code at right to see a detailed listing and descriptions of these useful sources. Briefly, they are as follows: **Geoff Bell Auctions** (New Brunswick); **Bowers and Merena** (Wolfeboro, New Hampshire); **Bowman** (*Canadian Patterns*); **Breton** (*Illustrated History of Coins and Tokens Relating to Canada*); **Canadian Numismatic Journal** (rcna.ca); **Charlton** (*Charlton Standard Catalogue*); **Cornerstone** (*The Cornerstone Collection*); **Haxby** (*A Guide Book of Canadian Coins and Tokens*); **Heaton Mint** (*A Numismatic History of the Birmingham Mint*); **Heritage** (Heritage Auctions, ha.com); **ICCS** (International Coin Certification Service); **MacLachlan** (*A Descriptive Catalogue of Coins, Tokens and Medals Relating to the Dominion of Canada and Newfoundland*); **NGC** (ngccoin.com/census/world/canada); **Newman Portal** (Newman Numismatic Portal, nnp.wustl.edu/library); **PCGS** (pcgs.com/pop/canadiancoins); **Richer** *(The Gold Coins of Newfoundland)*; **Stack's Bowers** (Stack's Bowers Galleries, stacksbowers.com); **TCNC** (The Canadian Numismatic Company, auctions.canadiancoinsandpapermoney.com); **Turner** *(Dies and Diadems: A Die Tracker's Guide to the Victorian Cents of Canada)*; **Turner** *(Past and Nearly Perfect)*.

Chapter 1

The Early Money of Canada

In this first chapter, I present 13 essays on the monetary situation of what is now Canada, well before Confederation. The main dynamic in this period was the struggle of early inhabitants, both European and Indigenous, to find specie of any sort in order to carry out meaningful trade. This led to a remarkable variety of solutions, from beads fashioned into belts to ordinary playing cards, to beaver skins, to military buttons, to various tokens. Some of these tokens were struck in Europe, while others were manufactured in Canada; the latter of these produced some of the most interesting and valuable tokens in the entire Canadian series.

No. 18 Early North American Wampum Belts

Standards—**Weight:** Variable. **Composition:** Generally beads made from shells. **Size:** Various. **Rarity:** Genuine wampum belts from more than 100 years ago are very scarce. There are a huge number of modern imitations.

Neither the Indigenous population nor the very earliest European settlers in North America had coins or paper money to use for commerce. Trade was carried out using a barter system of commodities such as beaver pelts, corn, and fish. Prior to contact with European settlers, the Native population of North America used white or purple shells to make what are now referred to as wampum belts. The word for the belts, "wampum" (originally *wampumpeag*), was adopted by European settlers from the language of the natives of southern Quebec and eastern Ontario.

Manufacture of these was hardly a simple task. The shells had to be cleaned and then drilled so they could be strung together on string made of plant or animal materials. The drilling process, done with small rocks, could easily shatter the shells. The shells had to be polished, then fashioned into belts, bracelets, headpieces—any number of adornments. The size, shape, and extent of wampum belts depended on the status of the wearer.

Before the arrival of the Europeans, the Native North Americans used wampum belts largely for decoration or for important ceremonies. These belts were generally on display when important treaties or settlements were negotiated. They were given as gifts on the birth of a child or a wedding. Belts were wagered in Native games that resembled football or soccer. The value of a belt was derived from the skill required for its manufacture, its size, and the spiritual message it conveyed.

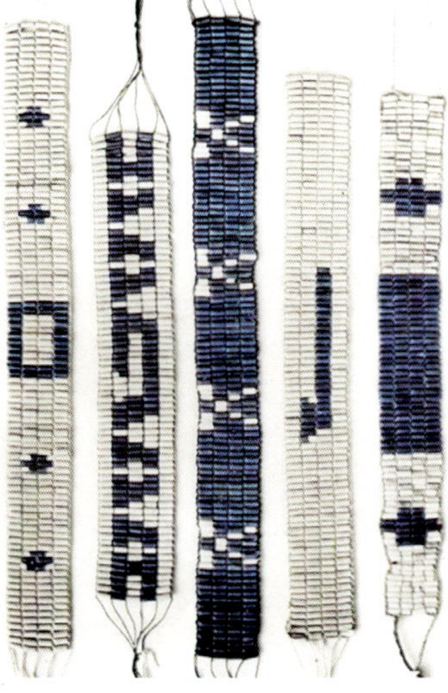

Some believed that the belts were so powerful that they could bring the dead back to life.

Due to a lack of European currency, wampum became a medium of exchange when the Europeans arrived. The Dutch were the first Europeans to appreciate the significance of wampum for the Native population. They started trading furs for wampum, then used the wampum for further transactions with Native fur traders. This influx of wampum attracted the interest of the more northerly Native fur-trading nations, which usually conducted business with French hunters and traders. The French had no wampum, so they suddenly found it difficult to compete with the Dutch for furs.

By the early seventeenth century, wampum was in widespread use in North America. Belts made of wampum were of particular significance in relation to treaties and covenants made between Indigenous peoples and European colonial powers. Some groups of Indigenous people indicated their assent to certain treaties by presenting wampum belts to European officials. Remarkably, wampum was even subjected to inflationary pressures. During the mid-eighteenth century, machines were developed (not by the Native population) to mass-produce wampum. Eventually, wampum became devalued and ceased to be used as money.

Although wampum beads are now mass-produced in various countries, Indigenous artists in the Canadian North still craft wampum from the same shells as their ancestors did 1,000 years ago. Wampum belts are present in private collections and in numerous museums in both Canada and the United States. Indigenous groups are attempting to repatriate these artifacts, while museums strive to preserve the history of these remarkable relics, arguably the first money in Canada.

No. 16 The Coinage of New France: Louis XIV 1670 5 and 15 Sols; Double

Standards (5 sols)—**Weight:** 2.3 grams. **Composition:** Silver. **Diameter:** 20.7 millimeters. **Edge:** Plain. **Designer:** Jean Warin. **Mint:** Paris (large "A" on reverse below crest). **Rarity:** Only about 100–150 examples known..

Standards (15 sols)—**Weight:** 6.69 grams. **Composition:** Silver. **Diameter:** 27.2 millimeters. **Edge:** Plain. **Designer:** Jean Warin. **Mint:** Paris (large "A" on reverse below crest). **Rarity:** Just 15 examples extant, 8 of which are permanently impounded in various museums.

Standards (double de L'Amérique Françoise)—**Weight:** 4.04 grams. **Composition:** Copper. **Diameter:** 23.4 millimeters. **Edge:** Plain. **Mint:** Paris (large "A" on both obverse and reverse). **Rarity:** Thought to be unique.

France was rather slow to the "colonial power" game in North America. After Spain, England, and Portugal established footholds there as early as 1492 (Christopher Columbus, Spain), 1497 (John Cabot, England), and 1502 (Miguel and Gaspar Corte-Real, Portugal), France finally awoke to the fact that territories in North America were there for the taking.

The kingdom sent Jacques Cartier to the New World, where he claimed the Gaspé region of Quebec for France in 1534 and Hochelaga (now Quebec City) and Montreal on another voyage in the following year. Cartier waited so long to return to France after the latter trip that he and his crew were forced to overwinter in 1535–1536. It was a brutally cold winter and Cartier and his entourage suffered terribly. Many developed scurvy, but his troops were largely spared by learning from the Native peoples how to use the bark of the spruce tree in a drink (a form of spruce beer) as a cure.

Commerce developed slowly in New France. As in most such colonial settings, there arose a need for a medium of exchange, which was met (rather unsuccessfully) with various kludges: wampum, playing card money, foreign coins, and tokens. In New France, low-denomination imported French bronze coinage sufficed originally, but as commerce developed within and external to the colony, more sophisticated and larger-denomination specie was required.

France never did mint coinage exclusively for any of its major colonies in the New World, which included the territory comprising what is now a large portion of Eastern Canada, plus a wide swath down the center of North America, including the Great Lakes and the area down to the Gulf of Mexico; it also held major territories in the Caribbean. While no coinage was provided exclusively for any one of these colonies, France did provide monies for "general circulation" in Canada and the Caribbean. The first of these were recycled hammered coins made of billion (a silver-copper alloy) that were stamped with a fleur-de-lis and shipped to the colonies.

On February 19, 1670, a royal edict declared that coins of 2 (copper), 5, and 15 sols (silver) should be produced at the Paris Mint for the Compagnie des Indes Occidentales en Amériques (West India Company in the Americas). These coins were meant to circulate only in the New World and were not to be used in France. The silver coins were duly produced. The 5- and 15-sol coins depict King Louis XIV on the obverse, with a crown and shield on the reverse. The "A" mintmark (for the Paris Mint) is seen at the bottom reverse of the coin. Surrounding the king's portrait on the obverse are the letters LVDXIIIID.G FR ET NAV REX ("Louis 14th Grace of God France and Navarre King"). Navarre was a French province in northern Spain that bordered on the Basque region, La Rioja, and Aragon. Its main city was Pamplona, currently of bull-running fame, an event held during the feast of San Fermin each July. The reverse of the 5- and 15-sol coins displays the date (1670) together with the Latin words GLORIAM REGNI TUI DICENT, which can be translated as "They will speak/tell the glory of your reign." The mintage for the 5-sol coin was 200,000, and 40,000 for the 15-sol piece.

The mintage of the copper double was to be 300,000 coins, but there were problems obtaining proper refined copper, and apparently very few were actually produced. This coin has quite a different design from the 5- and 15-sol coins. One point of great historical interest is that it is the only French colonial coin that bears a direct reference to French America, "La Merique Françoise." Comments in the Bowers and Merena catalog for the Norweb auction, which most recently featured this coin, suggest that this might have been an error by the die engraver—that it was intended to read "L'Amérique Françoise" but was misspelled. This, together with the difficulty in obtaining the copper needed to strike the coin, may have been responsible for the demise of the double. The large, crowned letter "L" on the obverse refers, of course, to King Louis XIV; the large letter "A" on both sides is for the Paris Mint. Louis XIV currently holds the record as the longest-serving monarch in any European country (72 years, 110 days). Queen Elizabeth II will surpass this record on March 19, 2024.

All these coins struck for the French colonies are very rare. The 5-sol piece is the most common, with 100–150 examples extant. An MS-63 example (a high grade for this series) realized US$19,975 in a 2016 Heritage auction. There were two lower-grade examples in the Partrick Heritage Sale in March 2021, with a VG example selling for US$2,040 and a VF-35 piece hammering for US$9,000. Additionally, Heritage offered a very rare 15-sol piece as part of the Partrick Sale, which went for US$60,000 in very active bidding.

The double is *the* rarity in the French North American colonial series. The coin is likely to be unique, and recent research seems to confirm this, at least to the extent that I have identified no other genuine piece. The only recent appearance of this coin at auction that can be traced was in the Norweb Collection of Canadian and Provincial Coins by Bowers and Merena in 1996. The Norwebs acquired the coin from John J. Ford Jr.; earlier, it had passed through American dealers/collectors Wayte Raymond and Burdette G. Johnson. The earliest owner that can be traced was Count Ferrari, whose collection was dispersed in 1922. Ford had the coin in his private collection and sold it to the Norwebs in 1954, apparently believing that another one would turn up. It never did.

The double realized US$82,250 in the Norweb auction, the third-highest price in the sale, surpassed only by an SP-67 1921 50-cent piece and a British Columbia $20 gold coin that John J. Ford Jr. dubbed "the Canadian 1822 $5." The double was bought by a New York coin dealer, held in his collection for a time, and then sold to another prominent American collector. As far as is known, the estate of this collector retains the coin to this day. There were rumors that the American Numismatic Society had an example, but in response to my inquiry, the society said that all they possessed was a "fake copper alloy." The Norweb piece thus appears to be unique, which is of course why John J. Ford Jr. never located another example.

No. 7 Playing Card Money

Standards—**Weight:** Variable. **Composition:** Paper. **Size:** Various, but typically 2 inches by 3 inches as a full card. **Rarity:** Extremely rare. Some researchers believe that no examples from the first emission in 1685 survive to this day.

In the early French colonies in Canada (collectively called New France), the commercial functioning of the colony in the latter part of the seventeenth century relied on a steady stream of low-denomination copper coins arriving from France. It was a lengthy and dangerous journey across the Atlantic Ocean, however, and many ships were lost or delayed. To make matters worse, France was involved in numerous wars at home, which tended to drain the national coffers, and even at the best of times it was not the most generous of colonial masters. All this put an enormous strain on the financial management of the colony, and by 1685 the situation in New France had become desperate.

In the late 1600s the unit of currency in New France was the *livre* (originally equal to one pound of silver, hence the name "livre," or pound), and 20 *sols* (or sous) was equal to 1 livre. The daily food cost for a person in New France around the year 1700 was about 10 sols. A daily laborer's salary at the same time was typically 30 sols, so a third of one's income went to pay for food. Today an equivalent number is more like 5 to 10 percent, so from this perspective an average family is far better off today than 300 years ago. There was also a circulating gold coin during this era, the louis d'or (the gold Louis), which was introduced by King Louis XIII in 1640 and featured his portrait. With a value of 20 livres, it was generally used to pay soldiers and civil servants but probably saw little circulation among the general public in New France due to its high monetary value.

Playing card money was a neat solution to the monetary problem in New France. Playing cards that had been requisitioned by the governor from the inhabitants became a substitute for money in the colony since there was never an adequate supply of specie for commerce. The cards were first introduced in 1685, and later issues remained in circulation in New France until the fall of Quebec in 1759. Originally, the cards were cut into quarters, with the seal of the Treasurer of New France (the king's representative) affixed with wax. Each quarter was then signed by the governor and by the intendant of the colony. The intendant was second in rank after the governor. He controlled the colony's entire civil administration, particularly its economic development and the administration of justice.

When coinage finally arrived from France in September 1685, each card was exchanged at par against metallic coins within just a week. One downside was that the cards were almost immediately counterfeited. There is even a record of one Louis Mallet and his wife being condemned to hang in Quebec for this offense. It is not known whether the sentence was actually carried out.

None of these original cards is thought to have survived to this day, but based on colonial records, it is believed that the first issues had denominations that included 15 and 40 sols. Later issues included half and whole cards as a means of providing different denominations. The cards were originally intended to be a short-term solution but were so well received that they continued to be issued in subsequent years. By 1714 more that 2 million livres of playing card money was in circulation in New France, with some cards having a value as high as 100 livres. That amount of money could purchase 100 gallons of wine, a cow, or fifty cords of wood in New France at the time. When a new shipment of coinage arrived, the cards were redeemed for real specie and were burned. In this way inflation in card money was avoided and the population had confidence in this form of money. For a time, card money actually traded at a premium with respect to hard coinage. French finances were never very stable during this period, however, and as they deteriorated so too did confidence in card money. In 1763, after the fall of New France, some 16 million livres in paper money was held by Canadians, but only 3.8 percent of this was in card money. After negotiations with the local governments France agreed to convert card money into government bonds, but by 1771 financial troubles in France had made these bonds worthless, thus ending the history of card money in Canada.

A superb example of a 1640 louis d'or.

After about 1730 the cards were printed on ordinary white cardboard, and some had their corners cut according to a fixed formula that determined the value of the card. Often, notes were written on the back of the playing card, as seen on the two cards shown in this essay. These notes sometimes expressed minor contracts between individuals. In this sense, playing cards were an early form of Post-it Notes, but without the adhesive! These notes provide a unique insight into life in early New France, but they are not always easy to decipher.

The cards shown in this essay are examples of those produced sometime after 1730, with each measuring approximately 2 by 3 inches. On the card shown on the previous page, only the first and last lines are important for our purposes, and they appear to constitute a receipt for merchandise received:

> *Bon pour avoir loger un demi corde ...*
> *payé 1.10.*
> Good for having lodged [delivered, stacked?] a half cord [of wood] . . .
> paid 1 livre 10 sol.

A cord of wood, when stacked as tightly as possible and with the individual pieces running parallel to each other, occupies a volume of 128 cubic feet. Thus, a half cord, for example, would be a pile 4 feet high, 4 feet wide, and 4 feet long. Wood was used extensively in New France as fuel for heating homes and providing a fire for cooking. A full cord of wood would last somewhere between six and ten weeks if used as the primary source of heating during winter.

On the card shown at right there is a clear mention of money, but it is difficult to translate as it may have been written in a dialect in use at the time. The fact that the grammar is generally incorrect makes it even more difficult to understand. The translation I provide here retains the grammatical errors. Nevertheless, even this one card provides some insight into the economics of New France near the middle of the eighteenth century.

On the bottom of the card shown at right, the French reads as follows, with the more or less literal translation shown after it:

> *et il â donner une lettre de change ouf! Le bon de 20 lui d'or neuf en déduction dés trante deux qu'il me devoir*
>
> "and he gave a letter of exchange phew! It is good for 20 new louis d'or which goes towards the reduction of the 32 that he owes me."

The reference here to "new louis d'or" is interesting. In 1726 France adopted a new monetary policy that fixed the weight of a louis d'or at 8.1580 grams, with a gold content of 0.24205 troy ounces. This is almost identical to the gold content of a U.S. $5 gold coin minted after 1837. The louis d'or was valued at 20 livres in 1726, and the French government pledged to maintain this valuation. This pledge did not last very long, and in 1740 a new valuation was declared at 24 livres per louis d'or. The person who wrote on this playing card and had his debt reduced by the payee wanted to make sure that he was paid 24 livres for each louis d'or that he was owed, not 20 livres. This dates the card to the period after 1740.

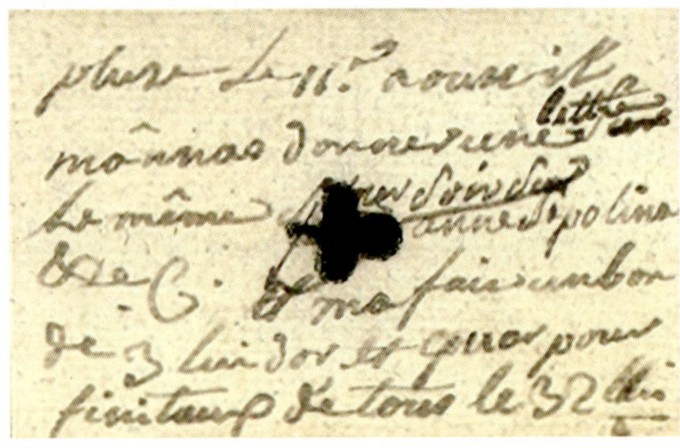

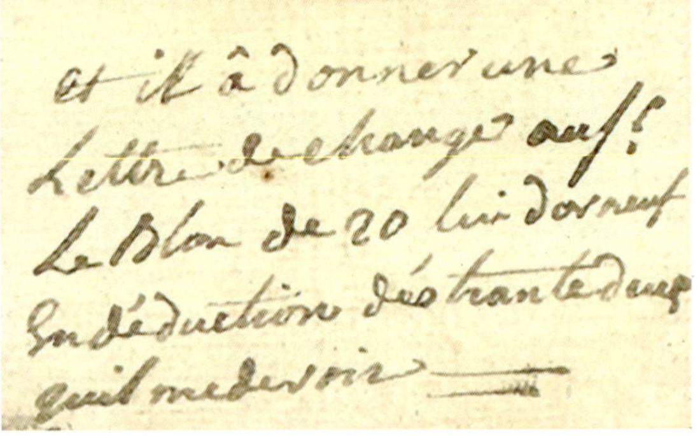

NO. 49 COPPER COMPANY OF UPPER CANADA 1794 HALF-PENNY TOKEN

Standards—**Weight:** 12.5 grams. **Composition:** Copper. **Diameter:** 29.1 millimeters. **Edge:** Plain. **Designer:** Noël-Alexandre Ponthon. **Issuing authority:** W. J. Taylor. **Rarity:** Only about 25 struck.

This half-penny token, an emission from a company called the Copper Company of Upper Canada, ended up as nothing more than an attempt by a late-nineteenth-century British coin dealer to create an artificially rare token and sell it off to collectors at a high price.

The history behind this token dates from the time of John Simcoe's appointment as lieutenant-governor of Upper Canada in 1791. Reflecting travel difficulties in that era, it took him until the summer of 1792 to arrive and finally get settled in the New World, after spending the winter of 1792 in Quebec City. Simcoe had enjoyed a fine career as a British officer in the American Revolutionary War. His immediate problem on arriving in Upper Canada concerned the Northwest Indian War, a conflict between the United States and a Native American confederation. The war had begun in 1785 and was still ongoing when Simcoe arrived. Even though much of his attention and energy were devoted to bringing an end to the conflict, as a strong administrator he realized that there were other important issues in the colony. One of these was the difficulty in carrying out commerce, due largely to a shortage of copper coinage. To address this, he contracted with the Soho Mint in England to produce a half-penny token that he hoped to deploy in the colony. Dies were prepared and a few pieces struck and sent to Canada for approval. Simcoe then approached the Home Office for permission to strike quantities of these as an aid in commerce. Approval was not given, and London sent a supply of worn halfpence from Ireland instead. It is likely that no more than about 25 pieces of this original token were produced.

The token itself is extremely well designed and beautifully executed. The obverse features Neptune reclining at full length, surrounded by flowing water-pots. He holds a four-pronged spear in his left hand and below him is the word "Ponthon," underneath which is the date 1794. "Ponthon" is believed to refer to the designer of the token, Noel-Alexandre Ponthon. He was an employee of the Soho Mint in the late eighteenth century and his tokens were distinguished by their unusually high artistic merit.

In the late nineteenth century the dies for this token apparently came into the possession of one J. Rochelle Thomas, numismatist, of Portman Square, London. He published an announcement that he was striking a limited number of proofs from the original dies, namely, 12 in silver and 50 in copper. Thomas was not shy in his asking price: 42 shillings for the silver and 12 shillings for the copper examples. A silver example of the token was equivalent to about two weeks' salary for a skilled seamstress at the time!

In addition, Thomas's claim that he struck only these limited quantities from the original dies was completely false on at least two counts. First, the restrikes have somewhat different die characteristics than the original coins. A simple diagnostic is the separation between the 7 and the 9 in the date. On the token shown on the previous page (an original striking), there is a fairly wide separation between these numbers, but on the example below (a restrike in gold), this space is much smaller. This proves that new dies were actually produced to strike these tokens. Second, of course, is that Thomas had the coins struck in more metallic varieties than simply silver and copper. Examples are currently known in aluminum, pewter, and gold, as well.

A Copper Company of Upper Canada 1794 half-penny token struck in gold. This is a restrike minted 100 years after the date on the token. Possibly unique.

Note the spacing of the date numerals on an original token and on a restrike.

Examples in any metal, whether originals or restrikes, are rare and avidly pursued by collectors. The example illustrated on the previous page, one of the finest original tokens known, realized US$8,225 in the Heritage 2017 auction of the Douglas Robins collection. A similarly graded restrike would command somewhat more than half this amount. The single known example in gold has a short but impressive pedigree that begins with Sotheby's July 21, 1903, sale of the Murdoch collection, with the token described as "brilliant . . . and struck from modern dies about 10 years ago." It sold for £5 12s 6d, or just under US$30, at the time. Its second appearance was in the John J. Ford Collection VII auctioned by Stack's, where it was bought by Douglas Robins. In 2018 the Robins collection was sold by Heritage and this token realized US$16,800.

No. 5 Prince Edward Island Holey Dollars and Dumps, and Canada's 1804 Silver Dollar

Standards (1808 holey dollar)—**Weight:** 22 grams. **Composition:** Silver. **Diameter:** 39.6 millimeters. **Edge:** Security edge. **Details:** Holey dollar counterstamped. Date on coin 1803, but issued in 1813. **Rarity:** These holey dollars, counterstamped for Prince Edward Island, are not particularly rare.

Standards (holey dollar dump)—**Weight:** 4.7 grams. **Composition:** Silver. **Diameter:** 16.8 millimeters. **Edge:** Plain. **Details:** Holey dollar (dump). **Rarity:** Few genuine examples known; this particular one is thought to be a counterfeit.

Standards (1804 holey silver dollar)—**Weight:** Original 26.6 grams. **Composition:** 0.902 silver. **Diameter:** 41.6 millimeters. **Edge:** Plain. **Details:** Holey dollar counterstamped. Issued by the Bank of England, Royal Mint, date on coin 1804, issued 1813. **Rarity:** Thought to be unique; the only known genuine specimen resides in the National Currency Collection of the Bank of Canada.

The arrival of the British in Canada did not necessarily mean an end to the barter system. For many decades the economy remained dependent on a medium of exchange that included dried fish, fur pelts, and other substitutes. Any coinage quickly found its way back to England and rarely remained in the colony.

However, more active and freer trade between the British colonies and their neighbors to the south led to an influx of

Spanish-American dollars (also called 8 reales). This coin had been minted since the early sixteenth century, and its manufacture continued until the 1820s. It was a result of the huge production of silver by the Spanish colonies, which was used to produce coins at various mints in Spain's New World colonies, including Bolivia, Chile, Colombia, Guatemala, Peru, and most importantly Mexico. The typical Spanish-American dollar depicted the reigning Spanish monarch on the obverse; the coin illustrated on the previous page shows Charles IV, who reigned from 1788 to 1808. The reverse generally featured twin pillars, with either two globes or the Spanish coat of arms topped by a crown. The valuation of the Spanish-American dollar was typically 6 shillings in the New World, although it varied in both time and location.

In Prince Edward Island (PEI) the 8 reales' valuation was only 5 shillings. The authorities used this dollar to provide a clever solution to the problem of a shortage of circulating currency: they made two coins out of a single Spanish-American dollar. A small piece (called a dump) was punched out of the center; this was given a value of 1 shilling, with the remaining ring (called a holey dollar) valued at 5 shillings. The idea behind these valuations was that since the ring and dump were each somewhat overvalued, they would both likely remain in the colony instead of being transported elsewhere. The dump and holey dollar were also counterstamped to indicate that they originated in PEI. On the dollar, a ring of 10 triangles was stamped near the monarch's forehead, exhibiting a sunburst pattern, as in the example shown on the previous page. Similar markings are seen on the dumps from PEI. In 1813 two holey dollars and a dump could get you a pair of shoes, but this was also about a week's wages, according to *The Holey Dollars and Dumps of Prince Edward Island*.

The dump turned out to be somewhat overweight for its 1-shilling valuation, and most were melted. There was also active counterfeiting of these small "coins." For these reasons, genuine dumps are much scarcer and generally more expensive than the rings. The one pictured on the previous page is from the National Currency Collection of the Bank of Canada and is thought to be a counterfeit.

Holey dollars from Prince Edward Island appear only infrequently at auction. Heritage sold one for US$2,990 at its Dominion Collection Sale in 2006. Christopher Faulkner, author of *The Holey Dollars and Dumps of Prince Edward Island*, could trace only five genuine dumps that have been listed for sale at auction. One was listed in a J&M Coin and Jewellery numismatic auction in 1989; it was estimated at US$7,500 but did not sell. A different dump likewise did not attract a buyer on a US$9,500 estimate in a 1989 TOREX auction. A genuine dump in a 2003 Jeffrey Hoare auction did sell at US$1,750.

Australia also has a series of holey dollars, but these are much scarcer and command much higher prices. A 2013 sale found a buyer who paid US$495,000 for an Australia holey dollar produced from an 8-real coin of the Lima Mint.

In the early years of the nineteenth century Britain herself experienced a shortage of circulating silver coins. As a quick fix, the Bank of England contracted the Soho Mint in Birmingham to overstrike Spanish-American 8-real coins, making 5-shilling (dollar) coins in their stead. A few of these coins eventually found their way to Prince Edward Island, where they presumably suffered the same fate as their Spanish cousins. The sole known genuine example of this coin, dated 1804, was actually issued by the Bank of England in 1813. Note the ring of triangles near the monarch's head, testifying to the fact that its counterstamp was from Prince Edward Island. This particular coin, denoted the Langstroth 1 Dollar, is featured in *The Holey Dollars and Dumps of Prince Edward Island*. With some veracity, we can state that Canada has its own 1804 silver dollar!

NO. 19 MAGDALEN ISLAND 1815 ONE-PENNY TOKEN

Standards—**Weight:** 17.25 grams. **Composition:** Copper. **Diameter:** 33.5 millimeters. **Edge:** Reticulated. **Manufacturer:** Sir Edward Thomason, Birmingham, England. **Issuing authority:** Sir Isaac Coffin. **Rarity:** Moderately rare; choice specimens attract impressive auction prices. **Breton number:** 520.

The Magdalen Islands are a small archipelago located north of Prince Edward Island and Nova Scotia in the Gulf of St. Lawrence. They are currently part of the province of Quebec and the inhabitants are largely French speakers. The population currently numbers around 13,000, and only 13 of the 15 islands making up the archipelago are inhabited.

The Magdalen Islands were discovered by Europeans in 1532, when Jacques Cartier first landed there. However, they had a Native presence (largely the Mi'kmaq Nation) for hundreds of years before this and were used as a hunting (mainly for walruses) and fishing venue. Basque fishermen also likely landed on the Islands prior to Cartier's arrival. The current name for the archipelago dates back to 1663, when François Honfleur christened them Îles de la Madeleine in honor of his wife, Madeleine Lafleur.

The later history of the Islands was strongly intertwined with the fortunes of Sir Isaac Coffin. Born in Boston in 1759, Coffin was an officer in the Royal Navy and, remarkably, was granted the Magdalen Islands by the British Crown after the American Revolutionary War. This gift came about after a chance remark he made to Lord Dorchester on the ship *Thisbe*, which Coffin was commanding.

Coffin had been ordered to transport Lord Dorchester and his family to Quebec City in 1786. Dorchester was on his way to the New World to take up the post of commander-in-chief over Quebec, Nova Scotia, New Brunswick, and Newfoundland, and someone of his stature would have had serious influence in the court of King George III. Sailing past the Magdalen Islands, Coffin remarked to Dorchester, probably not too seriously, that as a representative of the Crown, Dorchester could bestow the Islands upon him. This request was initially not received very favorably in London, but it was eventually granted in 1798. In his will, Coffin entrusted the Islands to various family members, including his sons, nephews, and cousins.

It was Coffin's plan to set up a feudal system on the Magdalen Islands. He claimed the right to coin money for the Islands and had one-penny tokens minted in Birmingham, England. The obverse of the token features a seal on a small iceberg; surrounding it are the words "Magdalen Island Token," with the date 1815 appearing below. The reverse features a filleted codfish and the words "Success to the Fishery" at the top and "One Penny" at the bottom. Breton claims (entry 520) that Coffin distributed the coins by way of loans among the chief inhabitants of the Islands during his sole visit in 1815. His arrogant manner did not endear him to the local populace, who sent him off with jeers of "Whip King Coffin." The token was neither appreciated nor much used by Magdalen Islanders. Many were eventually shipped to Nova Scotia, where they were often found circulating as one penny alongside Nova Scotia coins.

The hardships of life on the Islands have kept the population low over the years. They are now part of the province of Quebec, after being administered by Newfoundland until 1774. A ferry system, initiated in 1938, provides easier access to the mainland. The fishery and sealing have declined significantly in recent years, but tourism has grown to such an extent that the population of the Islands triples during the summer months.

The Magdalen Island tokens are not particularly rare or expensive unless they are in high grade. A VG example can usually be secured for about US$200. A coin graded MS-62RB realized US$3,360 in a 2018 Heritage auction. The highest price I was able to trace was for a PF-66 example that reached US$12,600 in the April 2018 Heritage auction of the Douglas Robins Collection.

Sir Isaac Coffin.

NO. 60 ANCHOR MONEY 1820–1822 HALF DOLLAR

Standards—**Weight:** 13.54 grams. **Composition:** 0.903 silver, 0.097 copper. **Diameter:** 32.2 millimeters. **Edge:** Reeded. **Designer:** William Wyon. **Rarity:** All denominations (sixteenth dollar, eighth dollar, quarter dollar, half dollar) are moderately scarce, with the half dollar being the rarest.

The Royal Mint struck the first coins for Canada (at that time the Province of Canada) in 1858. I highlight some of these coins in the next chapter of this anthology. As discussed in the previous essays, various types of monetary substitutes circulated prior to the coins, including wampum, tokens of various sorts, and specie from other countries, including Ireland, France, and Great Britain. This made commerce extremely difficult, as changing from one monetary type to another was rarely easy or satisfying to both sides in a transaction.

A Spanish 8-reales coin recovered from an 1818 shipwreck off the coast of Mauritius.

By 1820 the British Empire had finally achieved some stability. The Treaty of Vienna was signed in 1815 after more than 20 years of conflict, largely against Napoleon, and Britain took her place among the world's great imperial powers, a group that included China, France, the Ottoman Empire, and Russia. At that time the British Empire included Australia, the territories in North America, South Africa (including Mauritius), India, the Caribbean (including Jamaica and Barbados), and territories located along the north and east coasts of South America (including Trinidad and Demerara-Essequibo). It was not only North America that suffered from a shortage of coinage for commerce—all the British colonies did to some extent. Many of the conquered colonies had been wrested from Spain and had the Spanish real in circulation. The 8-real coin became known as the "Spanish-American dollar," and the U.S. dollar and eventually the Canadian dollar were based on this coin. It was a large (~38 millimeters), handsome silver coin, often featuring the Spanish monarch on the obverse and various designs (pillars, crests) on the reverse. Coins of smaller denomination were also produced (1, 2, and 4 reales in particular). The 1-real coin was termed a "bit"; hence, a quarter-dollar became 2 bits and the 4-real coin a half dollar.

In the early 1820s the British government conceived the reasonable idea of preparing a coinage that could be used across a number of colonies, potentially providing some stability to commerce. Following the tradition of the Spanish-American dollar, coins were struck in denominations of one-sixteenth to one-half dollar. They were designed and engraved by William Wyon and the original coinage was meant for Mauritius and Barbados. All the coinage for Mauritius was withdrawn from circulation in 1826 and sent to the West Indies. The Canadian connection here is that there was extensive trade between the West Indies and the North American colonies of Nova Scotia and New Brunswick, so "Anchor Money" entered Canada via this trade route, although there is no evidence that the coins were directly imported into the Atlantic colonies.

Anchor Money was minted in 1820 and 1822 only. It derives its name from the large anchor depicted on the obverse, with the date below. The reverse features the royal coat of arms with the legend surrounding it, including the monarch's name (George IV), D:G: (*Dei Gratia*—"By the Grace of God"), and REX F:D: (*Rex, Fidei Defensor*—"King, Defender of the Faith"). These coins always seem to command solid prices when they appear at auction. At a Heritage auction in 2021, the finest half dollar known realized US$6,900 in spirited bidding.

NO. 41 CANADA HALF-PENNY TOKEN: SHIPS COLONIES & COMMERCE

Standards—**Weight:** 5.94 grams. **Composition:** Copper. **Diameter:** 26.1 millimeters. **Edge:** Plain. **Designer:** Unknown. **Rarity:** This particular example is one of the rarest coins and tokens of Canada; likely only two examples known.

The extremely rare half-penny token illustrated above was likely struck sometime between 1830 and 1835. Tokens of this type, with a ship on the obverse and the inscription "Ships Colonies & Commerce" on the reverse, were minted in response to a shortage of coinage in pre-Confederation Canada. There are literally hundreds of different types of these tokens, but the one shown here is distinguished and owes its rarity to the lack of a poop deck (the roof of a cabin at the ship's stern) on the obverse of the token. The inscription on the reverse is attributed to Napoleon Bonaparte, whose 1811 statement that ships, colonies, and commerce were the advantages that the British had over the French, and these would defeat him in the end, turned out to be prophetic.

The first tokens in this series were produced in the United States and showed the Stars and Stripes flying. Later issues were produced in England; in these, the ship flies the Union Jack, as shown in this example.

First introduced in the 1820s, and originally intended for use in Lower Canada, these tokens eventually found their way to Prince Edward Island and Newfoundland, where they were worth more than a half cent due to a difference in the currencies of the colonies. A number of mints in England were involved in the manufacture of these tokens and there are so many varieties extant that Haxby devotes more than eight pages to their description. Breton assigns only five numbers (997, 998, 999, 1000, and 1002) for this entire series. The most comprehensive original listing of the numerous varieties of these tokens was carried out in 1926 by Judge W.A.D. Lees in *The Numismatist*, with new and updated listings in Christopher Faulkner's *Imperial Designs: Canada's Ships, Colonies & Commerce Tokens* in 2019.

The design on this token is similar to the one above, except that it includes a poop deck, seen at the far right under the sail.

The large token on the previous page, without the poop deck, was recently auctioned as part of the Douglas Robins Collection of Canadian Tokens and realized US$10,200. There is one other in the collection of the American Numismatic Society in New York, and both specimens can be traced back to the famous W.W.C. Wilson Sale of 1925. In the Heritage Douglas Robins auction, no fewer than 32 lots of Ships Colonies & Commerce tokens were available, attesting to the popularity and variety of these issues.

NO. 30 MONTREAL MILITIA TOKEN, CIRCA 1830

Standards—**Weight:** Around 9.4 grams. **Composition:** Brass. **Diameter:** Around 28 millimeters. **Edge:** Plain. **Rarity:** Although not particularly expensive, these tokens appear very infrequently at auction and thus should be considered moderately scarce.

It was not until the late 1850s that Canada had its own coinage struck in England, although somewhat earlier, starting in the late 1830s, a series of bank tokens were produced by Canada's fledgling banks. In the early 1830s, before these tokens entered commerce, the situation became so dire that individuals took it upon themselves to introduce their own version of specie. This resulted in a rich variety of privately struck tokens, such as the Wellington tokens, the Bust and Harp tokens, the Ship and Harp tokens, the Blacksmith tokens, and the Ships Colonies & Commerce tokens mentioned in the previous essay. There were many others, and they caused great confusion in the monetary system as to their value and legitimacy. No matter how many of these odd tokens were made, the commercial needs were never properly satisfied, so individuals resorted to their own solutions. One group, consisting of soldiers from various militia groups in Upper and Lower Canada, had a unique quick fix. The image at left shows a soldier's uniform for a battalion in the city of Montreal around 1812. Soldiers from a number of different battalions would have had similar uniforms. Note, in particular, the large number of metal buttons adorning the uniform. These buttons became a favorite substitute for coinage and a way for the soldiers to increase their wages. The buttons would be removed from the uniform, the stem cut away, and the button flattened to imitate the shape of a coin, which was then placed in circulation. A typical resulting size was about that of a British half penny, and it would have that value when used in commerce. Most of these buttons were displaced from circulation in the late 1830s when large quantities

Uniform from the 3rd Battalion of the city of Montreal circa 1812, similar to what a Montreal Militia soldier would have worn circa 1830. The buttons in this example do not appear to be engraved, however.

of heavier and properly denominated bank tokens were introduced. These bank tokens will be discussed in a later essay.

The buttons illustrated at the outset of this essay were made for the Montreal Militia, one of the largest militias in Lower Canada following the War of 1812. They bear the simple incuse legend "Montreal British Militia," and were struck in brass and originally finished in gilt. These tokens are not particularly rare or expensive. An example similar to that illustrated on the previous page sold for US$480 in the Donald G. Partrick collection Heritage sale of March 21, 2021. Both buttons shown in this essay are from the National Currency Collection of the Bank of Canada and earlier were in the collection of J. Douglas Ferguson. Clearly there were *at least* two types of these buttons made; note the difference in the style of the letter "s" in the word "British" on the two buttons shown. Though not high-priced items, they tell an important story of the paucity of specie in early Canada and the lengths to which people would go to rectify it. Looking at the button evokes the image of an underpaid soldier smashing one of the shiny buttons from his uniform against a cobblestone in Old Montreal in order to buy a pint.

NO. 31 NOVA SCOTIA "1382" COUNTERFEIT THISTLE HALF-PENNY TOKEN

Standards—Weight: Around 9 grams, but the bottom coin, which is a contemporary counterfeit, is generally underweight. **Composition:** Copper. Diameter: Around 27 millimeters. **Edge:** Plain. **Designer:** Unknown. **Rarity:** The counterfeit token (bottom) is very rare; the others are relatively common.

After the War of 1812, Nova Scotia emerged as a major trading center, and the general lack of coinage in the colony became a serious issue. Private tokens with varied designs distributed by local merchants appeared in circulation, with many of these having been manufactured in England. Between 1812 and 1820, the plethora of issues became a real nuisance. Tokens tended to be underweight, they were difficult to redeem, and the issuer was often unknown. The colonial government decreed that by 1820 all these private tokens had to be withdrawn from circulation. While a necessary measure, this plunged the colony again into a situation where small copper coinage for everyday commerce was scarce or unavailable.

Since Britain had control of the coinage for all her colonies, she would not have allowed a special coinage for Nova Scotia. Further, the local merchants had clearly demonstrated that they were incapable of supplying proper-weight copper tokens. All this put the Nova Scotia government in a terrible position. Its solution was to clandestinely order tokens made privately in England, without the knowledge or consent of the British government. This resulted in the "Thistle" tokens—half-penny and one-penny copper tokens of proper weight with an effigy of King George IV, the reigning monarch, on the obverse and a thistle on the reverse (see images above). These were clearly handsome, well-executed, and full-weight tokens that received strong support in the colony, solving, at least temporarily, its coinage shortage. The first of these tokens were dated 1823.

It was not until 1832 that Nova Scotia required a further issue of these tokens. By then, William IV was king, his brother George having passed away two years earlier. Apparently, the instructions to the minters in Birmingham were to make the new tokens identical to those minted in 1823 except for the new date. These suggestions were taken literally, so the 1832 issue again has the effigy of the now-deceased King George on the obverse (top images on the previous page) and not that of William IV.

There were numerous contemporary copies of the Thistle tokens. As expected, most were underweight, crudely designed, and poorly executed. One particularly amusing counterfeit is shown in the third piece, above. Not only is the token crudely executed but the date has been blundered, reading 1382 instead of 1832! Now that should have been an easy counterfeit to spot, but if a merchant was willing to accept it in payment for goods required, why look too carefully? More than anything else, this token illustrates the depths to which merchants in Canada's early colonies would go to facilitate commerce in the early nineteenth century.

The counterfeit 1382-dated tokens are scarce, popular, and moderately expensive. A 2019 Heritage auction featured a somewhat damaged half-penny example that sold for US$2,880, while an AU-53 example required a bid of US$6,600 to take the token home. Genuine 1832 tokens typically sell for much less; in similar grades they can be obtained for well under US$1,000.

NO. 22 SHIP / ST. JOHN'S HALF-PENNY TOKEN

Standards—**Weight:** 6.21 grams. **Composition:** Copper. **Diameter:** 27.24 millimeters. **Edge:** Plain. **Designer:** Unknown, but see caption under Montreal Ropery token below. **Rarity:** One of the rarest tokens of Canada, with only a single example known.

Readers who are not very familiar with Canada may not know that there is a city in the province of Newfoundland and Labrador (NL) called St. John's, and another in New Brunswick (NB) named Saint John. Spelling out "Saint" instead of abbreviating it is the correct rendering of the New Brunswick city's name. Both, of course, trace their name back to John the Baptist. Samuel de Champlain apparently sailed into Saint John Harbour on June 24, 1604, the feast day of Saint John the Baptist, providing the name for the city as well as the name of the river that feeds into the Atlantic Ocean there. Of course, the Native peoples had been living in this region for many centuries before Champlain arrived; their name for the river was Wolastoq. St. John's, Newfoundland, is even older, appearing on maps as early as 1519 after being "discovered" by Europeans when John Cabot sailed into its harbor in 1497. Vikings had landed in the north of the province even earlier, around A.D. 1000, and Native migration, likely from Siberia, arrived in Newfoundland and Labrador as early as 10,000 years ago.

Stories abound of confusion in referring to these two cities; one has an amateur sports team bound for St. John's instead watching what was supposed to be their match from a bar in Saint John. Clearly, the designer and minter of the illustrated token also got confused. Since there can be no confusion over "N.B.," meaning New Brunswick, it appears that this token (circa 1830–1839) was ordered by a merchant in Saint John, New Brunswick, for some undisclosed purpose, probably to promote his (unstated) business. The designer got the province right but rendered the city name incorrectly. It is interesting to speculate that perhaps "Saint John" could not be made to fit in the space allocated, so the designer shortened it to "St. John's" in the hope that no one would notice! On the other hand, it may have been just an egregious error. In any case, the token was probably rejected by the client after only a single test example was struck—which is precisely the number currently known of this token.

It is interesting that the ship on the reverse of the "Montreal Ropery" token, a very rare token in its own right and illustrated below, is almost the same as that seen on the St. John's N.B. half penny. Montreal Ropery operated in that city until the mid-1820s, and there is strong evidence that the dies for both tokens were cut by the same engraver.

The ship on the reverse of the Montreal Ropery token bears a distinct similarity to that on the St. John's N.B. one, although they are not identical.

The most recent sale of the possibly unique St. John's N.B. token was in the Douglas Robins Heritage sale in April 2018, when it fetched US$45,600. In 1976 it had appeared in the John McKay-Clements collection sale, where Douglas Robins acquired it. The National Currency Collection of the Bank of Canada does not have an example of this rarity, only a plaster cast.

NO. 15 BANK OF MONTREAL 1837–1845 TOKENS

Standards (half-penny token)—**Weight:** 9.37 grams. **Composition:** Copper. **Diameter:** 28.2 millimeters. **Edge:** Plain. **Designer:** Minted and likely designed at the Soho Mint, West Midlands, United Kingdom. **Rarity:** Side-view examples are quite rare; front-view examples are much more common.

Standards (penny token)—**Weight:** 23.48 grams. **Composition:** Copper. **Diameter:** 34.2 millimeters. **Edge:** Plain.

After the British defeated the French in 1759 at the Battle of the Plains of Abraham near Quebec City, they assumed the difficult task of governing their new territorial acquisitions. In 1791 Britain partitioned the territory of Quebec into the Provinces of Upper and Lower Canada, which was determined by geographical position along the St. Lawrence River. Upper Canada was upriver (further inland), while Lower Canada was closer to the mouth of the river, which fed into the Atlantic Ocean.

Upper Canada came to be largely populated by those who had remained loyal to the British Crown during the American Revolutionary War and therefore were required to flee the United States after the war. Lower Canada was predominately French-speaking and was renamed the Province of Quebec after Confederation in 1867.

The coinage situation in Lower Canada after 1791 was abysmal, particularly for the low-denomination copper coins frequently used in daily commerce. Beginning around 1800, old copper coins from Britain slowly seeped into the colony, as a new copper coinage minted for Britain near the end of the century made these old coins unnecessary. This alleviated the shortage only a little, as the quantity of half-pence coins thus made available was not nearly sufficient to meet the demand. The situation became so desperate that even old military buttons were flattened and used as a coinage substitute (see earlier essay on the Montreal Militia token, pages 13–14).

A half-penny bank token of 1837 from the City Bank in Montreal. These tokens are not particularly scarce and sell for under US$1,000 in the higher grades of Uncirculated tokens. In Proof, they can command up to US$3,000.

Beginning around 1813, private tokens from the British Isles and the United States, and some that were locally produced, found their way into the commerce stream of Lower Canada. As it was almost impossible to provide a value for this fiat money, the commercial situation became increasingly difficult. In 1835 the government decided to remove all the lightweight pieces from circulation, and the shortage grew acute. Things improved in the late 1830s when a number of the larger banks operating in Lower Canada were given official permission to issue their own tokens. These were of higher quality and copper content than most of the then-circulating tokens. By Gresham's law ("bad money drives out good"), the better tokens should have disappeared and been hoarded, but the bank tokens eventually predominated because the populace refused to accept the lower-quality ones, and the latter in time disappeared from circulation.

The first major issue of tokens from the Montreal banks appeared in 1837. The three major banks (City Bank, Bank of Montreal, and La Banque du Peuple) ordered half-penny and penny tokens from Boulton and Watt in England. The design consisted of a habitant (French Canadian farmer) on the obverse and the arms of the city of Montreal on the reverse. The name of the issuing bank was on a ribbon near the bottom, also on the reverse.

The issue of habitant tokens was so successful that the Bank of Montreal wanted a token issued with its own distinct design and for its exclusive use. In 1838 it placed an order with Cotterill, Hill and Company of Birmingham, England, featuring the same reverse design, with "Bank of Montreal" on the ribbon, and a view of the bank itself on the obverse. The perspective of the bank building is from the side, hence the name "Side-View" tokens (see first coin image on the previous page). This shipment was rejected by the bank because the metal content of the tokens was considered inferior and the perspective of the bank on the token unrealistic. A new minting dated 1839 was also rejected for similar reasons. In 1842 the bank ordered tokens from Boulton and Watt in Birmingham, featuring the same reverse design as on the habitant token, with "Bank of Montreal" on the ribbon, together with an obverse featuring a "Front-View" of the bank. These were deemed acceptable and were widely distributed and extensively used in commerce.

Officially rejected by the Bank of Montreal, the "Side-View" tokens never saw wide circulation in Lower Canada. They were likely extensively melted and are therefore quite rare. A beautiful MS-62 example sold for US$10,200 in a recent Heritage auction.

The Bank of Montreal as seen in 1893.

The great rarity in the Bank of Montreal token series is the half-penny token of 1845 (Breton 527). Breton knew of only a single specimen, whereas currently around four are believed to exist. The reason for the scarcity of this issue is unclear, but the most likely explanation is that dies dated 1844 were used for most of the production. The only recent auction appearance I was able to trace was a Proof example in the Geoff Bell Auction, associated with the Toronto Coin Expo of October 2015. The auction catalog stated that this was the only example in collectors' hands. The token sold for a hefty CAD$61,200. The extensive description in the Bell auction catalog is useful reading for those interested in the history and earlier ownership of these tokens. The National Currency Collection of the Bank of Canada also houses an example of this extremely rare token.

NO. 20 "PRO BONO PUBLICO" 1837 HALF-PENNY TOKEN, LOWER CANADA

Standards—**Weight:** 5.97 grams. **Composition:** Copper. **Diameter:** 27 millimeters. **Edge:** Plain. **Designer:** Likely engraved by Jean-Marie Arnault of Montreal. **Rarity:** This token is thought to be unique.

The Pro Bono Publico half-penny token does not reveal much about why it was struck and who had it manufactured. There is no bank name, and the only clue is the word "Montreal" on the reverse, suggesting that one of the city's banks had it produced. This would mean either the Bank of Montreal, the City Bank of Montreal, or the Banque du Peuple. The fact that the legends are in English likely excludes the Banque du Peuple as the source of the token. This bank's clientele was largely French speaking, and the bank flourished in a financial world dominated by the English-speaking majority in Montreal. To express its ties to the French community more strongly, the bank changed its name from that of its founders, Viger DeWitt et Compagnie, to Banque du Peuple. The fact that the inscriptions on the token were in English and the denomination shown as "1/2 Penny" instead of the more usual "Un Sou" might explain why so few were struck, as such a token was unlikely to see very wide circulation.

The obverse of the token likewise contains few hints as to why it was struck. It contains the banal words "Trade & Agriculture" and "Lower Canada," which say little about the purpose of this token. The one truly interesting inscription is "Pro Bono Publico" (for the public good), seen on the reverse. This was not the first time this legend was seen on coins; the British Conder tokens, for example, contained numerous examples, as did other minor coinage struck in Great Britain. It indicates that the token was struck for the public good since small-denomination coinage was in short supply, and perhaps this token could help alleviate the shortage. But that, of course, does not explain why so few were made!

An example of a British "South Wales" copper farthing, 1793. On the reverse, the Prince of Wales crest is on the shield and "Pro Bono Publico" is at the top.

The Pro Bono Publico token is assumed to be one of Canada's rarest, with only a single example extant. It currently resides in the National Currency Collection of the Bank of Canada and was previously held by the Château de Ramezay in Montreal. The Bank of Canada purchased the Château's collection in its entirety in 1974. P.N. Breton, in his 1894 publication *Illustrated History of Coins and Tokens Relating to Canada*, indicates that at that time the token was in the collection of R.W. McLachlan and was earlier in an 1884 New York auction, where it sold for the remarkably high price of US$62.

By comparison, using a catalog from 1884 (E.T. Howard Collection, auctioned by Bangs and Company, May 15–16, 1884) and the Heritage Auctions website, I calculate roughly a factor of 2,850 between several 1884 sale prices and current realizations. Thus, if this token were auctioned today, it would likely realize about US$177,000. This seems reasonable, as the second-rarest example in this series, Breton 673, realized US$44,062 in Stack's 2013 American Numismatic Association auction. There are an estimated four or five examples extant of Breton 673, which is a bank token with the same obverse as the piece shown on the previous page (and presumably the same engraver, Jean-Marie Arnault of Montreal) but possessing a different reverse.

NO. 8 HUDSON'S BAY COMPANY TOKENS

Standards (made-beaver)—**Weight:** 7.89 grams. **Composition:** Brass. **Diameter:** 29.77 millimeters. **Year issued:** 1857. **Edge:** Reeded. Issuing authority: Hudson's Bay Company, Eastmain District. **Rarity:** Readily available, but quite scarce in choice Uncirculated grades.

The Hudson's Bay Company (HBC) received its charter from King Charles II of England on May 2, 1670. The original and official name of the company was as grand as its history has been in Canada: "Governor and Company of Adventurers of England Trading into Hudson Bay." The Company was granted enormously wide powers, including a monopoly on trading rights in the vast region whose rivers drained into Hudson Bay, a territory comprising almost 40 percent of what is now Canada. It remains to this day the oldest incorporated company in the English-speaking world. Its history is deeply intertwined with that of Canada, and the Company's fur trading, which was its only business for most of its history, tells much of the story of the colonization of British North America.

The Company established a series of trading posts across Northern Canada, most of them located at the mouths of major rivers around the shores of James Bay and Hudson Bay. These included Rupert's House on the southeast corner of Hudson Bay and Moose Factory at the south end of James Bay. The French explorers and traders Pierre-Esprit Radisson and Médard Chouart des Groseilliers had discovered that there was a vast amount of wealth in the fur of beavers, fox, and other animals native to Northern Canada. Many of the rivers and lakes where the beavers lived were accessible through Hudson Bay. The HBC plan was to build forts that had relatively easy access to England when the ice was out and let the Natives come to them in the winter to trade for furs. The French attitude was more aggressive: they set up trading posts along rivers further south, effectively intercepting the Native traders before they got as far north as Hudson Bay. By the middle of the eighteenth century, the HBC began establishing forts further south and west as a result of this strong competition from the French, leading to the founding of some of the great northwestern river cities in Canada: Winnipeg, Calgary, and Edmonton.

In exchange for fur pelts, the HBC originally offered simple manufactured goods such as metal knives, needles, and blankets. The iconic Hudson's Bay point blanket, still available and cherished today, dates from this era. After about 1857, the HBC began to trade pelts (mainly beaver) for tokens that they produced. Native traders brought their furs to one of the HBC trading posts and received in exchange tokens denominated in "made-beavers." One made-beaver was equal in value to the prepared skin of a healthy adult beaver, and both the skins and manufactured objects were rated in that currency. In terms of buying power, one made-beaver

Standards (half made-beaver)—**Weight:** 6.91 grams. **Composition:** Brass. **Diameter:** 27.3 millimeters. **Year issued:** 1857. **Edge:** Reeded. **Issuing authority:** Hudson's Bay Company, Eastmain District. **Rarity:** Readily available, but quite scarce in choice Uncirculated grades.

Standards (quarter made-beaver)—**Weight:** 4.3 grams. **Composition:** Brass. **Diameter:** 24.8 millimeters. **Year issued:** 1857. **Edge:** Reeded. **Issuing authority:** Hudson's Bay Company, Eastmain District. **Rarity:** Readily available, but quite scarce in choice Uncirculated grades.

purchased two pounds of sugar. Other fur pelts were also denominated in made-beavers: two marten pelts were equal to one beaver pelt, for example. The Natives could select items from the HBC store until their tokens were exhausted. These tokens, about the size of a 25-cent coin, came in four denominations stamped on the reverse: 1, half, quarter, and one-eighth made-beavers. The obverse featured the HBC coat-of-arms with the Latin inscription "Pro Pelle Cutem" ("A pelt for a skin"), the Company's motto. The reverse contained a major error. The letters translate as follows:

HB:	Hudson's Bay
EM:	East Main (an HBC trading post located on the east coast of James Bay; by 1730 it had become the Company's main headquarters)
1, 1/2, 1/4, 1/8:	the denomination of the coin in made-beavers
NB:	Made-Beaver (the die cutter made an error here, cutting an "N" instead of an "M")

At auction, Uncirculated examples of these tokens typically sell for under US$1,000. Other tokens were used by the HBC in different areas of Canada. Aluminum tokens were

Standards (eighth made-beaver)—**Weight:** 2.54 grams. **Composition:** Brass. **Diameter:** 24.8 millimeters. **Year issued:** 1857. **Edge:** Reeded. **Issuing authority:** Hudson's Bay Company, Eastmain District. **Rarity:** Readily available, but quite scarce in choice Uncirculated grades.

introduced relatively recently (1941) and used until about 1961 for arctic fox in the Far North. This was a decimal coinage and the pieces were valued in cents (5, 10, 25, 50, 100) (see images on the next page). These tokens are not particularly rare and sell at auction for just a few hundred dollars. The two examples discussed here—brass tokens denominated in made-beaver and aluminum ones in cents—are just two of the many different tokens created by the HBC both for the fur trade and for retail commerce.

Overall, the fur trade was not a positive influence on the Indigenous peoples of Canada. Because of its lure, with its promise of wealth and a better way of life, many Natives abandoned their traditional hunting and fishing practices and came to rely on manufactured goods for their survival. Some also moved beyond their traditional territories in search of elusive furs, often coming into conflict with other tribes. With the Europeans also came diseases, such as smallpox, to which the Native population had no immunity.

A station of the Hudson's Bay Company, 1877.

Recent Hudson's Bay Company aluminum tokens.

NO. 46 WEIR & LARMINIE 1862 ENCASED POSTAGE STAMP

Standards—**Weight:** 2.52 grams. **Composition:** Brass, mica, and paper. **Diameter:** 24.5 millimeters. **Edge:** Plain. **Designer:** John Gault. **Rarity:** The cent example is purportedly the rarest of all four denominations known (1, 3, 5, and 10 cents), but all are quite scarce.

It is debatable whether an encased postage stamp—with an embedded U.S. stamp, of all things—is an appropriate entry anywhere in this Canadian anthology. Further, is this point in the narrative the correct place to locate this essay? Of course, I would answer yes.

Encased postage stamps were an emergency medium of exchange in the United States due to an endemic shortage of small coinage early in the American Civil War, so they definitely were a form of money. They have a place in a Canadian anthology because the company that actually had these particular stamps encased operated out of Montreal. Furthermore, this first chapter deals with fiat money of various types: wampum, tokens, playing card money. Encased postage stamps certainly fit into this category. Similar to the tokens produced by banks in Lower Canada because of a lack of coinage, encased postage stamps were a response to insufficient specie for commerce in the United States. This fiat money appeared somewhat later (1862–1863) than those discussed earlier, but their similarity of purpose demands that the subject be taken up here in our narrative.

In 1792 the U.S. Coinage Act established the price of silver at $1.29 per ounce. For the next 70 years, this hardly varied at all. During the U.S. Civil War, however, it spiked to almost $4. Even though Canada's rates generally closely followed those of the United States, there was a modest difference in price for precious metals between the two countries. The firm of Weir & Larminie, formed in 1862, was a private banking and precious-metal broker in Montreal, and the government charged its senior partner, William Weir, with exploiting this price difference for the flood of U.S. silver coins being dumped into Canada during the war. Born in Scotland, Weir emigrated to Lower Canada in 1842 and rose to become an important financial figure, although many years after the end of the Civil War he was involved in a banking scandal that resulted in his conviction and imprisonment.

Early in the Civil War, gold and silver coins and even copper-nickel cents were hoarded. To keep some coinage available for everyday commerce, the U.S. Mint produced, almost exclusively, low-denomination copper-nickel cents in large numbers during this era: 10 million in 1861, 28 million in 1862, and 50 million in 1863. But even this did not properly satisfy the demand. In July 1862 President Abraham Lincoln authorized the use of postage stamps as a medium of exchange, and the U.S. government carried this idea further by actually printing stamps on banknote paper. This was not an entirely acceptable solution, however, as stamps were fragile and easily lost or damaged. A clever Boston inventor, John Gault, developed a device to hold the postage stamp in a brass case with transparent mica, which allowed the stamp to be viewed. This evolved into a mica-covered stamp set in a metal disc, on which an advertisement for some company could be impressed. The encased postage stamp was a purely American commodity designed to satisfy a need for coinage in that country; they were not used at all in Canada. However, Weir & Larminie had a number of these produced in New York, most likely simply for promotional purposes.

The small number of Weir & Larminie encased postage stamps known today indicates that they were never intended as a medium of exchange. In fact, Weir & Larminie stamps are among the rarest of all encased stamps issued. Extant examples are known in four denominations: 1, 3, 5, and 10 cents, with the 1-cent encased stamp thought to be the rarest. There are supposedly 20 to 30 known 10-cent encased stamps, and likely around one-third the number for the 1-cent stamps. The Stack's Medio / Da Costa Gomez Collections Sale (June 2004) contained a total of six examples (lots 625–630) of Weir & Larminie encasements: three 1-cent examples, a single 3-cent piece, and two 10-cent pieces. The cent examples sold for between US$3,700 and US$4,350. The auction record for Weir & Larminie pieces of any denomination, as far as I was able to trace, was for a 3-cent example from the same sale (lot 628). This encased postage stamp sold for US$19,800, with the auction description claiming that only two existed in this denomination. A more recent sale of a 1-cent stamp (ex Douglas Robins Collection of Canadian Tokens) at a 2018 Heritage auction required a bid of US$8,400 to win the lot, with a 3-cent example in the same sale selling for US$7,200. A 10-cent example sold for US$5,760 in a 2021 Heritage sale.

William Weir at about age 40.

No. 12 Canadian Indian Chiefs 1871–1877 Peace Medals

Standards (1872 medal)—**Weight:** 350 grams. **Composition:** Silver-plated electrotype. **Diameter:** 96.6 millimeters. **Rarity:** About 25 were produced.

Standards (1871 Treaty No. 1 medal)—**Weight:** 350 grams. **Composition:** Silver. **Diameter:** 76 millimeters. **Designers:** Joseph Shepherd and Alfred Benjamin Wyon. **Rarity:** Perhaps as few as ten produced.

While not a direct form of currency to be used for commerce, the Canadian Indian chiefs peace medals were a method of payment and giving thanks to the chiefs of various tribes upon ratification of a treaty between them and the Government of Canada. The earliest record of such medals dates back to 1670, when a Caughnawaga chief was presented with a medal from King Charles II of England.

In 1871 two important treaties (Treaty 1 and Treaty 2) were signed by the Government of Canada and the Chippewa and Cree tribes of southern Manitoba. Each treaty stipulated that every one of the chiefs should receive "a suit of clothes, a flag, and a medal as a mark of distinction." The medals were items of great value to the chiefs, who considered it a tremendous honor to wear a medal bearing the portrait of the British sovereign. The aim of the Aboriginal peoples in signing these treaties was to protect and preserve their traditional lands and provide a livelihood for their families, while securing help in their difficult transition to an unfamiliar way of life. From the

King George III medal in copper presented by the Hudson's Bay Company to Native chiefs around 1820.

perspective of the Canadian government, treaty making was a way to expedite settlement of the West and assimilation of Indigenous peoples into Canadian society.

Treaties 1 and 2 attempted to incorporate these quite divergent aims but unfortunately left a legacy of unresolved issues, as the terms of the treaties were perhaps purposely left vague and ill defined. The legacy of these ultimately unsuccessful treaties is still felt today, as relations between Indigenous peoples and the Canadian government remain fraught with suspicion, lack of trust, and confrontation. The situation is not much better today than 150 years ago.

The medal illustrated at the outset of this essay mirrors the government-Indigenous relationship beautifully. Canada wanted to "wow" the Natives and overwhelm them with a trinket in exchange for their land and loyalty. The medal would certainly have been magnificent had it been made of solid silver, but it was actually an electrotype with silver plating. It was lovely on the surface but worthless at the core, perhaps mimicking the newly signed treaty. The Indigenous people were not fooled by this sham, however. There was a long tradition in the United States, stretching back to the late eighteenth century, of Native American peace medals struck in solid silver. Canadian Natives were well aware of the fine quality of some of these medals and demanded much the same from Canada beginning as early as 1873, only two years after the signing of Treaty 1. The struck solid silver medal seen above replaced the electrotype one, with space for engraving the date and treaty number. The theme was much more appropriate, featuring a Native encampment at sunset with a Canadian military officer in full uniform shaking hands with a Native leader wearing a headdress and leggings. A tomahawk is buried in the ground at their feet, perhaps signifying an end to hostilities.

It was not just governments that presented medals to Indigenous leaders. Private companies trading in the New World often made similar gifts, and none was more profligate with medal-giving than the Hudson's Bay Company. In the early 1800s numerous companies operated in the fur trade in the Montreal area. They competed bitterly with each other but also had the common goal of destroying the Hudson's Bay Company's monopoly over the trade with Indigenous peoples. To entice Native traders to bring furs to their respective trading posts, many of the companies provided tobacco, alcohol, and other gratuities. Among the favors presented by the Hudson's Bay Company to the Native chiefs were grand medals. The example illustrated at right, likely presented to Native chiefs around 1820, was a handsome medal in bronzed copper bearing King George III's portrait on one side and the Company's coat-of-arms on the other. It was impressive in its size and weight, measuring 48 millimeters across and weighing 56.2 grams.

Many of the medals presented to Native Canadians are currently very rare. One reason for this is that the medals were worn and sometimes melted to make silver choker necklaces and amulets. But the main reason is that the medals were made in extremely limited quantities. For example, the medal shown at the outset of this essay had a mintage of only 25 pieces, and there are only about ten known examples of the 1871 Treaty No. 1 medal. An example of this medal sold for US$14,400 in a March 2021 Heritage auction. A 2018 auction of a silver medal of the same type but from Treaty No. 6 (signed in 1876) realized US$6,750.

Chapter 2

Pre-Confederation and Related Coinage of Canada and the Provinces

In this chapter, I present 12 essays on the early official coinage struck for various locations in Canada. With one exception (British Columbia gold coins), all were produced at either the Royal Mint or the Heaton Mint in England. Most of the issues discussed are pre-Confederation. The chapter begins with the 1858 emission for the Province of Canada, followed by a number of Canadian and provincial pattern coins produced around that time. The impression one comes away with is that of both Canada and the Royal Mint trying to decide what would work as coinage and what might not. The 20-cent coin minted in 1858 is a prime example of one that didn't quite work. While the 1858 coinage pieces are generally considered the first true Canadian coins, in reality they were still a colonial emission, since Confederation had not yet occurred. The copper coinage of Nova Scotia, some beautiful patterns made for this province, and the substantial emission of both copper and silver coins for New Brunswick are given due weight later in the chapter. Before concluding, we go west across the continent to discuss the British Columbia gold coins (perhaps the most valuable and desirable of all Canadian coinage), then back east to the single emission of Prince Edward Island coinage and a group of very odd Proof New Brunswick issues. The chapter concludes with an 1871 20-cent coin from Canada, for which trial pieces were made without any plan to actually produce the coin for circulation. Newfoundland is not mentioned here at all, as its coinage will be discussed in full in chapter 3.

No. 10 First Coinage of the Province of Canada, 1858

Standards (cent)—**Weight:** 4.54 grams. **Composition:** 0.950 copper, 0.040 tin, 0.010 zinc. **Diameter:** 25.4 millimeters. **Edge:** Plain. **Designer:** Leonard C. Wyon. **Rarity:** Moderately scarce, but historically very significant.

Standards (5 cents)—**Weight:** 1.167 grams. **Composition:** 0.925 silver, 0.075 copper. **Diameter:** 15.5 millimeters. **Edge:** Reeded. **Designer:** Leonard C. Wyon. **Rarity:** Moderately scarce, but historically very significant.

Standards (10 cents)—**Weight:** 2.32 grams. **Composition:** 0.925 silver, 0.075 copper. **Diameter:** 17.8 millimeters. **Edge:** Reeded. **Designer:** Leonard C. Wyon. **Rarity:** Moderately scarce, but historically very significant.

Stadards (20 cents)—**Weight:** 4.648 grams. **Composition:** 0.925 silver, 0.075 copper. **Diameter:** 23.27 millimeters. **Edge:** Reeded. **Designer:** Leonard C. Wyon. **Rarity:** Moderately scarce, but historically very significant.

Unfortunately, the W.W.C. Wilson auction catalog I had access to did not include prices realized. We do know, however, what it realized in the Norweb Sale: US$6,160, an incredible bargain for an important and unique pattern. The uniface examples (there were three of them in the same sale, lots 706–708) garnered bids ranging from US$3,300 to US$4,400.

No. 67 Province of Canada 1858 Pattern 20 Cents

Standards—**Weight:** 4.62 grams. **Composition:** 0.925 silver, 0.075 copper. **Diameter:** 23.27 millimeters. **Edge:** Plain. **Designers:** Obverse designed by Leonard C. Wyon, reverse by either Leonard C. Wyon or George William Wyon (see below). **Rarity:** About ten examples known. Bowman 6.

Although this coin is dated 1858, it may have been struck several years later. Equally in doubt is whether it really was a potential design for the Canadian 20-cent piece. The obverse is the same as that on the officially produced 20-cent coin of 1858, but the reverse is entirely different and was used on the regular-issue Province of New Brunswick 20-cent pieces dated 1862 and 1864, as illustrated below.

An MS-66 (PCGS) example of the 1862 20-cent coin from New Brunswick. Note that the reverse is *identical* to that of the 1858 Canadian pattern except for the date.

Aesthetically, this pattern is much less satisfying than the regular-issue 1858 20-cent coin. The wreath on the reverse seems much too bold for the delicate obverse, and the digits in the date on the reverse are large and not as delicately formed as on the adopted design. The lettering in CENTS is sloppily executed; in particular, the letter T leans somewhat to the right and is too close to the N. As can be seen in the examples shown here, these deficiencies were present on both the pattern and the regular-issue New Brunswick coins, which, of course, is to be expected as they used the same reverse die.

Although this pattern might have been a test coin for the Province of Canada, there appears to be a consensus that it was more likely made as a cabinet piece or mint-sport for no special purpose other than to demonstrate the capabilities of the Royal Mint, perhaps for potential customers. The Deputy Master of the Royal Mint, Charles W. Fremantle, was known to have produced a number of these pieces (see the final essay in this chapter, "New Brunswick 1870–1875 Trial/Pattern 5, 10, and 20 Cents").

The obituary medal for George W. Wyon, exhibiting the reverse of the New Brunswick 20-cent coin of 1862.

The 1858 Canada 20-cent pattern coin is very rare, with likely fewer than ten examples extant. Neither Pittman nor Belzberg had an example, while the Norwebs had two (lots 712 and 713 in the Bowers and Merena 1996 sale of their collection). The National Currency Collection of the Bank of Canada possesses two examples. Also in this collection is an obituary medal for George W. Wyon, a member of the famous Wyon family of coin engravers at the Royal Mint. George was the son of James Wyon (1804–1868), chief engraver at the Royal Mint from 1851 until his retirement. In 1862 George replaced his father as chief engraver, but unfortunately died just two years later at the age of 26. There is an additional obituary medal in the PCGS population report, which displays the reverse of the New Brunswick 1862 20-cent coin, while the obverse contains the obituary information. The existence of this medal has prompted some to surmise that it was the young George W. Wyon who designed the reverse of the New Brunswick 20-cent coin.

The 1858 Canada 20-cent pattern appears only very infrequently at auction. The two examples in the Norweb Sale realized US$6,380 and US$4,400. In the 2014 Heritage auction of the Prager Collection, an SP-62 coin was bid to US$10,575. The same coin had appeared previously as lot 712 in the Norweb Sale.

No. 23 Province of Canada 1859 Brass Cent

Standards—**Weight:** 4.29 grams. **Composition:** Brass. Likely 0.640 copper, 0.340 zinc, but copper content could be up to 90%. **Diameter:** 25.75 millimeters. **Edge:** Plain. **Designer:** Leonard C. Wyon. **Rarity:** Perhaps two dozen known. The example illustrated above is the second-finest known at PCGS, a VF-30 example.

The mintage of the 1859 cents for the Province of Canada was an enormous 9.6 million. This was so large that no further cent pieces would be required by Canada for another 17 years. Due to the massive quantity of coins produced, a large number of dies were used to strike the entire mintage. The initial 1859s were generally overdates of 1858 coins, where a wide punch for the 9 was used in an attempt to obliterate the final 8 of that date. Most of the 1859 cents were not overdates, however, and generally a narrow 9 punch was used for the final digit in the date, but since it was hand-punched, the digit's position varied from die to die. There are so many of these varieties (e.g., narrow 9 with various orientations of the numeral; wide 9 over 8 with coin axes parallel; wide 9 over 8 with axes anti-parallel) that most standard catalogs do not even attempt to list them all. A useful counterexample here is Haxby's 2012 *Guide Book of Canadian Coins and Tokens*, which lists most of the varieties known, together with convenient images of each. These minor differences do not result in much variation in price, and the exact characteristics of the date are often not even mentioned in many auction listings of 1859 cent pieces.

In addition to all these die variations, there is a curious metal variation that is extremely rare. A small number of 1859 cents are known to be made of brass, an alloy containing roughly two-thirds copper and one-third zinc. This mixture can vary quite widely, however, with compositions as extreme as 90 percent copper and 10 percent zinc still referred to as brass. Normal cents of this era were made from bronze: 95 percent copper, 4 percent tin, and 1 percent zinc. Coins struck in brass can often be distinguished from a bronze example by their yellowish hue, but this is not definitive since chemically cleaning a bronze coin will give it a similar color. The purpose of minting the coin in brass is not known. Was it a pattern, a trial strike, or something else? No definitive decision seems to have been reached on this.

There is one last curiosity regarding this coin. When encountered, it is always well circulated and often has surface issues such as mild corrosion. It is as though the entire coinage had been placed into circulation, and only much later was it discovered that they formed a rare subgroup of the entire population. The highest grades assigned to this coin at PCGS are a single piece in VF-35 and another in VF-30. No Mint State examples are known from any grading service. PCGS has graded a total of nine examples of this rarity. In 2017 a VF-20 example sold at a Heritage auction for US$17,625; in 2018 a slightly impaired example attracted a winning bid of US$14,400.

No. 54 Province of Canada 1859 Pattern Cent

Standards—**Weight:** 5.63 grams. **Composition:** Copper alloy, with either nickel or bronze. **Diameter:** 25.4 millimeters. **Edge:** Plain. **Designer:** Leonard C. Wyon. **Rarity:** Only two examples known. Bowman 5.

There is some controversy surrounding this extremely rare and highly artistic coin. Some regard it as a Canadian pattern and others as a British one. This is understandable, as the obverse die was from an 1858 or 1859 Province of Canada cent, while the reverse is similar to a British half-penny pattern, showing Britannia seated, facing right, with shield, trident, and helmet. Another uncertainty is the source of the weight of the coin. It has the same diameter as an 1859 Canadian cent (25.4 millimeters), but that coin weighs only 4.54 grams, compared with 5.63 grams for this pattern. Perhaps it is alloyed with a heavier metal, such as nickel. Yet another odd thing about this piece is that the date is presented in Roman numerals, MDCCCLIX, the only classic Canadian coin to express it in this manner. The die with this reverse design was used on pattern pieces for British farthings, half pennies, and pennies.

It is also not at all clear why this coin was struck. Most likely, it was simply a fantasy piece: the obverse and reverse dies were available at the Royal Mint and someone mated the two unrelated dies and struck a few examples.

This pattern is extremely rare, with only two examples currently identified. Earlier, Bowman (entry #5 in his *Canadian Patterns*, 1957) mentioned the existence of only a single example which had appeared in the Parson's Collection in 1936. There are no examples in the National Currency Collection at the Bank of Canada. The finest known is the

Norweb example (graded SP-63), whose last recorded sale was in the 1996 Norweb Canadian auction cataloged by Bowers and Merena, where the copper-nickel example sold for US$7,260. The Norwebs had obtained this coin from A.H. Baldwin & Sons in April 1956. A much lesser example (SP-45) made from bronze sold for US$8,338 in the Heritage Belzberg Sale in January 2003. The current *Charlton Standard Catalogue of Canadian Coins* lists this pattern at US$35,000 in SP-63.

NO. 53 NOVA SCOTIA 1861 CIRCULATION-STRIKE AND PATTERN CENT

Standards—**Weight:** 5.67 grams. **Composition:** 0.95 copper, 0.04 tin, 0.01 zinc. **Diameter:** 25.5 millimeters. **Edge:** Plain. **Designer:** James Wyon, obverse. **Rarity:** Circulation strikes are common; about ten examples of this pattern coin are known. Bowman 7.

In 1860 Nova Scotia adopted a decimal system of coinage, a serious break with the British system, which had been in use for many decades. However, it tempered the shock of a new monetary system somewhat by adopting a simple relation between the Nova Scotia dollar and the British pound, namely, $5 was equivalent to £1. This made the Nova Scotia coinage formally incompatible with those of Canada and New Brunswick, both of which rated the sovereign at $4.8666, but it allowed British coins to continue circulating in the colony with little difficulty. Since there were 20 shillings in a pound, a Nova Scotia dollar was, conveniently, exactly 4 shillings, allowing a 50-cent coin to be 2 shillings, a 25-cent coin to be a shilling, and a sixpence (half a shilling) to be equivalent to 12-1/2 cents. All that was needed in the way of new coinage, then, was a cent coin and a half-cent piece, the latter making change for the sixpence. After some delay in the manufacture of these coins in Britain, as the Royal Mint was extremely busy during this era, coins finally arrived in the colony in 1861.

The obverse of the circulation-strike cents for Nova Scotia (the first of the two examples on the previous page) and its physical size are the same as those of a British half penny, establishing yet again the propensity of the Royal Mint to recycle old dies, presumably in order to cut costs. The second of the two coins pictured is a rare pattern cent. There are two varieties of the obverse of this pattern coin, Large Bust and Small Bust. The first example is the Large Bust variety; the Small Bust design is on the pattern shown below it. The simplest diagnostic, besides the size of the portrait, is the width of the ribbon behind the queen's head. The Large Bust variety has a broad ribbon, while the Small Bust has a narrower ribbon, as seen below. The circulation strikes are clearly of the Small Bust variety.

An example of the Small Bust portrait of Her Majesty Queen Victoria on an 1861 pattern cent of Nova Scotia (Charlton NS-6). This coin may be unique.

The reverses of the two patterns shown depict a wreath of roses surrounding a crown in the center, with lettering and the date near the periphery. In his pamphlet *Canadian Patterns*, Fred Bowman writes that this very attractive pattern was rejected because the mayflower (or trailing arbutus, *Epigaea repens*) had recently been adopted as the flower of Nova Scotia, although it was not *officially* adopted as the provincial flower until 1901. Apparently, it was felt that a ring of British roses, as appears on the reverse here, would thus be an unacceptable design. Unofficially, the mayflower had been used as decoration on various Nova Scotia elements since the 1820s. It appeared on the front page of the *Nova Scotian* newspaper for many years, was celebrated in song and poetry, and often appeared on pre-Confederation stamps of the province.

Nova Scotia, along with New Brunswick, had been given control over its post offices by London in 1851 and issued its first three stamps in the same year. These were diamond-shaped issues featuring three flowers from Britain and the mayflower from Nova Scotia (the floral symbol seen at the top of the 1-shilling or 12-pence stamp illustrated here).

Both the Large Bust and Small Bust patterns are extremely rare coins. Fred Bowman lists both varieties, Nos. 7 and 8, in his *Canadian Patterns*. In an article on Canada's ten rarest coins, he lists only a single known example of the Small Bust pattern cent, with the latest sale known (to him) being a New Netherlands auction of 1960. An example of the Small Bust coin (unknown whether it was the same coin) later appeared in the Norweb Sale of 1996, graded only MS-60 (the Small Bust pattern illustrated), and sold for US$1,045. One should pay attention to auctions, as the same coin recently appeared in a Heritage auction on May 28, 2020. It was correctly attributed to Norweb and described as very rare, but hammered for a paltry US$1,140—a small sum for a potentially unique coin! An example of the Large Bust cent also appeared in the Norweb Sale; it was graded SP-65 and fetched US$5,500. A more recent auction (Heritage, 2017) of a gorgeous SP-65 red example of the Large Bust pattern realized US$4,465.

Finally, PCGS has two examples of the Small Bust pattern (NS-6) listed in its population report: the MS-60 coin shown in this essay and an MS-65RB example. The latter coin has been misattributed and is actually an NS-4 variety, a Large Bust example in Specimen. It is in fact the second coin shown at the outset of this essay—clearly a Large Bust example. Hence, the Small Bust pattern may truly be unique.

NO. 56 NEW BRUNSWICK 1861 HALF CENT

Standards—**Weight:** 2.84 grams. **Composition:** 0.95 copper, 0.04 tin, 0.01 zinc. **Diameter:** 20.65 millimeters. **Edge:** Plain. **Designer:** From a model by C. Hill, engraved by Leonard C. Wyon. **Rarity:** A moderately scarce coin.

The 1861 New Brunswick half cent is a coin that really should not exist. To understand why, we need to consider what was happening in Nova Scotia and New Brunswick in the late 1850s.

In 1859 Nova Scotia adopted a decimal system for its currency. British coins circulated there to a greater extent than in the other colonies, and the new system reflected these close monetary ties by allowing British coins to continue circulating. The Nova Scotia dollar (so called, although a dollar coin was never actually minted) was set at 5 to 1 British pound. This meant that British silver coins could continue circulating in Nova Scotia after decimalization, as they fit neatly into the new decimal system. In the British system, 1 pound (5 Nova Scotia dollars) was equal to 20 shillings, so 2 shillings was exactly 50 cents, 1 shilling was 25 cents, and 6 pence (a real, circulating British coin) was valued at 12-1/2 cents, as 12 pence was equal to 1 shilling. In order to properly make change between British coins and the new decimal system, Nova Scotia thus required a half-cent coin. Since British coins continued to circulate widely after 1860, all Nova Scotia needed to achieve a fully functioning decimal system was for the Royal Mint to produce cents and half cents for its use. These were intermittently minted for the province by London between 1861 and 1864, almost up to Confederation, after which the coins of the new Dominion of Canada became legal tender in Nova Scotia.

When New Brunswick contemplated its own coinage in 1860, it decided to follow the lead of the Province of Canada, which in 1858 had also ordered coins from the Royal Mint in decimal denominations. In order to keep costs at a minimum, the mint used an obverse die earlier employed on British farthings and a reverse die almost identical to that employed to strike Nova Scotia cents (see the regular-issue Nova Scotia cent example in the previous essay).

In New Brunswick the relation between the pound and the dollar differed from that in Nova Scotia, however. The dollars of New Brunswick and Canada were tied to the value of the U.S. dollar instead of the British pound. Thus, there was no need for a half-cent coin, and in 1861 New Brunswick ordered bronze cent coins together with silver coins from the Royal Mint. Apparently, the Royal Mint became confused (since Nova Scotia ordered half cents, it seemed logical that New Brunswick would do the same) and struck half-cent pieces for New Brunswick that had never been ordered. This emission is thought to have numbered 222,800. When the error was discovered before the coins were shipped, most were melted. Those that do exist are believed to have been mixed in with half-cent pieces struck for Nova Scotia and shipped to Halifax.

The coin shown above is one of the finest known (MS-65RB) for this emission, with only three better in MS-66RB. In 2010 an SP-65 brown example sold for US$3,450 in a Heritage auction. In the same sale, an MS-64RB coin achieved a winning a bid of US$1,495. If one of the MS-66RB examples were to come on the market, a price well in excess of US$5,000 would be required to buy it today.

No. 58 New Brunswick 1862 Pattern 10 Cents

Standards—**Weight:** 2.29 grams. **Composition:** Silver. **Diameter:** 17.7 millimeters. **Edge:** Plain. **Designer:** Leonard C. Wyon. **Rarity:** Perhaps only two known. Bowman 20.

The New Brunswick 1862 10-cent pattern is extremely rare. In his *Canadian Patterns*, Fred Bowman identified just two examples, both in the W.W.C. Wilson Collection. There is currently one in the National Currency Collection at the Bank of Canada, the example illustrated above; another appeared in the Norweb Sale auctioned by Bowers and Merena in 1996 (lot 722), where it sold for the very modest price of US$2,860.

The reverse design is entirely different from the regular-issue New Brunswick 10-cent coin of the same date pictured at right. There are no maple leaves on the pattern; instead, an arabesque border surrounds the denomination and date. The reverse bears a strong resemblance, but is not identical, to the reverse of the Newfoundland 10-cent coins of the same era (see images at right). The arabesque design is more ornate on the Newfoundland coin, which also has larger lettering.

A reverse design bearing many similarities to the New Brunswick pattern was also used on a pattern 1862 10-cent coin from Hong Kong, illustrated at right. Large numbers of Hong Kong pattern coins were prepared either at the Royal Mint in London or at a branch mint established in Hong Kong in 1866. This particular pattern was manufactured in London. The similarity between the New Brunswick and Hong Kong patterns suggests that it was the practice of the Royal Mint to reuse dies for many different issues. The designer, Leonard Wyon, clearly had his reverse design used for locations at opposite ends of the world.

Left: The reverse of a regular-issue 1862 New Brunswick 10-cent coin. Right: The reverse of an 1865 Newfoundland 10-cent coin.

Hong Kong 1862 10-cent coin with a reverse design similar to that of the New Brunswick 1862 10-cent coin.

NO. 2 BRITISH COLUMBIA 1862 GOLD $10 AND $20

Standards ($10)—**Weight:** 11.2 grams. **Composition:** 0.90 gold, 0.10 copper. **Diameter:** 27.1 millimeters. **Edge:** Reeded. **Designer:** Albert Küner. **Issuing authority:** Government of British Columbia. **Rarity:** Excessively rare; only three known. None are publicly available. Bowman 37.

Standards ($20)—**Weight:** 23.68 grams. **Composition:** 0.90 gold, 0.10 copper. **Diameter:** 34.1 millimeters. **Edge:** Reeded. **Designer:** Albert Küner. **Issuing authority:** Government of British Columbia. **Rarity:** Extremely rare; only five known. Bowman 36.

Coins were being struck not only in eastern Canada in the late 1850s and early 1860s but even in remote British Columbia, effectively a colony of Britain between 1858 and 1871. The coins minted in the colony were neither approved nor authorized by the British government, however, which accounts for their rarity.

In January 1848 gold was discovered at Sutter's Mill near present-day Coloma, California. This initiated the 1849 California Gold Rush, which lasted for about seven years and drew more than 300,000 people in search of gold and their fortunes. This huge influx from other parts of the United States, Europe, and Asia reinvigorated the sluggish American economy, but it had a deleterious effect on the Native American population, whose land, rivers, and lakes suffered the effects of toxic prospecting chemicals and the loss of fish and game habitat.

History repeated itself almost a decade later when, in 1857 and 1858, gold was discovered in the Fraser River and Cariboo regions of the interior of British Columbia. Miners, mainly Americans from the California gold fields, surged northward. British Columbia possessed neither the facilities to assay the gold nor a mint to turn it into coins, so much of the gold was shipped south to San Francisco for processing. British Columbia governor Sir James Douglas was appalled by this and in 1862 purchased minting equipment capable of producing $10 and $20 gold coins. A mint was established in

New Westminster, now a municipality in Metro Vancouver. Albert Küner, a highly regarded engraver who had made coin dies for various San Francisco mining companies—including Moffat and Company; Norris, Gregg & Norris; and Wass, Molitor and Company—was hired to engrave dies for the British Columbian coins. Within a year, however, Douglas changed his mind and the equipment was temporarily placed in storage. It was eventually used to strike only a few pattern pieces in gold. Trial examples in silver were produced in San Francisco, with a few retained by Küner. Some gold and silver examples were sent to the 1862 International Exhibition in London, and a few were distributed to local dignitaries. Britain was not pleased with this development in one of her colonies, as only the Crown had the legal right to strike coinage. The mint was eventually dismantled, and while there is no record of exactly how many pieces were produced, five $20 gold pieces and three $10 gold pieces are currently known. All of the $10 gold issues are located in museum collections and unavailable to the collecting public. Thus, these coins are the rarest of all the North American Gold Rush coins. The dies are stored at the Royal British Columbia Museum in Victoria.

An 1860 illustration in *Harper's Weekly* depicting people boarding a ship for the Fraser Canyon Gold Rush.

Of the five known $20 coins, one is in the British Museum in London, one (a holed example) is in the Royal British Columbia Museum, and one is held by the Canadian Imperial Bank of Commerce. Until recently, only two were publicly available, and both have appeared at auction in the past 25 years. One was sold in the John Jay Pittman Sale of August 1999, cataloged and auctioned by David Akers Numismatics, Inc. This was the coin from the collection of King Farouk of Egypt, a prolific collector of coins and many other valuables from cars to watches. Pittman bought this coin from A.H. Baldwin and Son for US$4,500 after the 1950 Farouk auction in Egypt, at which it had realized 1,500 Egyptian pounds, the second-highest single coin lot in the entire auction. Only the U.S. Ultra High Relief 1907 double eagle sold for more in the Farouk auction. Before this British Columbia $20 gold coin came into Farouk's possession, it had been in the Virgil Brand Collection. Brand had purchased it for US$1,650 in the Count Ferrari Sale of January 27, 1922, with Spink acting as his agent. In the 1999 Pittman Sale, this same coin was bought jointly by a trio of U.S. coin dealers for US$149,500! It is currently in the possession of a Vancouver coin dealer and remains the only one in the public domain. This same coin dealer also owns an example of each of the $10 and $20 British Columbia pieces in silver.

The other $20 British Columbia gold coin that was, until recently, publicly available boasts an illustrious pedigree running from Brand to Norweb to Belzberg. Brand acquired it for US$1,500 in Sotheby's Lieutenant Colonel Leslie Ellis auction in 1919, together with a $10 piece in gold, for which he paid US$1,000. These two gold coins most recently appeared in Heritage Auctions' 2003 Belzberg Sale as part of a complete set of four British Columbian coins that also included the $10 and $20 pieces in silver. The set did not sell in that auction and was eventually acquired by a prominent Canadian dealer. In 2017 the gold coins were traded to the National Currency Collection of the Bank of Canada and now reside proudly in Canada's national collection.

New Westminster, 1865.

NO. 25 PRINCE EDWARD ISLAND 1871 CENT

Standards—**Weight:** 5.67 grams. **Composition:** 0.95 copper, 0.04 tin, 0.01 zinc. **Diameter:** 25.40 millimeters. **Edge:** Plain. **Designer:** Leonard C. Wyon; reverse from a model by William Theed. **Rarity:** Not rare, but of interest as the only coin issued by this province.

In 1867 three of the British North American colonies—Canada (basically Ontario and Quebec), New Brunswick, and Nova Scotia—united to form the Dominion of Canada. The Province of Canada had coins struck in London in 1858 and 1859, while New Brunswick and Nova Scotia obtained coinage from the Royal Mint beginning in 1861. Manitoba joined Confederation in 1870, but not with all the land that it has today, and British Columbia in 1871. Neither of these two provinces had coinage officially struck for them before Confederation, although, as seen in the previous essay, British Columbia had tried to strike its own gold and silver coins in 1862, only for these to be eventually rejected by Britain.

Prince Edward Island, known as St. John's Island until 1799, was granted colonial status by Britain in 1769. In 1871 it adopted a decimal currency, with its dollar valued identically to that of Canada and New Brunswick. It had a single bronze coin minted in England, a cent dated 1871 with a rather unique design. After it joined Confederation in 1873, Prince Edward Island's coins were those of Canada.

The design of its single pre-Confederation coin is quite dramatic. The obverse features a portrait of Queen Victoria that was to appear on Canadian cent pieces from the 1870s onward. The coin is "Godless," with neither the expression *Dei Gratia* nor its abbreviation, D.G. The reverse incorporates the Latin phrase *Parva Sub Ingenti* ("The small beneath the great") and portrays a large oak tree (England) sheltering three smaller ones (the three counties in PEI).

The Royal Mint was occupied with other coinage when these cent pieces were requested by PEI, so the contract was let to the Heaton Mint. In an unusual turn, Heaton failed to incorporate its normal "H" mintmark anywhere on the coin. The Heaton Archives retained a total of 257 of these coins, which were disbursed in the 1970s when other Heaton coins were released. This is why there are so many superb examples of this coin, including 15 in MS-67 recorded by PCGS alone. However, some Uncirculated examples have a large fingerprint on the obverse, as though someone with a sweaty hand had counted through the hoard.

While not a rare coin, its wonderful design has made it a favorite with collectors. One of the finest known PEI cents, grading MS-67+, realized US$2,232.50 in a 2015 Heritage auction.

NO. 29 CANADA 1871 TRIAL/PATTERN 20 CENTS

Standards (1871 trial 20 cents)—**Weight:** 4.65 grams. **Composition:** 0.925 silver, 0.075 copper. **Diameter:** 23.3 millimeters. **Edge:** Plain/reeded. **Designer:** Leonard C. Wyon. **Rarity:** About ten examples known. Bowman 39.

In the catalog of the James Mossman Collection of Canadian Coinage (2015), and earlier in the Belzberg catalog (2003), Heritage Auctions wrote that the coin illustrated above was purchased by London coin dealer B.A. Seaby in 1960 from the family of Sir William Grey Ellison-Macartney, a past master at the Royal Canadian Mint. As a minor footnote, Seaby also purchased the 1911 Canadian dollar, once called the world's most valuable coin, at the same time from the same family. There are reports that both of these coins were displayed at the 1960 Canadian Numismatic Association annual meeting in Sherbrooke, Quebec. I attended this, my first major coin show, as a teenager, but have no recollection whatsoever of the momentous events swirling all around me.

In his *Canadian Patterns*, Fred Bowman points out that this pattern can be found with both a plain and a reeded edge. The reeded-edge variety is generally thought to be the rarer of the two, but population reports suggest that both versions are equally scarce. In Bowman's compilation and this coin's two most recent auction appearances, the coin was listed as a pattern piece. This is likely a misnomer; "trial strike" is more appropriate. The coin was definitely not a suggestion for a 20-cent coin that would circulate after Confederation. There was never going to be an 1871 20-cent coin for Canada, which, while still the Province of Canada, had learned its lesson regarding the 20-cent piece that it produced for only a single year in 1858. That coin was apparently often confused with a U.S. 25-cent coin and later with the Canadian 25-cent pieces struck beginning in 1870. It is remarkable that there could be confusion with the American coin. Portrayed below is an 1870 U.S. quarter dollar. It is significantly heavier (6.22 grams versus 4.65 grams) and somewhat larger (24.3 millimeters versus 23.3 millimeters) than the 1858 Canadian 20-cent piece. Even the Canadian 25-cent coin is more substantial than the 20-cent coin, at 5.81 grams and 23.62 millimeters.

An 1870 U.S. quarter dollar.

The 1871 coin was struck by the Royal Mint purely for exhibition purposes. The date was irrelevant; the mint's intention was simply to exhibit the design for advertising or promotional purposes.

In the PCGS population report, nine examples are listed for the 1871 20-cent coin: five with a reeded edge and four with a plain edge. Heritage lists three recent auction sales ranging in price from US$9,987.50 for an SP-62 example to US$22,800 for the SP-65 gem shown here, which was sold in the 2019 George Hans Cook Collection Sale.

NO. 64 NEW BRUNSWICK 1870–1875 TRIAL/PATTERN 5, 10, AND 20 CENTS

Standards (5 cents)—**Weight:** 1.16 grams. **Composition:** 0.925 silver, 0.075 copper. **Diameter:** 15.49 millimeters. **Edge:** Both plain- and reeded-edge Proofs are known. **Designer:** Leonard C. Wyon. **Rarity:** Perhaps only two or three known. Bowman 19.

Standards (10 cents)—**Weight:** 2.31 grams. **Composition:** 0.925 silver, 0.075 copper. **Diameter:** 18.03 millimeters. **Edge:** Both plain- and reeded-edge Proofs are known. **Designer:** Leonard C. Wyon. **Rarity:** Perhaps only two or three known of each. Bowman 20.

Standards (20 cents)—**Weight:** 4.63 grams. **Composition:** 0.925 silver, 0.075 copper. **Diameter:** 23.2 millimeters. **Edge:** Both plain- and reeded-edge Proofs are known. **Designer:** Obverse Leonard C. Wyon, reverse likely Leonard C. Wyon. **Rarity:** Perhaps only two or three known. Bowman 24.

To call the coins portrayed here patterns may be a misnomer. New Brunswick had joined with Ontario and Quebec (collectively the Province of Canada) and Nova Scotia to form the new Dominion of Canada in 1867. Prior to this, both New Brunswick and Nova Scotia had coins produced for them at the Royal Mint in London, and the Province of Canada had an issue of coinage in 1858, prior to Confederation. After Confederation, Canada had its own emission of coinage beginning in 1870, so there clearly was absolutely no need for the provinces to produce their own coins after that year. So why were these pieces struck?

The first point to note is that these coins are all identical in design to the actual ones struck for New Brunswick in 1862 and 1864—only the dates are different, as well as impossible. They cannot be properly called patterns, as there was no possibility that a new issue of coins would be struck for New Brunswick after Confederation. A better term for these is "display" or "fantasy" pieces. They were likely produced simply to exhibit the style of the coins or the capabilities of the Royal Mint. They might have been used to show potential clients the quality of coinage the Royal Mint was able to produce.

In addition to the coins illustrated on the previous page, Fred Bowman lists in *Canadian Patterns* a New Brunswick 5-cent coin dated 1870 and a 10-cent piece dated 1871. The latter came from the Montagu Sale (lot 251) and later appeared in Sotheby's Caldecott Sale as part of lot 384. The Montagu Sale also contained a 20-cent piece dated 1871 (lot 250) and a 5-cent piece dated 1875. Both the 1875 5-cent piece and the 1870 10-cent piece later appeared in the W.W.C. Wilson Sale of 1925. The 1871 20-cent coin is known with both a reeded edge (as with the coin illustrated on the previous page) and a plain edge. In the auction occurrences listed here, there are certainly multiple appearances of the same coins. More recent auctions of any of these coins are extremely rare, and very few could be traced for the last 50 years. I was able to locate an SP-60 1871 20-cent coin that realized US$3,450 in the January 2003 Belzberg Heritage sale. Other New Brunswick pattern coins were also featured in the 1996 Norweb Sale, where 5-cent examples for 1870 and 1875 appeared together with an 1870 10-cent coin.

In the 1996 Norweb Sale catalog, Dave Bowers compared these coins to the Class I 1804 U.S. dollars. Those coins were struck well after the date that appears on them (likely around 1835), and what was important was the coin type, not the date. They were made for display and for distribution to diplomats, dignitaries, and royalty. Much the same can be said of the New Brunswick coins with regard to their purpose, but the date on these New Brunswick coins does seem to be the year in which the coins were actually produced. The similarity to the 1804 U.S. dollars ends here—certainly from a pricing perspective. In the Norweb Sale of 1996, the 1875 New Brunswick 5-cent pattern sold for a very solid US$7,480, while the 1870 10 cents (with a plain edge, which may be rarer than the reeded-edge variety) commanded US$17,600. In contrast, D. Brent Pogue, a famous American collector, bought an 1804 U.S. silver dollar for US$4.14 million in 1999. Auction values remain strong for the 1804 U.S. dollar, one of which topped US$3.36 million in December 2020.

The New Brunswick Legislature building.

Chapter 3

The Coinage of Newfoundland

This chapter discusses coinage related only to Newfoundland, which remained a colony of Great Britain until 1949, not joining Confederation for a full 82 years after Canada was founded. This means that it has its own extensive and rich coinage history, one that is substantially different from that of the other provinces and Canada after Confederation. Newfoundland minted gold coins 47 years before Canada did, and continued producing 20-cent coins until 1912, 42 years after Canada had abandoned this denomination in favor of a 25-cent piece. Some of the Newfoundland coins are among the most beautiful and rarest of any minted for what is now Canada.

No. 35 1864 Pattern Coins

Standards (Cent)—**Weight:** 5.45 grams. **Composition:** Bronze. **Diameter:** 25.4 millimeters. **Edge:** Plain. **Rarity:** About ten examples known. Bowman 26.

Standards (5 cents)—**Weight:** 1.40 grams. **Composition:** Bronze. **Diameter:** 15.5 millimeters. **Edge:** Plain. **Rarity:** Probably unique. Bowman 28.

Standards (10 cents)—**Weight:** 2.95 grams (estimated). **Composition:** Bronze. **Diameter:** 15.5 millimeters. **Edge:** Plain. **Rarity:** Probably unique. **No coin image is available.**

Standards (20 cents)—**Weight:** 6.2 grams. **Composition:** Bronze. **Diameter:** 22.95 millimeters. **Edge:** Engrailed. **Rarity:** Only a few examples known. Bowman 31.

Standards ($2)—**Weight:** 2.39 grams. **Composition:** Bronze. **Diameter:** 17.7 millimeters. **Edge:** Plain. **Rarity:** Only a single example extant, housed in the National Currency Collection of the Bank of Canada. Bowman 32.

In 1864 the Royal Mint struck a complete set of patterns in preparation for the regular-issue coinage of Newfoundland that appeared in 1865: cent, 5-cent, 10-cent, 20-cent, and $2 pieces, all of which are very rare, with the cent pattern being somewhat more available.

The 1864 cent (of which about a dozen are thought to exist) was included in the double Proof sets of 1864–1865, with all the other denominations bearing the 1865 date. It was produced with the same basic design, except for very minor differences, as the circulation-strike coins dated 1865. An example of this double Proof set was sold in the Wayte Raymond 1925 sale of the W.W.C. Wilson Collection and earlier in the Caldecott sale of 1912 (lot 368). This may have been the same set. An additional pattern cent of this date, bearing the inscription VICTORIA QUEEN surrounding the monarch's portrait instead of VICTORIA D: G: REG:, is somewhat scarcer.

The 1864 5-cent coin may be unique. The design is a mule of provincial dies, with the obverse being the design eventually adopted for Newfoundland 5-cent coins and the reverse being that of a New Brunswick 5-cent coin. There have been two recent appearances of this coin at auction: in the Norweb (1996) and Prager (2014) sales. At the latter auction the coin attracted a winning bid of US$11,550, compared with US$5,060 in the earlier Norweb sale. The Norwebs obtained this coin from the William B. Tennant Collection in 1953 (likely with John J. Ford Jr. as intermediary). It had appeared earlier in the Sotheby auction sales of the Murdoch (1903, lot 457) and Caldecott (1912, lot 370) collections.

Like the 5-cent coin, the 10-cent and 20-cent coins have obverses identical to those eventually adopted, while the reverses are the New Brunswick designs for the respective coins. No image is available for the 10-cent coin, which is also thought to be unique. No recent auction appearances have been recorded. The 20-cent coin also has no recent sales, but an example appeared in both the Murdoch and Caldecott sales (lots 457 and 369, respectively) in the early twentieth century.

The Royal Mint in England made a number of early patterns for the anticipated Newfoundland $2 gold issue. Presumably the copper pattern illustrated on the previous page (also known as Bowman 32) is the first of these, as it is dated 1864, one year before the regular-issue coins were struck. The coin is believed to have been designed by Leonard Charles Wyon, the eldest son of the former chief engraver of the Royal Mint, Charles Wyon. This pattern clearly shows the coin's derivation from 10-cent coins of other provinces, as the Royal Mint was interested in producing coinage for the colonies as cheaply as possible. The obverse is identical to the 10-cent coins from Canada (still a province in 1864) and New Brunswick, except for the name of the province. The number of denticles and the crown and leaves on the reverse are also identical to those from the other two provinces. The only major design changes here are the new denomination, TWO DOLLARS, and the date. In the end, this reverse format was not adopted, and an entirely new reverse was designed and used for this series beginning in 1865.

Bowman 32 first appeared at auction in 1892, and after appearances in Sotheby auctions of the Montagu (1892, lot 245) and Murdoch (1904, lot 456) collections it eventually found its way into the Virgil Brand Collection in 1912. Brand paid Spink US$35 for the coin at the time, after it had sold in Sotheby's 1912 Caldecott Sale (lot 367) for £7, with Spink acting for Brand at that auction. In the late 1940s or early 1950s it was acquired by John J. Ford Jr., likely through one of Brand's two brothers who had inherited his collection. Ford eventually sold the coin in 1973 to the Bank of Canada for its national collection, where it remains today.

NO. 11 1865 GOLD PATTERN $2

Standards—**Weight:** 3.328 grams. **Composition:** 0.9167 gold, 0.08333 copper. **Diameter:** 17.983 millimeters. **Edge:** Plain. **Rarity:** Unique. Also known as Bowman 34.

In 1865 the Royal Mint began producing the iconic Newfoundland $2 gold coins for circulation in the colony. The original suggestion was for a $1 gold coin, as there was a desire in Newfoundland to be consistent with coinage in the United States, which had a circulating gold coin of this denomination. After much discussion, a $2 coin was chosen instead, as it was felt that a coin as small as a $1 gold piece could be easily lost by local fishermen and other laborers. The U.S. $1 gold coin from 1865, on which a Newfoundland $1 gold coin would certainly have been modeled, has a diameter of just 15 millimeters, has a weight of 1.672 grams, and contains a mere 0.04837 ounces of gold. Nevertheless, the loss of such a coin would have been keenly felt in contemporary Newfoundland, as $1 equaled about a week's wage for a constable in one of the small towns that dotted the Newfoundland coast.

In the end Newfoundland opted for a gold coin that weighed 0.107 troy ounces, containing 0.0981 ounces of pure gold. With the value of gold in that period fixed at $20.67 per ounce, the gold value of the coin was $2.0277 in U.S. dollars and $1.9973 in Newfoundland dollars, so these coins contained their full face value in gold.

Cod fishing off the Newfoundland coast.

As with the minor coins, the Royal Mint prepared patterns for the emission of Newfoundland circulating gold coins. There are two 1865-dated patterns, both struck in the metal-of-intent for the coin, and their designs differ significantly from those of the circulation-strike coins, an example of which is shown below.

The 1865 circulation-strike Newfoundland $2 gold coin, the first date of this type minted for circulation. Note that the denomination is indicated in three different ways—dollars, cents, and pence—as an aid to currency conversion for the Newfoundland populace. This is a unique aspect of these coins.

One of these patterns is unique and the other has two known examples. Both were actually struck in the metal intended for the circulation pieces, unlike the 1864 copper pattern. In the example illustrated at the beginning of this essay, the design differs dramatically from that of the circulation-strike coins. On the obverse the portrait of Queen Victoria is smaller than on the coins intended for circulation, and it is surrounded by a circle of beads. This portrait is as it appears on the 5-cent coins of Newfoundland, or earlier on the coin of the same denomination from Canada dated 1858, or on the 1862 and 1864 5-cent coins from New Brunswick. The lettering on the pattern is in block type on both obverse and reverse. There is only a single example known of this rarity. It currently resides in a private Canadian collection but was earlier in the Brand, Farouk, Norweb, and Temple collections. The first public offering of this coin, also cataloged as Bowman 34 by Fred Bowman in his book on Canadian patterns, was in the Spink Circular of May 1910, where it was offered for £10, quite a high price at the time. By comparison, in the same circular Spink offered an 1889 Australia sovereign in FDC (fleur de coin—a perfect coin in the same condition as when it left the Mint) for £2, a coin with a current valuation of US$40,000. The 1865 pattern was acquired by Virgil Brand from Spink in 1910 and later found its way into the Farouk and Norweb collections. In 1996 it sold for US$39,600 in the Bowers and Merena Norweb Canadian auction, and later in a 2014 Heritage auction for US$102,815, currently the highest price paid at auction for any Newfoundland coin.

The pattern 1865 Newfoundland $2 coin in the Bank of Canada's National Currency Collection (Bowman 33). The obverse is identical to circulation-strike issues, but the reverse is in block type as in Bowman 34.

The other 1865 $2 gold pattern (Bowman 33, illustrated above) has two known examples. One is housed in the National Currency Collection of the Bank of Canada, the other in the British Museum. The coin has the identical reverse design (including the block type) as Bowman 34, while the obverse is the same as on the normal circulation strikes. As far as is known, neither of the two Bowman 33 coins has ever appeared publicly at auction.

NO. 95 1871-H 10 CENTS

Standards—**Weight:** 2.27 grams. **Composition:** Silver. **Diameter:** 18.05 millimeters. **Edge:** Reeded. **Designer:** Leonard C. Wyon. **Rarity:** Perhaps only two known.

Newfoundland's 1871-H 10-cent coin is very rare, with some estimates stating that only two examples are known, both in the National Currency Collection of the Bank of Canada. It is also unique among Canadian coins, as there is a Heaton Mint "H" mintmark on both the obverse and reverse. How did this coin come to be?

In 1871 no 10-cent pieces were struck for Newfoundland at either the Royal Mint or Heaton. The Royal Mint provided 10-cent coins for the colony in 1870 (no mintmark) and Heaton minted 1872 10-cent coins with its standard "H" mintmark on the *obverse* of the coin. For Canada, *both* Heaton and the Royal Mint provided 10-cent pieces for 1871, with no mintmark on the Royal Mint issue but an "H" on the *reverse* for those struck at the Heaton Mint in Birmingham. The fact that both mints produced 10-cent coins for Canada in 1871 lies at the heart of the reason this odd coin exists. It is clearly a "mule error," using an obverse die from Newfoundland (mintmark on the obverse) and a reverse die from Canada (mintmark on the reverse). The error must have occurred at the Heaton Mint because no 1871-H normal Newfoundland 10-cent coins were struck in that year by Heaton, but the 1871-H Canadian 10-cent coin struck there is the most common coin in this series from the Victorian era, with 1,870,000 pieces produced. The staff at the Heaton Mint likely thought they were striking Canadian 10-cent coins and paid little attention to a Newfoundland obverse die that was inserted by mistake.

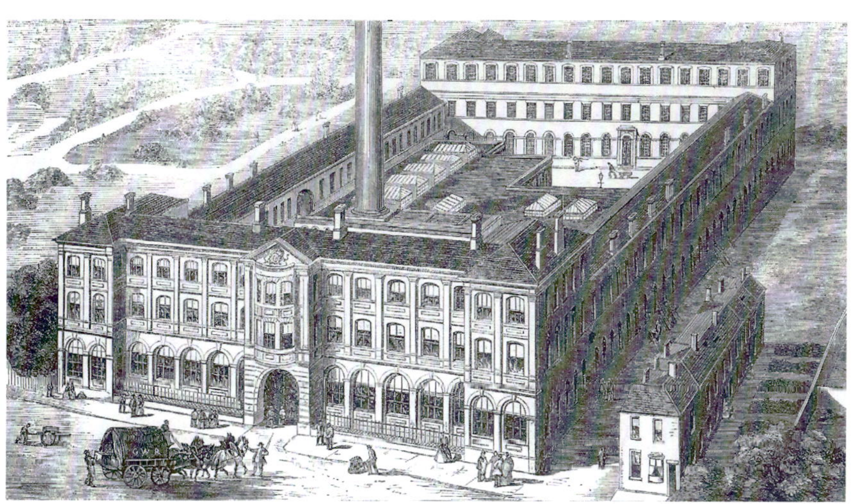

The Heaton Mint in 1862.

Given that this coin has a Newfoundland obverse and a Canadian reverse, there is some debate over whether it is part of the Newfoundland or Canadian series. Nowhere does it say Canada on the coin, however, so it has commonly been considered part of the Newfoundland series of Victorian 10-cent pieces.

In his 1894 book, *Illustrated History of Coins and Tokens Relating to Canada*, P.N. Breton claimed that he knew of only a single specimen that had been found in circulation by R.W. McLachlan. I have not been able to located any recorded public sales of the coin, so an estimate of its value is not possible except by way of a current advertisement from a Canadian East Coast dealer who is offering "upwards of $100,000" for it.

No. 98 1872-H 20 Cents

Standards—**Weight:** 4.713 grams. **Composition:** 0.925 silver, 0.075 copper. **Diameter:** 23.19 millimeters. **Edge:** Reeded. **Designers:** Leonard C. Wyon. obverse; Horace Morehen, reverse. **Rarity:** Not a particularly rare coin, but scarce (unique?) in the condition illustrated here.

In 1978 I published an article in the *CN Journal* (the journal of the Canadian Numismatic Association, now the Royal Canadian Numismatic Association). I was living in Sweden on sabbatical at the time and had stopped in at the British (London) and Ashmolean (Oxford) Museums while in England, on my way to Uppsala. I cataloged the Canadian and Newfoundland collections of both institutions and was absolutely smitten by the beauty of some of the coins I saw. Many pieces, particularly in the Ashmolean collection, had not been handled very much. This is not so much the case today, when many coins exhibit handling marks and some have even been switched for more common or lower-grade examples. In the late 1970s a large proportion of the two museums' collections was absolutely pristine, with beautiful toning in the various colors that silver can assume when exposed to air.

The Ashmolean Museum in Oxford.

I commented in my 1978 article that the coin series that impressed me most with its artistic beauty, stunning design, and overall quality of execution was the set of 15 Newfoundland 20-cent coins from the Victoria era. On these coins, each design element stood out dramatically, including the wreath in the monarch's hair and the details in the youthful bun tied at the back of her head. This was the highest art in coinage design and fabrication, and it beautifully exhibited the genius of Leonard Wyon. Samples of these coins from the Heaton Hoard, of which the one featured here is certainly an example, have retained all the original beauty envisioned by the designers.

This coin is the finest known of the type in the PCGS population report, the only one grading MS-68. It is practically flawless and possesses a lovely grey-gold tone with highlights at various locations on both obverse and reverse. The strike is full and every detail of Leonard Wyon's magnificent design is fully on display. Even the details of the monarch's hair around her ear are sharply defined, avoiding a deficiency often seen on many other large coins with this portrait of the queen (see "First Coinage of the Province of Canada" on pages 26–28). The current PCGS population of this coin in all grades of Mint State is 13 examples, with all but one grading MS-65 or higher, reflecting the moderately large number of hoard coins, so it is not so rare even in very high grades. While lightly circulated examples can be obtained for less than US$200, examples such as the one illustrated on the previous page can command high prices. The Canadian Numismatic Company auction in June 2018 featured a stunning MS-67 example that required a winning bid of CAD$7,475 to take the coin home.

No. 71 1873-H 5 Cents

Standards—**Weight:** 1.18 grams. **Composition:** 0.925 silver, 0.075 copper. **Diameter:** 15.49 millimeters. **Edge:** Reeded. **Designer:** Leonard C. Wyon. **Rarity:** By far the rarest of the Newfoundland Victorian 5-cent coins.

The rarity of this coin can be judged by the number of examples currently in the population census. Only a single coin is listed in the PCGS population report: the coin illustrated here, an MS-64 example, earlier in the Norweb Collection. There is no record of a coin of this date in the Heaton Mint Archives (even though it bears an "H" mintmark), there is no example in the Royal Mint Museum, and none of the great Canadian collections earlier than the mid-1950s contained an example of it. So, what is the history behind this coin?

A plausible scenario was presented by R.C. Willey in a May 1991 article in the *CN Journal*. In 1872 the Heaton Mint had struck all the silver coinage for Newfoundland, inserting its "H" mintmark prominently on all these coins below the queen's bust, just above the second N in NEWFOUNDLAND, as can be seen on the 5-cent coin pictured here. It is important to note that between 1872 and 1876, if Heaton struck the coin for Newfoundland, the mintmark was placed on the obverse. In 1882 Heaton was again called upon to strike the coins for Newfoundland, but this time the mintmark was placed on the reverse of the coins. In late 1872 or early 1873, after using the dies to strike the 1872 coins (with an "H" on the obverse), Heaton returned the dies to the Royal Mint. Willey's hypothesis is that the Royal Mint then used the same obverse dies to strike the 1873 coins by mistake—with the Heaton "H" on the obverse. If it had been a few years later, this accident would probably not have occurred, as the mintmark would have been on the reverse and visible with the date. It is not officially known how many were inadvertently struck with the "H" mintmark, but estimates are somewhere between 50 and 100.

In an October 2015 *CN Journal* article on the 1873-H 5-cent coin, Robert Forbes suggests an alternative theory in which the Heaton Mint actually struck the coin. In 1873 the Royal Mint contracted with Heaton to provide bronze blanks for the Newfoundland cent coinage for that year. The Heaton Mint's invoice for these blanks was about 10 percent too high, so the hypothesis is that Heaton must have delivered something in addition to the blanks—the 1873-H 5-cent coins, perhaps? From the amount of overcharge, Heaton could have struck and delivered about a thousand 5-cent coins to the Royal Mint. This suggestion, however, leaves open the question of why Heaton would have struck these coins without authorization, and then, having done so, turned around and charged the Mint for them?

This coin rarely appears at auction, and when it does it is almost always in circulated condition. A VF-30 example reached US$3,055 in 2013, and an AU-53 coin garnered US$9,775 in 2010. The Belzberg/Norweb coin—the finest known—realized US$16,100 in a January 2003 auction.

No. 83 1874 Specimen 50 Cents

Standards—**Weight:** 11.78 grams. **Composition:** 0.925 silver, 0.075 copper. **Diameter:** 29.85 millimeters. **Edge:** Reeded. **Designer:** Leonard C. Wyon. **Rarity:** Only two Specimen strikes known.

The Newfoundland 50-cent coin was not part of the original emission of coinage for the colony in 1865. It was not until 1870 that this denomination was struck for circulation. The portrait of Her Majesty, designed by Leonard Wyon, is unique for this denomination: no other colony, or Britain itself, used a similar rendition of Queen Victoria. The 50-cent coin proved to be particularly popular in Newfoundland, being the largest silver denomination available, which is one reason that Mint State examples of all dates are rather scarce.

Among the 50-cent coins of Newfoundland, the 1874 is by no means the scarcest. Eighty thousand were struck for circulation in that year, about average for the colony during the Victorian era. However, after the 1894 failure of Newfoundland's two major banks, the Commercial Bank and the Union Bank, a serious crisis developed. The $2 coins, the highest denomination available and made of gold, were likely hoarded extensively. This put additional pressure on the 50-cent coins to meet much of the commercial needs of the colony, making Uncirculated coins of this denomination scarce. In fact, three dates—1873, 1874, and 1888—have no circulation-strike Uncirculated examples at all in the population reports.

It was therefore all the more remarkable when two absolutely superb, mirror Proof Specimen examples of the 1874 50-cent coin appeared in the 1990s. They surfaced in England and both were initially graded SP-66. The pieces have a wonderful pedigree, which attests to their beauty and desirability. They have been in the Temple, Belzberg, and Cornerstone collections. Dr. John Temple, a sophisticated collector of Canadian coins and patterns, hailed from Franklin, Michigan. The husband-and-wife team of Sid and Alicia Belzberg of Toronto assembled one of the finest collections of Canadian and provincial coins, and it was sold for over US$3.1 million by Heritage Auctions in 2003. The Cornerstone Collection was assembled by the Rogozinsky family of Montreal and consisted solely of superb Specimen coins. One of the 1874 Specimen 50-cent pieces was owned by Jay Parrino, a prominent American coin dealer who once owned a 1913 U.S. Liberty Head 5-cent coin. Parrino's coin company was called The Mint, after The Mint casino in Las Vegas, where he apparently worked as a young man. He was certainly famous for owning some of the most expensive coins in the U.S. series.

In the Belzberg Sale (2003), one of the 1874 50-cent specimens (originally from Temple) sold for US$32,200, and the same coin was later listed at CAD$75,000 in the Cornerstone Collection (2019). It reappeared in a January 21, 2021, Heritage sale, where it went for US$60,000.

A Newfoundland fishing boat in 1872.

NO. 39 1880 GOLD SPECIMEN $2

Standards—**Weight:** 3.328 grams. **Net Weight:** Total weight 0.107 troy ounces, 0.0981 ounces pure gold. **Composition:** 0.9167 gold, 0.08333 copper. **Diameter:** 17.983 millimeters. **Edge:** Reeded. **Rarity:** Two examples known.

The Newfoundland $2 gold coins were issued for circulation in eight non-consecutive years between 1865 and 1888. The mintages were always modest; the total number produced for circulation was 92,500, with the smallest issue being 2,500 in the year 1880, making this date the rarest coin in the series.

The $2 gold coins of Newfoundland possess a number of unique features. The denomination is shown in three different ways on the reverse, a feature meant to help Newfoundlanders adapt to decimal coinage after almost 300 years of the British system of pounds, shillings, and pence. Newfoundland was also the only British colony in North America to have a gold coin minted for it. Thomas Graham, the master of the Royal Mint when the coinage was first being contemplated, approved of the plan for a gold coinage, as he felt it would help coinage remain in the colony after the fishing fleets had left in the fall. A scarcity of coinage was one of Newfoundland's constant problems in the early nineteenth century and was a real detriment to a successful economy. Graham suggested that the fineness of the $2 gold coinage should be 0.900, the contemporary U.S. value, instead of the British standard of 0.917. Perhaps he was anticipating closer ties between Newfoundland and the United States, something that almost came to pass during the Second World War, when thousands of young Newfoundland women married U.S. army personnel and closer economic ties between the two jurisdictions were contemplated.

Two dollars was a reasonably large amount of money in mid-nineteenth-century Newfoundland, where typical laborer's wages averaged about $1 per week (without board and lodging). The original plan to mint $1 gold coins (as in the United States) was deemed to be unreasonable because such a small-sized coin of relatively large value would be easy to misplace. The plan was to develop a $2 coin instead, one that was virtually the same size as the then-current 10-cent piece of Canada or the United States. Putting $2 worth of gold (of 0.917 fineness) into such a coin meant that it would be rather thin and subject to bending. The reader may wish to peruse the earlier essay on the 1865 $2 pattern gold coins (on pages 45–46) for more details on the physical characteristics of these coins.

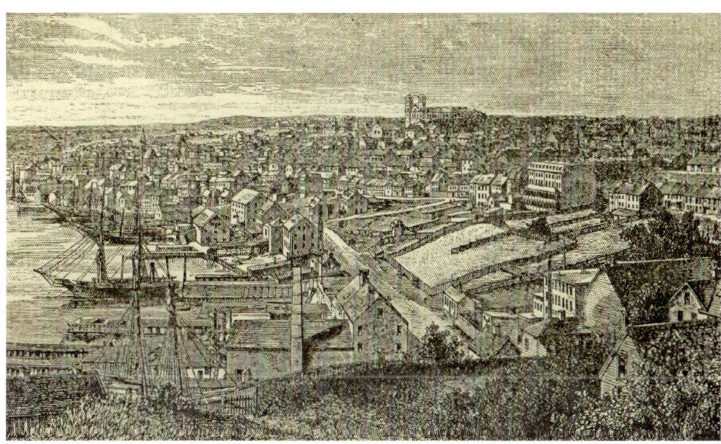

St. John's, Newfoundland, in 1885.

To obtain new coinage in the 1800s, the government of Newfoundland (and other colonies) would make a formal request to the Secretary of State for the Colonies, a member of the British cabinet, who would then contact the Lords Commissioners of the Treasury, who in turn would petition the Royal Mint for new coinage. As far as we know, these requests were never denied or altered. The Royal Mint incurred no monetary outlays, since the costs were borne entirely by the colony. (Of some importance for Canadians, the colonial secretary between 1882 and 1885 was Lord Stanley, who donated the trophy [the Stanley Cup] that is currently emblematic of professional hockey excellence.) This request process worked well in Newfoundland, which was able to acquire the coinage it requested from the Royal Mint. However, no coinage had been requested by the colony for the years 1877, 1878, and 1879, so perhaps the government of Newfoundland had forgotten the proper procedure. In 1880 Charles Fremantle, the master of the Royal Mint, received a coinage request directly from the Newfoundland government. Although he chastised the colony for this breach of protocol in a letter dated February 14, 1880, he acceded to the request, which included 2,500 \$2 gold coins, the smallest mintage by far in the series. The next smallest had been for the year 1872, when 6,000 coins were minted.

During the heyday of the British colonial era, the Royal Mint was apparently willing to produce variants of circulating coins in response to special requests from governments and individuals. One such example was the 1880 Newfoundland \$2 Specimen gold coin. The Mint did not normally strike Specimens of these coins, but it received a special order from the deputy master of the Royal Mint in Australia, V. Delves Broughton, for a sample of all colonial coinage that was struck at the Royal Mint in 1880. The reason for this was that the Australian government wanted to mount a numismatic display as part of the Sydney International Exhibition of 1879–1880. The shipment was enormous, weighing over 200 pounds, and Australia paid only face value for the coins.

An illustration of the Sydney International Exhibition in the *Illustrated Australian News*.

Part of the shipment comprised two complete sets of all the 1880 Newfoundland coins (1, 5, 10, 20, and 50 cents and \$2 in gold) produced by the Royal Mint. Presumably, two of each coin were requested so that both the obverse and the reverse of the coins could be exhibited. Fremantle, who was deputy master of the Royal Mint at that time, had the \$2 gold coin produced from a die that was not used to strike any circulation coins, as it was somewhat mismade. As can be seen in the image on the previous page, the last three letters of DOLLARS (ARS) on the reverse were set too high, and the second 8 in the date was punched over a 7. No 1880 \$2 gold coins struck for circulation purposes present these particular die characteristics (see the image below for such an example). After the Sydney International Exhibition, the coins found their way to the Victoria Museum in Melbourne. By then one of the \$2 gold coins had been sold by the museum; the other remains in the museum's collection to this day. There is thus only a single 1880 \$2 Specimen gold coin available to collectors.

An 1880 Newfoundland \$2 gold coin that was struck for circulation. Note the distinctly different die characteristics from the Specimen coin: ARS in DOLLARS is on the same level as DOLL, and the second 8 in the date is not punched over a 7.

The single traceable early public auction offering of the Specimen coin was in the Sotheby-Murdoch Sale of 1903, where it sold for £1 14s. This lot also included an 1865 Newfoundland \$2 Specimen gold coin. Since the face value of these coins was 8 shillings 4 pence, the lot sold for only about double the face value of the coins! The 1880 \$2 Specimen coin next appeared in the April 1937 Spink Circular, where it was listed for £3, and it was probably bought by the Norwebs. The last public auction in which this coin appeared was in the Bowers and Merena Norweb Canadian auction in 1996, so the Norwebs kept it in their collection for about 60 years. It was the fourth highest-priced coin in the Norweb Sale, realizing US\$70,400. Today this coin would have a valuation of at least US\$250,000 if it were put on sale.

As noted in the Bowers and Merena catalog of the Norweb collection (lot 688), John J. Ford Jr. commented that if he "were going to buy a single coin in the Norweb sale, it would be this one."

No. 85 1882-H Specimen Set

Standards (5 cents)—**Weight:** 1.18 grams. **Composition:** 0.925 silver, 0.075 copper. **Diameter:** 15.49 millimeters. **Edge:** Reeded. **Designer:** Leonard G. Wyon. **Rarity:** Probably about eight produced.

Standards (10 cents)—**Weight:** 2.36 grams. **Composition:** 0.925 silver, 0.075 copper. **Diameter:** 17.98 millimeters. **Edge:** Reeded. **Designer:** Leonard G. Wyon. **Rarity:** Probably about eight produced.

Standards (20 cents)—**Weight:** 4.71 grams. **Composition:** 0.925 silver, 0.075 copper. **Diameter:** 23.19 millimeters. **Edge:** Reeded. **Designer:** Leonard G. Wyon. **Rarity:** Probably about eight produced.

Newfoundland $2 gold coin had to be devalued by 1.4 percent, and high-denomination Newfoundland coinage in both silver and gold was subsequently hoarded, although there have been very few discoveries of such hoards.

The only verified hoard of $2 gold coins known to me surfaced in 2008 and consisted of just 16 examples, all dated 1885 and all in the lower grades of Uncirculated condition: MS-62 and MS-63. These coins were in the possession of the scion of a prominent Newfoundland family that owned the Palace movie theater in Corner Brook. The owner of the hoard believes that at least some of the gold coins were collected as admission to the movies in the 1930s and 1940s. This would have been remarkable and indeed unlikely, particularly as Canada had officially gone off the gold standard in October 1931 and the Newfoundland colony followed in December, so by the spring of 1932 paper money was no longer convertible into gold.

It is not unreasonable, however, that the coupon of this bond would have been redeemable in gold because when the bond was issued in 1930, the Newfoundland government could not have known that Newfoundland or other jurisdictions would go off the gold standard in 1931 or 1932. Certainly, notices would have been published stipulating that the interest on the bond could no longer be redeemed in gold. It is therefore very unlikely that the aforementioned hoard was assembled from movie ticket fees late into the 1930s; a more plausible scenario is that it was obtained from an individual who had hoarded gold after the banks failed, or from an individual who fortuitously redeemed a bond like this one before Newfoundland went off the gold standard. Regardless of the situation, the existence of the bond does indicate that the Newfoundland $2 gold coins were still in active circulation at least into the beginning of the 1930s.

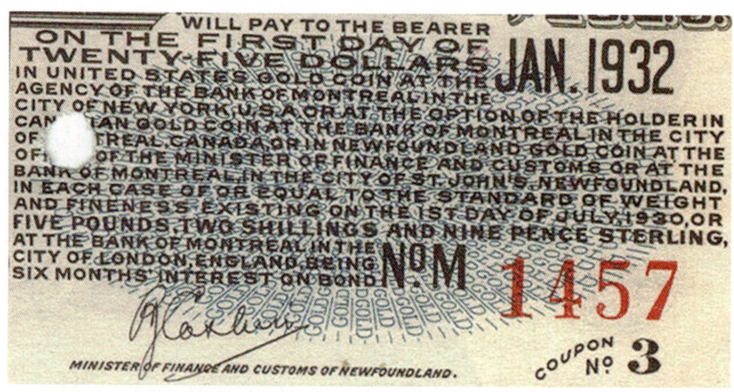

WILL PAY TO THE BEARER
ON THE FIRST DAY OF JAN. 1932
TWENTY-FIVE DOLLARS
IN UNITED STATES GOLD COIN AT THE
AGENCY OF THE BANK OF MONTREAL IN THE
CITY OF NEW YORK, U.S.A. OR AT THE OPTION OF THE HOLDER IN
CAN IAN GOLD COIN AT THE BANK OF MONTREAL IN THE CITY
OF TREAL, CANADA, OR IN NEWFOUNDLAND GOLD COIN AT THE
OF OF THE MINISTER OF FINANCE AND CUSTOMS OR AT THE
BANK OF MONTREAL, IN THE CITY OF ST. JOHN'S, NEWFOUNDLAND,
IN EACH CASE OF OR EQUAL TO THE STANDARD OF WEIGHT
AND FINENESS EXISTING ON THE 1ST DAY OF JULY, 1930, OR
FIVE POUNDS, TWO SHILLINGS AND NINE PENCE STERLING,
AT THE BANK OF MONTREAL IN THE
CITY OF LONDON, ENGLAND, BEING
SIX MONTHS' INTEREST ON BOND No. M 1457
MINISTER OF FINANCE AND CUSTOMS OF NEWFOUNDLAND.
COUPON No. 3

An expanded view of the various options available to the bondholder for redemption. All involve receiving gold coins denominated in U.S., Canadian, or Newfoundland dollars, except for the option of receiving pounds sterling.

In 1932 the price of gold was $20.69 per ounce, so redeeming this bond in "Newfoundland Gold Coin" would have yielded slightly more than 12 Newfoundland $2 gold coins, as each coin contained just under 0.1 ounces of gold. With common-date coins currently averaging around US$600 in About Uncirculated condition (AU), if the $25 bond had been redeemed in Newfoundland $2 gold coins, the $25 would be worth around US$7,200 today—equivalent to a return of 6.5 percent compounded annually for 90 years. This is, in fact, about the average rate of return over the past 90 years, so this would have been a decent but not outstanding investment. By contrast, taking the redemption in Canadian $5 gold coins (which was an option), whose value in About Uncirculated condition is around US$700 today, would have yielded only about US$3,500, not a very good return. Cashing the bond in United States $5 gold coins (also available to the bond holder), with a current value of less than CAD$600 each, would have yielded even less.

No. 91 1938 Cent

Standards—**Weight:** 3.24 grams. **Composition:** 0.955 copper, 0.030 tin, 0.015 zinc. **Diameter:** 19.05 millimeters. **Edge:** Plain. **Designers:** Percy Metcalfe, obverse; Walter J. Newman, reverse. **Rarity:** Not a rare coin, but of considerable historical importance.

A coin as common as the Newfoundland 1938 cent may seem an odd choice to include in a compilation of Canada's greatest coins. But this coin has a wonderful story to tell—"The Revenge of the Newfoundlanders"—and that in itself makes it worthy of inclusion in this anthology.

The story begins in 1864, when the coins for Newfoundland were first being designed. Queen Victoria herself had chosen a representation of a pitcher plant to appear on the colony's cent coin. The pitcher plant was *not* the official flower of Newfoundland at that time. Apparently, Newfoundland did not have an official floral emblem until 1990, when the Floral Emblem Act designated the pitcher plant as the provincial flower. These plants were common in Newfoundland, flourishing in its boggy soil. A pitcher plant is carnivorous. It traps rainwater in its tubular base and drowns and digests spiders and insects such as flies, moths, and mosquitos that show up there to drink.

An example of an 1865 Newfoundland cent graded MS-65RD by PCGS. There are four examples in this grade in the PCGS population report.

Pictured above is a regular-issue 1865 cent for Newfoundland with the reverse designed in 1864 by Horace Morehen. It features a rendition of a pitcher plant surrounding the crown and date. Morehen apparently attended a number of botanical exhibitions in and around London to see these plants for himself and help in his design. Nonetheless, it is obvious that the pitcher plant is not very well rendered here. It has an unnatural shape as a result of being forced to surround other elements of the design. For over 70 years, up to the end of the rein of George V in 1936, Newfoundlanders had to live with this quite inferior design.

In 1937 the Newfoundland government began considering switching from a large cent to a smaller one. From its first regular coinage in 1865 until 1936, Newfoundland had large cents of the same size and weight as those that Canada had produced only up to 1920. A small cent would be cheaper to produce and would also allow for a redesign of the pitcher plant. For the 1938 cent, a beautiful, elegant, and realistic version of the plant appeared on the reverse, engraved by Walter J. Newman, the principal engraver of the Royal Mint at the time. The eventual design was the result of extended negotiations between the Newfoundland government and the Royal Mint throughout 1938. The coin was produced late in 1938, bears no mintmark, and was shipped to the colony very late in the year. The remainder of the small-cent series for Newfoundland was coined in Ottawa to avoid the risk of an ocean crossing during the Second World War. All these (except for the 1940 and 1942 issues) have a small letter "C" for Canada on the reverse, to the right of the T in CENT, as illustrated below on a 1941 example. The last coinage in this series was in 1947, two years before Newfoundland joined Confederation.

Reverse of 1941 Newfoundland cent. Note the small "C" to the right of CENT.

The mintage of the Newfoundland 1938 cent was 500,000 pieces, so it is not particularly scarce. The coin shown at the beginning of this essay is the finest Specimen (specially struck, SP-67) known, and realized US$6,325 in a 2010 auction. An MS-65 red example can be obtained for around US$500.

Pitcher plants in Newfoundland.

NO. 70 1946-C 5 CENTS

Standards—**Weight:** 1.17 grams. **Composition:** 0.800 silver, 0.200 copper. **Diameter:** 15.49 millimeters. **Edge:** Reeded. **Designers**: Percy Metcalfe, obverse; G.W. DeSaulles, reverse. **Rarity:** Scarce, with a very low mintage.

As discussed in the previous essay, in 1938 Newfoundland replaced its large cent, which had been struck since the first coinage of the colony in 1865, with a small cent of the same weight, size, and composition as those struck for Canada. Newfoundlanders did not like the design of the reverse of the large cent, as it was a totally unrealistic version of the pitcher plant, by then the floral emblem of the province. At the same time, Newfoundland also considered replacing its small 5-cent silver coin with a nickel coin of the same physical characteristics as its Canadian counterpart. However, the government did not relish introducing two new coins simultaneously to a rather conservative populace, so the 5-cent coin remained basically the same except for the change in monarch. The last 5-cent coin had been minted in 1929, almost a decade before the first George VI coins were struck in 1938. In 1940 the size of the coin was reduced from 15.69 to 15.49 millimeters, and after 1944 the silver content was changed from sterling (0.925 silver) to 0.800 silver, bringing Newfoundland silver coinage in line with that of Canada. The last coin in this series was minted in 1947; after Newfoundland joined Confederation in 1949, all its circulating coins were those of Canada. All the George VI 5-cent coins, with the exception of one year, had a small "C" near the bottom of the reverse, indicating that they were struck at Canada's Ottawa Mint. The 1938 issue does not have this mintmark because it was produced at the Royal Mint in London.

Mintages were always modest for the Newfoundland George VI issues of this denomination, ranging from a high of 612,641 in 1941 to a low of 38,400 in 1947, except for the odd issue of 2,041 coins in 1946. Mint reports indicate that no 5-cent coins were actually struck in that year. In *A Charlton Standard Catalogue of Canadian Coins* it is suggested that those minted with this date were actually produced in 1947, the last year of production. Between ten and fifteen specially struck Specimen coins are also believed to have been produced.

Compared with other Canadian coins, the Newfoundland 1946 5-cent coin seems significantly underpriced. A very nice MS-63 example sold recently at auction for just under US$2,000, while a superb SP-67 coin reached US$7,800 in a 2019 Heritage auction. Compare this with a 1948 Canadian silver dollar, which sells for a comparable price despite a mintage about nine times that of the Newfoundland coin. Several recent MS-63 examples of the silver dollar reached around US$2,000 at auction, while a wonderful SP-67 coin reached US$17,625 in a 2014 Heritage auction. Newfoundland coins of comparable rarity consistently sell for significantly less than their Canadian cousins. A familiar adage is that Newfoundland coins are generally rare, and the only thing rarer are collectors of Newfoundland coins.

Chapter 4

Canadian Coins in the Victorian Era

In this extensive chapter (15 essays), I present a chronological discussion of Canadian coinage during the Victorian era. This is an extremely rich and artistic component of the Canadian series, running for 43 years between 1858 and 1901. Only the coinage of Queen Elizabeth II (1954 to at least 2022—68 years) covers a longer time span. Many of the great rarities in the Canadian series were minted during this era (1870 No LCW 50 cents, 1875-H coinage, 1889 10 cents, 1890-H 50 cents, and 1893 Round Top 10 cents), all of which are discussed in the following pages. The coinage of Canada during this era was blessed with the work of possibly one of the most talented engravers ever—Leonard C. Wyon—who designed and engraved virtually all of these coins.

No. 17 1870 No LCW 50 Cents

Standards—**Weight:** 11.62 grams. **Composition:** 0.925 silver, 0.075 copper. **Diameter:** 29.72 millimeters. **Edge:** Reeded. **Designer:** Leonard C. Wyon. **Rarity:** One of the great rarities in the Canadian series.

The first coins were struck for Canada in 1858. At that time it was the Province of Canada, as Confederation had not yet taken place. The denominations struck at the Royal Mint in London were the cent, 5 cents, 10 cents, and 20 cents. No higher denominations were produced, and it seems a serious omission that no 50-cent or $1 silver coins were introduced at the time. The United States, by contrast, was striking its Liberty Seated half-dollar and dollar silver coins during this era, as well as a full suite of five different denominations of gold coins.

Since the 1870 Victoria 50-cent coins were the first half dollars ever struck for Canada, new dies were required. Like most Canadian coins of the era, they were designed by Leonard Charles Wyon, the eldest son of William Wyon, chief engraver at the Royal Mint from 1828 until his untimely death in 1851. Well-taught by his father, Leonard took over the position at the young age of 25. Born on the grounds of the Royal Mint in 1826, he lived and breathed the activities at the Mint. He learned die engraving from his father, and by the time he was 16 years old he had already produced several medals that were eventually placed on display at the British Museum. In 1844, at only 18 years of age, he became the second engraver at the Mint, after his father.

The new 1870 Canadian 50-cent coin is an extremely handsome example of Wyon's great skill. The portrait of the crowned queen is youthful, although she was 51 at the time, and her crown is a small, elegant tiara. Her hair is in a bun at the back, held in place by a small ribbon. The reverse features St. Edward's crown at the top with maple boughs around the periphery, tied together at the bottom by a ribbon. There are two different obverse types for 1870 half dollars, one with the engraver's initials (LCW) at the truncation of the queen's neck just above the D in CANADA, the other without initials. The full coin illustrated above is the No LCW type, while the initials are seen below it in an enlargement of an example of the LCW obverse. There are other, more minor differences between these types (details in the crown, for example), but the main diagnostic is the presence or absence of the designer's initials.

The total mintage was 450,000 pieces. A very small, unknown number were of the No LCW type. The auction price differences between these types are a good indicator of their relative rarity. An MS-65 LCW example sold for US$25,000 in a Heritage auction in 2010. The Belzberg SP-64 plain-edge No LCW coin brought US$103,000 in 2003, while the example illustrated above, graded MS-64+, garnered US$70,500 at auction in 2016. Even lower-graded No LCW coins command strong prices—MS-62, US$22,800; EF-45, US$5,040; F-12, US$1,320—approximately reflecting the PCGS population statistics: three LCW coins in all grades of Uncirculated, with the highest being MS-64+, and 27 No LCW coins graded MS-61 to MS-65, with two of them MS-65.

No. 36 1875 No H 5 Cents

Standards—**Weight:** 1.16 grams. **Composition:** 0.925 silver, 0.075 copper. **Diameter:** 15.5 millimeters. **Edge:** Reeded. **Designer:** Leonard C. Wyon. **Rarity:** Likely only two examples known.

A small silver 5-cent coin for the Dominion of Canada first began circulating in 1870. Earlier, in the single year 1858, the Province of Canada had a virtually identical coin minted. This coin was half the weight of a Canadian 10-cent piece and was similar in size to the U.S. half dime that was minted intermittently between 1792 and 1873. This small

1792-dated coin is often considered to be the first circulation-strike U.S. coin made for commerce.

Virtually all the 5-cent coins of Canada dated 1875 have a small "H" on the reverse, as seen in the example below. This testifies that the coin was struck at the Heaton Mint (Ralph Heaton and Sons) in Birmingham, England, the largest sub-contractor to the Royal Mint. The mintage for this coin is not known, as a clerical error at the mint combined the mintage for the 1874 (also struck by Heaton) and 1875 5-cent pieces in the mint report, for a total of 1.8 million examples for the two years. What is clearly understood, however, is that the mintage for the 1875-H 5-cent coin was much smaller than for the 1874-H, as the former turns up much less frequently and is priced four to five times higher than the latter.

The reverse of an 1875 5-cent coin with the "H" mintmark below the bow.

The 1875 5-cent coin with no "H" mintmark is a great rarity in the Canadian series. I have been able to trace only two examples, one housed in the National Currency Collection of the Bank of Canada and the other from the Norweb Collection, which earlier came from the King Farouk Sale of 1954 (lot 2363). The Bank of Canada coin was purchased in 1973 from John J. Ford Jr. Images from both these sources confirm that they are not the same coin. John J. Pittman, who assembled one of the finest Canadian collections ever, did not have an example of this coin. Both known 1875 pieces are Specimen strikes. The Norweb coin sold for US$17,600 in 1996, and as far as is known, this is the only recent public auction sale registered for the coin. It did appear in 2019 in the fixed-price Cornerstone Collection offered by an East Coast Canadian dealer, indicating that the Rogozinsky family of Montreal had had it in their collection for at least part of the 23-year interval between 1996 and 2019. The asking price in the Cornerstone Collection was a cool US$95,000.

In the Norweb catalog, Dave Bowers discusses whether or not the 1875 No H 5-cent piece is properly called a pattern. He states that the *Charlton Catalogue* (DC-16) classifies it as a pattern, but this is not strictly correct. In *Charlton*, it is listed as a trial piece *after* the section on patterns. This seems like a reasonable classification. As Bowers states, "the presence or absence of a mintmark on a design does not constitute a pattern." Perhaps some new dies for this or a later date were being tested at the Royal Mint and a few Specimen trial pieces were struck before the mintmark was inserted. It may be relevant that 5-cent coins for Canada were struck in 1875 but then none were produced until 1880. After the hiatus, the Mint may have used a five-year-old die to test the striking procedures for such a small coin, resulting in this extremely rare emission.

No. 59 1875-H 10 Cents

Standards—**Weight:** 2.32 grams. **Composition:** 0.925 silver, 0.075 copper. **Diameter:** 18.03 millimeters. **Edge:** Reeded. **Designer:** Leonard C. Wyon.
Rarity: Among the top four rarest Victorian 10-cent pieces of Canada.

The year 1875 was an important one for Canada. In that year the Supreme Court of Canada was created and construction commenced on the Canadian Pacific Railway. The completion of Canada's first transcontinental railway fulfilled a promise to British Columbia, Canada's westernmost province, made in 1871 when it became part of the Dominion of Canada. The railway was the only mode of long-distance passenger travel in Canada for many decades and was critical to the opening up of Western Canada to trade, commerce, and settlement.

The Canadian Pacific Railway bridge over the Fraser River.

Around the time Canada was beginning its nation-building railway construction, the Royal Mint was suffering through a number of serious equipment failures. It had to stop production for 12 weeks in 1873, six weeks in 1874, four weeks in 1875, and over four months in 1876. During these difficult times, the Heaton Mint was called upon to help with the Royal Mint's coinage contracts. Heaton provided blanks and bars, struck a major portion of the colonial coinage, and provided South Africa with its first gold coin: the Burger pond of 1874. Except for the single year of 1882 in the Newfoundland $2 series, this was the only gold coinage produced by the Heaton Mint over its entire history. Because of the Royal Mint's difficulties, Heaton was asked to strike the silver coinage for Canada in 1874 and 1875, including the rare 1875-H 10-cent piece.

Remarkably, it is not known how many 10-cent coins were actually struck for Canada in 1875. What is known, of course, is that they were struck at the Heaton Mint (note the small "H" at the bottom of the reverse, below where the leaves are tied together in a bow). Heaton had also struck Canada's 10-cent pieces in 1874, and through a clerical error the mintages for both years were combined together, for a total of 1.6 million coins. The 1875-H 10-cent piece is considerably rarer and always commands a much higher price at auction than its 1874-H cousin. Presumably many fewer 1875-dated coins were actually produced.

Recently one of the highest-graded 1875-H 10-cent pieces (MS-64) sold forUS$20,400 in the 2019 Heritage Cook Sale. Even a Good (G-6) coin will typically command a bid of US$200. By contrast, one of the finest 1874-H 10-cent pieces known (MS-65) achieved a much lower price of US$4,320 in a 2020 Heritage auction. The PCGS population report indicates that there are 26 examples of the 1874-H coin in Mint State, with four having attained the highest grade of MS-66. The 1875-H entry indicates only 11 in Mint State, the loftiest being MS-65.

NO. 62 1875-H SPECIMEN 25 CENTS

Standards—**Weight:** 5.81 grams. **Composition:** 0.925 silver, 0.075 copper. **Diameter:** 23.62 millimeters. **Edge:** Reeded. **Designer:** Leonard G. Wyon. **Rarity:** Very rare, particularly if struck as a Specimen, as illustrated here.

One of the most transformative events in Canadian numismatics of the past century, or perhaps ever, was the release in the 1970s of hundreds of Canadian coins, either in Mint State or as specially struck Specimen coins, from the Heaton Mint Archives. The Specimen coins revealed all the intricate detail of the designers' genius in producing minor works of art that challenged those in any media from any period of history. The coins had obviously been treated with great care, perhaps lying untouched on velvet trays, and many were absolutely superb, with spectacular multicolored toning.

As mentioned earlier, the Heaton Mint was the largest subcontractor to the Royal Mint. With the expansion of the British Empire in the nineteenth century, there arose a need to provide coinage for many widely dispersed lands. Unable to keep up with the demand, the Royal Mint called on the services of Heaton, which was already providing coinage internationally, eventually minting currency for around 100 countries. For coinage in the British colonies, the Royal Mint provided the dies while Heaton contributed the metal and struck the coins. Coins struck by Heaton were often (but not always) identified by a small "H" somewhere on the coin (seen on the reverse, below the bow joining the maple leaves together). For Canada, I estimate that Heaton was involved in minting 79 distinct coinage types and dates both pre- and post-Confederation.

The 1875-H 25-cent coin of Canada is a rarity, although due to a clerical error that combined the totals for the 1874 and 1875 coinages in one mint report, it is not known exactly how many were produced. It is the highest-priced 25-cent piece of the Victorian era. A decent circulated coin in Fine (F-15) can be secured for an outlay of between US$400 and $700. In Uncirculated and Specimen grades it commands quite high prices, such as US$15,000 for one in MS-63. For the superb Specimen coin illustrated above (SP-68, the finest known), a buyer was willing to pay US$70,500 in a 2015 Heritage auction. There are a total of five Specimen coins graded SP-65 or better in the PCGS Population report. Mint state 1875-H 25-cent coins in high grade are perhaps even rarer, with only six listed by PCGS above MS-62. The finest of these (MS-64) sold at Heritage in 2010 (Canadiana Collection) for US$63,250.

NO. 44 1876-H PATTERN CENT

Standards—**Weight:** 5.67 grams. **Composition:** Bronze. **Diameter:** 25.5 millimeters. **Edge:** Plain. **Designer:** Leonard C. Wyon. **Rarity:** Only four examples known. Bowman 38.

The coins issued by the Province of Canada in pre-Confederation times were inherited by the Dominion of Canada in 1867, when Canada became independent of Great Britain. More than 10 million 1858 and 1859 copper cents had been struck for Canada, a remarkably large number for a population of only 3.4 million. By comparison, coinage of cent pieces for the remainder of the Victoria era (up to 1901) averaged only about 2 million coins per year. Not surprisingly, a large proportion of the 1858 and 1859 cent coinage remained unissued at the time of Confederation. Exhibiting sound fiscal policy, post-Confederation Canada decided to use up the remaining pre-Confederation coins, and the 1858 and 1859 cent pieces were slowly released into the commercial stream. It was not until 1876 that a need for a new issue of copper coins arose.

Queen Victoria in 1882.

The 1876-H pattern cent is an important coin in that it reveals some of the thinking of those making coinage decisions almost a decade after Confederation. The obverse is the same as on the 1858 and 1859 cents of the Province of Canada, so the government was clearly contemplating use of the same portrait on the post-Confederation coins. In 1858 Queen Victoria was 39 years old, and a design showing her as a very young woman might have been acceptable then. By 1876 however, she was 57 years old and apparently rather plump, and such a youthful portrait hardly seemed appropriate. For some reason, the Government of Canada originally wanted a portrait of a young monarch on its first post-Confederation copper coins, either simply for continuity and familiarity (Canadians were used to this coin) or to save money (no new dies would have to be cut—probably an unlikely reason).

In his recent book *Past and Nearly Perfect* Rob Turner points out that the Royal Mint had suffered a major machine failure in July 1876, and this is likely why the contract was given to the Heaton Mint. He lists four extant examples of this very rare pattern, one in the National Currency Collection of the Bank of Canada (the coin illustrated here) and three held in private collections.

No. 82 1876 No H Cent

Standards—**Weight:** 5.67 grams. **Composition:** 0.950 copper, 0.040 tin, 0.010 zinc. **Diameter:** 25.4 millimeters. **Edge:** Plain. **Designer and engraver:** Leonard C. Wyon. **Rarity:** Very rare in the Victoria cent series; roughly 20 examples known.

The only coins minted for Canada in 1876 were cent coins. The Royal Mint subcontracted this mintage to the Heaton Mint, with an agreement for Heaton to strike 4 million coins in bronze (a copper-tin-zinc alloy), the first time this denomination was struck for the Dominion of Canada. A large quantity of cents had been produced in 1859 for the Province of Canada (9,579,000 coins), after a modest emission of only 421,000 in 1858. The 1859 mintage proved to be much larger than was actually required, and most had not yet been distributed by 1867, the year of Confederation. Even after about 2 million pieces had been sold to the Province of New Brunswick in 1860 and the Bank of Upper Canada had offered them at a 20 percent discount off face value, many still languished in the bank's vaults in the early 1870s.

The Bank of Upper Canada.

In preparing the dies for the 1876 coin, the Royal Mint designer, Leonard C. Wyon, updated the portrait of the queen from the youthful one used in 1858 and 1859 (see image below) to a more mature one more closely aligned with her age, 57. The new obverse was a slightly modified version of that used on the 1869 Jamaican half penny and the Prince Edward Island cent of 1871. Additionally, the Province of Canada cent pieces of 1858 and 1859 had not found much favor with the public since they were rather thin and prone to bending, so the Mint increased the weight by about 25 percent without increasing the diameter, resulting in a coin that was thicker and about the same weight as the British half penny.

Heaton Mint records indicate that even though the coin bearing the "H" mintmark was dated 1876, it was actually minted in 1877. The reason for striking the No H Specimen coin has been hotly debated. An example appeared in the 1996 Norweb Sale by Bowers and Merena, whose catalogers suggested that it was a trial coin made for exhibition purposes. Others have theorized that the coins were meant to test the dies, which would be reasonable given that it was a new design with a thicker planchet. A most interesting idea came from Michael J. Hodder, again writing in the Norweb auction catalog: he suggests that the Royal Mint may have had some concerns about quality control at the Heaton Mint, so it struck a small number of 1876 cents with no mintmark in order to compare their quality with that of the Heaton products.

A census of extant 1876 No H cent pieces suggests that perhaps two dozen or so were produced. All are specially manufactured Specimen strikes. PCGS lists seven examples in its population report. The 1876 No H cent in the 1996 Norweb Sale realized a modest US$2,970 for an SP-64 example.

The obverse of an 1859 cent exhibiting a youthful portrait of Her Majesty (left). This was changed to the more mature portrait seen at right.

No. 74 1884 Specimen Cent

Standards—**Weight:** 5.67 grams. **Composition:** 0.95 copper, 0.04 tin, 0.01 zinc. **Diameter:** 25.4 millimeters. **Edge:** Plain. **Designer:** Leonard C. Wyon. **Rarity:** Very rare; may be unique in collectors' hands.

The story of the 1884 Specimen cent of Canada provides an example of what *not* to do in numismatics.

The coin pictured here is a very rare (perhaps even unique in collectors' hands) Royal Mint Specimen coin with full mirror surfaces. Two other, non-collectable examples of this specimen exist, one in the Royal Mint Museum in Wales and the other in the British Museum. The coin has a lovely red and brown coloration, with all features very sharply detailed. When it appeared in the Eric P. Newman Collection, Part III, in 2014, fierce bidding drove the price to a very healthy US$55,812.50. The coin also has a wonderful pedigree, which includes Colonel E.H.R. Green, Newman, and B.G. Johnson. It was graded Specimen-65 Red Brown by Numismatic Guaranty Corporation (NGC).

The same coin, although now almost entirely unrecognizable as such, appeared in a Heritage auction in August 2019, only five years later. It is pictured above. It had been harshly cleaned and was now graded UNC Details (Cleaned) by PCGS. The auctioneer set a starting bid for this fantastic rarity at only US$150. However, there were enough bidders in the audience who understood the coin's rarity to drive it to a final price of US$6,000, a huge evaluation for such an impaired coin.

This is the same coin that is pictured above. Sometime between 2014 and 2019, the coin was badly cleaned, reducing its value by a factor of about ten.

Colonel E.H.R. Green was the fabulously wealthy son of famous Wall Street investor Hetty Green, and a compulsive collector.

The buyer of the coin at the 2014 Newman auction obviously decided that he did not like its color and so cracked it out of the NGC holder, cleaned it very badly, and had it re-slabbed by PCGS. That grading company took full account of the damage that had been done, clearly stating this on the holder.

To destroy a part of history like this is almost criminal. All collectors of coins, stamps, art, and other collectibles of historic interest are only custodians of these treasures for a short period of time. It is their duty to preserve them as well as they can and pass them on to the next generation of collectors to enjoy.

No. 65 1884 10 Cents

Standards—**Weight:** 2.33 grams. **Composition:** 0.925 silver, 0.075 copper. **Diameter:** 18.03 millimeters. **Edge:** Reeded. **Designer and engraver:** Leonard C. Wyon. **Rarity:** Among the top three rarest coins in the Victorian 10-cent series.

The 1884 10-cent piece is among the rarest of all Canadian coins of this denomination in high grade. In the Victorian series, it is about as rare as the 1875-H and the 1889 and 1893 Round Top coins, and it is comparable to the George V 1913 Broad Leaves, but, as all 10-cent pieces do, it fades in comparison with the 1936 Dot coin, of which only about four are known.

Victorian 10-cent pieces were minted by the Royal Mint for the Province of Canada in 1858 and then in 1870 and 1871. In 1871 the Heaton Mint also coined 10-cent pieces for Canada, and from then until 1883 it was the only source of this denomination for Canada, although the denomination was not minted every year. In 1884, for the first time in 13 years, the Royal Mint produced the 10-cent pieces for Canada, minting only 150,000 examples, the smallest number *ever* for this denomination. This makes the 1884 10-cent coin a genuine rarity in the Canadian series.

The coin was rather sloppily produced by the Royal Mint. As seen on the 1884 coin below, all the digits in the date are "leaning" towards the right. Such imperfection was more or less standard fare for the Mint. In the image of the 1894 coin below, it is equally sloppy, perhaps even more so. The 1 again leans to the right, and the Mint employee used too large a punch for the 9 and 4.

Digits in the date leaning right in an 1884 and an 1894 10-cent coin produced by the Royal Mint.

The total certified population of this coin by PCGS (January 2022) is 88, with 13 in various grades of Uncirculated. There is one MS-66 example, and an additional coin in MS-65, and six in MS-64. The finest known example (then graded MS-65 by PCGS) appeared most recently at a Heritage auction in 2012 and was earlier in the famous Canadiana auction (2010) carried out by Heritage. It realized US$34,500 in the Canadiana Sale and attracted a winning bid of US$31,050 two years later.

A harshly cleaned example of the rare 1884 10-cent coin. The coin appears almost pristine and would likely have graded high in the MS category, attracting a strong bid at auction, had it not been badly tampered with.

There is one example of a tragedy involving an 1884 10-cent piece, similar to that which befell the 1884 Specimen cent discussed previously. In a 2019 Heritage auction, a high-grade 1884 10-cent coin was up for sale. It was graded as UNC Details (Cleaned) and described thus: "Extremely sharp with needle-fine details, lustrous and appealing despite the grade." Remarkably, the coin attracted a winning bid of US$6,000. Imagine what the price would have been had someone not tried to improve the coin with a cleaning!

No. 96 1885 5 Cents

Standards—**Weight:** 1.167 grams. **Composition:** 0.925 silver, 0.075 copper. **Diameter:** 15.5 millimeters. **Edge:** Reeded. **Designer:** Leonard C. Wyon. **Rarity:** About average rarity for the Victoria 5-cent series.

Above are images of the reverses of two different Canadian 1885-dated 5-cent coins. The obverses of both coins are identical to that seen in the example illustrated at right. Before reading any further, examine the images above and see if you can find any differences between them in the strike or design of the coins (not in the toning or number of abrasions). There is an important distinction, but it is subtle and difficult to see. At the end of this essay, an enlargement of the relevant area of the coins and a short discussion is provided. But first, a little background.

The obverse of the 5-cent coin shown at the left above. The two coins shown above have identical designs for their obverses.

In the second of the two images below, the 5 in the date is punched over a digit beneath it. The first mention of this die variety, as noted by J.C. Levesque in a 1979 article in the *CN Journal*, was in the New Netherlands Coin Company's 58th auction catalog (September 22–23, 1964). Listed as lot number 306, the coin was described as "1885 small 5 recut, the 5 in the date is boldly doubled-punched, the first figure having been cut too high and too far to the left." The official number of 1885 5-cent coins minted is 1 million. With 15 reverse dies used by the Royal Mint to strike these coins, only 6.7 percent (or about 67,000) of all 1885 5-cent coins were struck from each die. Since there was almost certainly only a single die that contained this re-punched 5, we can take this as the number of 1885/5 (1885, 5 Over 5) 5-cent coins minted, making it an important rarity in this Canadian Victorian series.

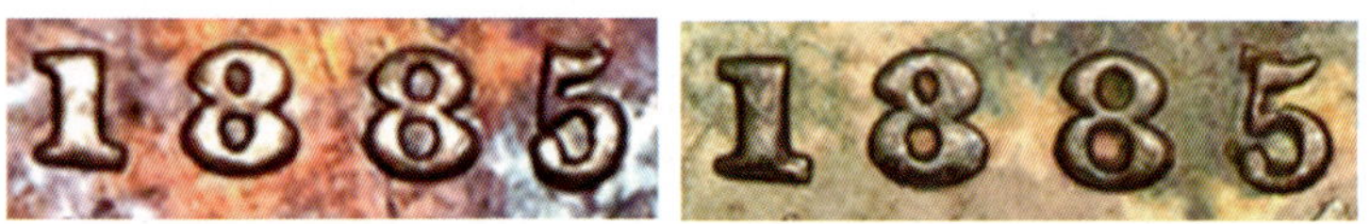

Enlargements of the reverses, focusing on the dates in the two 5-cent coins shown at the beginning of this essay. Note the presence of a digit underneath the 5 on the right coin.

The current population of these coins is of course very much smaller than the estimate of 67,000. The PCGS population report lists a total of 149 coins in all grades, with 15 1885/5 examples. This works out to 10.1 percent, which is in reasonable agreement with the 6.7 percent expected. In all grades of Uncirculated coins the agreement is even better, with an 1885/5 population of four out of a total PCGS Uncirculated sample of 70, or 5.7 percent.

In a 2010 Heritage auction, the 1885/5 coin (MS-64) illustrated here sold for US$4,168.75, compared with a top bid of US$3,220 for a similarly graded 1885 with no re-punching. Clearly the auction results do not reflect the rarity of the re-punched date.

Below is a magnified view of the region around the date on the two 1885 5-cent coins featured in this essay. Without much imagination, it is possible to see that there is something under the 5 on the right coin. This is New Netherlands' mis-punched 5, later corrected with an overpunch. Hence, the correct title for this essay should be "Canada 1885/5 5 Cents."

NO. 92 1887 25 CENTS

Standards—**Weight:** 5.81 grams. **Composition:** 0.925 silver, 0.075 copper. **Diameter:** 23.62 millimeters. **Edge:** Reeded. **Designer:** Leonard C. Wyon. **Rarity:** Arguably the most difficult date in the Victorian 25-cent series in Uncirculated grade.

If we were to take a poll of knowledgeable Canadian numismatists regarding the most difficult Victorian 25-cent piece to acquire in Mint State, the likely answer would be an 1889 example. It has the smallest mintage in the series at 66,340, followed by the 1887 and 1893 dates at 100,000 each. There are many minor varieties among the Canadian Victorian quarters, such as the placement of the digits in the date and overdates. The 1887 date alone has at least six. (I don't consider these here, however.) Some would argue that the 1875-H is the scarcest, as it always brings high prices at auction despite its mintage of 1 million coins, but the data support the 1887 quarter as the winner.

As of February 2021, the PCGS population report showed that the 1875-H has six coins in various grades of Mint State, the 1887 has three, the 1889 has seven, and the 1893 has eleven. It is difficult to compare auction prices, as not many high-grade examples of these coins have sold publicly in recent years. A gorgeous 1875-H MS-64 example sold for an astonishing US$66,250 in 2010. This was the highest-graded example of this date at the time, but there are now three others at this level (none higher).

The 1887 population consists of an MS-65 example (the coin illustrated above), an MS-65+, and an MS-62. The MS-62 example has seen the auction block twice in the past 20 years. In 2006 it was in an MS-61 PCGS holder, had a lovely olive-green patina, was quite attractive, and could boast that it was the only Mint State example in the population reports at that time. It attracted the strong winning bid of US$29,900 in a Heritage auction. In 2019 the coin appeared again at a Heritage auction, now in a PCGS MS-62 holder, but by this time it had likely been cleaned or wiped, and it took a bid of only US$11,100 to win the lot. Its most recent appearance was in 2020, again with Heritage, where it drew a successful bid of only US$7,800.

The 1889 25-cent piece, likely everyone's choice for the rarest Victorian quarter, has had several MS-63 appearances at recent auctions. One example realized US$13,800 in 2010, while an earlier auction in 2006 required a winning bid of US$14,950 for an equally graded example.

The 1893 quarter is distinguished by having the highest-graded example to have sold recently at auction. In 2010 a lovely MS-66 coin crossed the block for a solid US$34,500. A few years later, an International Coin Certification Service (ICCS) MS-64 example attracted a winning bid of US$5,288.

These are the data, then, for these four Victorian 25-cent coins. Readers can decide for themselves which they consider the rarest.

Queen Victoria.

No. 42 1889 10 Cents

Standards—**Weight:** 2.33 grams. **Composition:** 0.925 silver, 0.075 copper. **Diameter:** 18.03 millimeters. **Edge:** Reeded. **Designer:** Leonard C. Wyon. **Rarity:** One of Canada's rarest and most sought-after coins.

While the official mintage for the 1889 10-cent coin was 600,000 pieces, only the tenth-lowest for this Victorian series, most of these were probably dated 1888. Although we do not know exactly how many 1889 10-cent coins of Canada were actually produced, estimates seem to have converged on 10,000–20,000, making it by far the lowest mintage for any regular-issue 10-cent coin of Canada.

Very early on, it was appreciated by some that this was likely to be a very rare coin. In the Bowers and Merena Norweb catalog of Canadian coins (November 15, 1996), the catalogers quote the Canadian Antiquarian issue of January 1890, only a year after the coin was minted, as follows: "Specimens of the coinage of 1889 are still scarce in this vicinity (Montreal) indicating that it must have been issued from some of the distant offices of the receiver-general." But this analysis seems to have had little effect on the collecting community, and because the coin was not recognized as a rarity, very few were saved. By 1950 only 16 pieces had been accounted for and, as pointed out in the Norweb catalog, this was also the last year in which an example was found in circulation. At that time the coin was valued at only a few dollars in most catalogs. This all changed as its rarity was recognized, and in 1964 an Uncirculated example brought CAD$3,300 in the Canadian Numismatic Association Sale held in Halifax, Nova Scotia. The coin is so rare and desirable that it is one of the few coins to have been stolen from the British Museum collection. The slot that was meant to house this coin—and likely did so for many years after the museum obtained it from the Royal Mint around the time it was struck—has now had the original occupant removed and replaced with a circulated 1858 10-cent example.

The coin illustrated above is by far the finest known example (PCGS MS-66), with the next highest being a single coin graded MS-64 and an additional four examples in MS-63. The MS-66 coin sold most recently for US$86,250 as part of the Canadiana Collection offered by Heritage Auctions in January 2010. Several of the MS-63 examples have also recently crossed the auction block at around the US$20,000 price level.

Ambassador and Mrs. R. Henry Norweb both were discerning collectors of valuable coins, including many rarities like the 1889 10-cents. Their son Henry Jr. inherited the coin-collecting gene.

No. 14 1890-H 50 Cents

Standards—**Weight:** 11.62 grams. **Composition:** 0.925 silver, 0.075 copper. **Diameter:** 29.72 millimeters. **Edge:** Reeded. **Designer:** Leonard C. Wyon. **Rarity:** Very rare and key to the Victorian 50-cent series.

The Victorian 50-cent series of Canada abounds with rarities, especially in high grades. For the entire series, there are only 104 examples graded MS-63 or better at PCGS, and of these a paltry 17 have been graded MS-65 or better, with a single MS-67 example dominating the series. This last is an 1871-H example and very probably was part of the Heaton Hoard, released by that mint in 1974 and 1975.

Only six Victorian 50-cent issues have mintages in excess of 100,000 pieces, and four had 50,000 or fewer coins issued. The smallest mintage, a mere 20,000, was for the 1890 coin. This coin was manufactured not at the Royal Mint but at the Heaton Mint, attested to by the "H" on the reverse, below the ribbon. The coin shown above can likely be traced to the Heaton Hoard, as records indicate that two high-grade examples of this date were included in the release. The Heaton Mint had retained a rather large sample of coinage that it had minted for various countries, including Australia, British West Africa, China, Colombia, and Canada. The coins were generally in pristine condition, and Heaton retained these for almost a hundred years before selling most of them to the Paramount International Coin Corporation, which dispersed them into the wider collector market.

There are a number of minor variations on the obverse of Victorian 50-cent coins. These varieties are well described in the *Charlton Standard Catalogue, Canadian Coins* (for example, see pages 181–184 in the 74th edition from 2021). The 1890-H obverse is distinguished by having a large crease at the corner of the monarch's mouth (easily seen in the image above), resulting in the appearance of a puffy cheek.

The PCGS population reports indicate that there are only three Mint State examples extant: one each in MS-64, MS-65, and MS-66. The illustrated example, graded MS-66, is the finest known of this exceedingly rare date and has no known records of public sales. Any example of an 1890-H 50 cents usually leads to competitive bidding at auction. A lowly VG-10 example reached US$881.25 at a 2017 auction, while the third-finest known, an MS-64 example, sold for an impressive US$149,500 in the Heritage auction of the Canadiana Collection in 2010. The Canadian Numismatic Company holds the record as the highest price realized at auction for the 1890-H 50-cent piece, with an MS-65 achieving a winning bid of CAD$261,000 in their August 2019 sale.

Ralph Heaton, of the Heaton Mint.

No. 77 1891 Cent

Standards—**Weight:** 5.67 grams. **Composition:** 0.950 copper, 0.040 tin, 0.010 zinc. **Diameter:** 25.4 millimeters. **Edge:** Plain. **Designers:** Leonard C. Wyon, obverse; Leonard C. Wyon then George W. DeSaulles, reverse. **Rarity:** All varieties are scarce, with the Large Leaves, Small Date, variety being particularly so.

Three coins are shown above. All three have the common obverse shown at the top left. The coin whose reverse is at the top right is Large Leaves, Large Date. The coin at the bottom left is Large Leaves, Small Date. The coin at the bottom right is Small Leaves, Small Date. The best way to determine these varieties is to examine the 9 in the date—in the Small Date varieties, there is a greater separation between it and the preceding 8. The Small Leaves varieties have a better definition within the veins of the leaves, and the connecting vine is also reduced in width.

The first large cents were struck for the Dominion of Canada in 1876. These were manufactured at the Heaton Mint using dies prepared at the Royal Mint. The portrait of Her Majesty was completely updated from the Province of Canada issues of 1858 and 1859, showing a more mature monarch wearing a diadem instead of laurel wreaths. By contrast, the reverse displays only minor modifications from the earlier issues. These differences involve the size and placement of the leaves around the reverse rim of the coin, and the size of the numbers in the date.

On the coins minted between 1876 and 1882, the same reverse as on the Province of Canada issues was employed, except for repairs to minor defective areas in the wreath. In 1884 a somewhat modified reverse was used. The main difference was that the leaves on the reverse were made larger and the detail within the leaves made less distinct. With their increase in size, some of the leaves now touched the denticles as well as the vines. These features are nicely illustrated by the reverse of the coin at the top right above. The use of this Large Leaves reverse continued into 1891, when a number of additional changes were introduced. There were now two versions of the date: a Large Date variety, as had been used previously (top right), and a Small Date variety (bottom left and bottom right). In addition, the Mint reworked the dies and produced a Small Leaves variety, where the leaves did not touch the denticles or vines and had better definition within them, making for a more attractive design. All three of these designs were used in the same year. The result was a dizzying number of varieties for the collector to consider, especially since there were also two obverses used (I do not consider the obverse variations here, since they are rather minor).

There is no information on the number of coins struck for each reverse design. What is known is is that the total mintage for all varieties was 1,452,000 coins, at the low end but not extreme for cent coins of that era. Of the three reverse designs, the Large Leaves, Small Date, is the rarest. In Mint State Red, there is only a single coin in the PCGS population report (MS-64RD), while the Large Leaves, Large Date, variety has ten (MS-63 to MS-65) and the Small Leaves, Small Date, variety has nine (MS-64 to MS-65). All three varieties appeared in the 2003 Heritage Belzberg auction, providing a good calibration of relative values. Both the Small Leaves, Small Date, and Large Leaves, Large Date, varieties were represented by PCGS MS-65RD examples and attracted bids of US$2,070 and US$2,185, respectively. The rarest variety (Large Leaves, Small Date) was the solo finest (MS-64RD), and a bid of US$3,680 was required to win the lot.

NO. 84 1892 50 CENTS

Standards—**Weight:** 11.62 grams. **Composition:** 0.925 silver, 0.075 copper. **Diameter:** 29.72 millimeters. **Edge:** Reeded. **Designer:** Leonard C. Wyon.
Rarity: Rare in the Victorian 50-cent series; only two Uncirculated examples in the PCGS population report.

The Canadian Victorian 50-cents series did not begin until 1870. No coins were struck for the Province of Canada, likely because 50 cents in mid-nineteenth-century Canada was a considerable sum with a buying power equivalent to about CAD$20 today, hence the coin would have been unlikely to see wide circulation. Just before Confederation, the population of the Province of Canada (Upper and Lower Canada) was 2.5 million. By 1870, a few years after Canada was formed, the total population had jumped to 3.5 million, due in part to the addition of five new provinces, and a more extensive set of coinage was required to satisfy commerce. Even so, the 50-cent coin was never produced in large numbers during the Victorian era because demand remained low. In some years none were minted at all. The coin was produced for Canada from 1870 to 1872, followed by a hiatus of almost ten years until the next emission in 1881. After this mintage (from the Heaton Mint), none would be made until 1888, followed by two-year intervals for the next six years (1890, 1892, 1894). Production averaged only about 120,000 examples in the 12 years in which the coins were produced. This denomination remained the highest-value silver coinage of Canada until silver dollars were first produced in 1935.

There are a number of interesting die varieties in the queen's portrait among the Victorian 50-cent coins. At least four distinct portraits have been identified, which revolve around the characteristics of the queen's cheek, the shape of her upper lip, and how the lower eyelid connects to the upper eyelid. On the 1892 emission there is a deep crease near her mouth and the cheek is puffy. All these features can be seen in the image above. There are also variations as to the presence or lack thereof of a shamrock behind the first jewel in the queen's crown. Note on the 1892 image that the shamrock is present, but on the 1870 No LCW example shown on page 61 the shamrock is absent. The shamrock is there on the 1870 With LCW coins. A nice presentation of all these varieties with images can be seen on a website developed by the Saskatoon Coin Club (see bibliography).

The most celebrated rarity among the Victorian 50-cent issues of Canada, as discussed earlier, is the 1890-H coin, with a minuscule mintage of only 20,000 examples. There are only three coins graded as Uncirculated by PCGS (one each in MS-64, MS-65, and MS-66). By contrast, the 1892 50-cent emission was a robust 151,000 coins, the third highest for the entire series. However, its Mint State population at PCGS is only two examples: an MS-62 piece and the spectacular MS-65 coin illustrated above. The latter coin attracted a winning bid of US$86,250 in the same auction where the 1890-H appeared. Most of the 1892 production likely went directly into circulation after the lean years in 1888 (60,000 minted) and 1890, making Uncirculated examples extremely rare. The 1890 and 1892 coins have the same total populations across all grades at PCGS (76 examples).

When the illustrated 1892 example was auctioned in 2010, the cataloger commented that the coin could potentially be a special Specimen strike given its prooflike surfaces. If this speculation is correct, the Mint State population of the 1892 50-cent piece is reduced to a single MS-62 example, making it the scarcest Victorian 50-cent date in Mint State.

No. 21 1893 10 Cents, Flat Top and Round Top 3

Standards—**Weight:** 2.33 grams. **Composition:** 0.925 silver, 0.075 copper. **Diameter:** 18.03 millimeters. **Edge:** Reeded. **Designer:** Leonard C. Wyon. **Rarity:** The Flat Top variety is moderately scarce; the Round Top variety is a major rarity.

Dies that are used to strike coins have a limited lifetime. Immense pressure is applied to force a design into a planchet (often hundreds of tons per square inch). There are two dies for each coin struck, one for the obverse and the other for the reverse. The reverse die, called the hammer die, is generally stationary. In the striking process, the obverse die is smashed into the hammer die with a metal disk (planchet) between them, and an inverse image of each die is transferred to the planchet, producing the coin. The hammer die suffers excess pressure in this process, and though made of hardened steel, even in the Victorian era, many eventually fail. This failure often takes the form of minute cracking, producing raised lines on the final coin. Mintage output was carefully monitored at the Royal Mint and any sign of die wear meant the die would be replaced with a fresh one.

By 1893 the Royal Mint had been striking 10-cent coins for the Dominion of Canada for 23 years, although there was not a coinage emission every year. For the 1893 coinage, two different obverse dies were manufactured. These differed only slightly from that of earlier years, but in the left image below the queen is portrayed with a slightly doubled chin, the details in her lips and eyes are less prominent, and the overall impression is that of an older monarch. A second obverse die (the right image below), produced after the death of the chief engraver at the Royal Mint, Leonard Wyon, in 1891, restored some youthfulness to Her Majesty's portrait, with a more prominent upper lip, more detail in the monarch's hair near her left eye, and a more prominent forehead.

In like fashion, the Royal Mint produced a number of reverse dies for the 1893 10-cent coinage. Most of these had a small 9 in the date and a 3 with a flat top. Only one or two dies had a large 9 and a 3 with a rounded top. The total number of 10-cent coins produced in 1893 was 500,000, an unknown but very small proportion of which was struck from dies with a round-top 3. This resulted in a major rarity in the Canadian Victorian 10-cent series, certainly among the top three rarest of any date. The only comparably scarce coins of that series are the 1884 and 1889 10-cent pieces.

Any 1893 Round Top 3 10-cent coin appearing at auction is a major event in Canadian numismatics. Flat Top examples in MS-65 have recently attracted winning bids of US$4,080 and US$5,040 (Heritage, 2019), while the finest known MS-67 commanded a winning bid of US$17,250 in 2010. By contrast, in the same 2019 Heritage auction an example of a Round Top 3 in a lower grade of Uncirculated condition (MS-61) realized US$12,600. The PCGS population report for the Round Top variety lists only three coins in Mint State: two in MS-64 and one in MS-61. The website CoinsandCanada.com lists a price of US$49,000 for an MS-63 example of a Round Top 3 coin. Neither of the PCGS MS-64 examples appears to have sold publicly in recent years.

A diagram of a Royal Mint coining press.

Two obverse regal portraits used to strike the 1893 10-cent coinage. The one on the left shows a somewhat older-looking monarch, while the one on the right restores some youthful features, such as detail in her hair, a more prominent forehead, and a better-defined upper lip.

Chapter 5

Canadian Coins from the Reigns of King Edward VII and King George V

This chapter presents the top Canadian coinage selections from the reigns of King Edward VII and King George V, covering the years 1902 to 1936. It specifically excludes any discussion of Canadian gold coins, even though they were developed during this era. They have such a unique and distinctive history that the following chapter is entirely devoted to their evolution.

In 1902 Canadian coinage went through a major design change. Queen Victoria had passed away the previous year, the end of a 43-year-long Canadian coinage regime. Canada had known no other monarch since its establishment as a dominion in 1867, and the familiar coins were replaced with new designs portraying a different monarch. This happened first in 1902, when the Edwardian coinage was introduced, and again only nine years later, following the accession to the throne of George V.

Edward VII was Queen Victoria's son and George V her grandson, so the royal line remained firmly entrenched during this era, which saw a number of dramatic coinage emissions and emergencies due to the untimely death of Edward VII at age 68, the First World War, and the abdication of Edward VIII in 1936. Of course, one of the most singular numismatic events was the opening of Canada's own mint in 1908. This was a strong expression of independence from Britain, although the Royal Mint continued to engrave the dies for Canadian coinage for many years thereafter, even as the coins themselves were struck in Ottawa. Some of Canada's greatest and most iconic rarities were coined during this era.

No. 68 1905 50 Cents

Standards—**Weight:** 11.62 grams. **Composition:** 0.925 silver, 0.075 copper. **Diameter:** 29.72 millimeters. **Edge:** Reeded. **Designer:** G.W. DeSaulles ("DES" below the bust on the obverse). **Rarity:** The scarcest of the Edward VII 50-cent coins.

Beginning in 1902 with the change of monarch, there was a foundational design difference in Canada's circulating coinage. For the first time in history, Canadian coinage would feature a monarch facing to the right. George V reversed this variant back to a left-facing portrait when his coinage first appeared in 1911, as did George VI starting in 1936, but Elizabeth II reverted back to the rightward-looking design of her great-grandfather, Edward VII. There is much speculation as to why all these changes took place. The consensus is that the monarch chooses based on which direction provides a better profile. Perhaps the United States had stricter guidelines on this, as Abraham Lincoln's was the only right-facing effigy on a circulating American coin until very recently.

The year 1905 was a pivotal one for Canada. The provinces of Alberta and Saskatchewan were created, opening the west to immigration and agriculture. British troops were finally withdrawn from Canadian soil, forcing Canada to concern itself with and pay for its own defense. The British closed two important garrisons at opposite ends of the country: in Esquimalt, British Columbia, and in Halifax, Nova Scotia. By 1905 immigration into Canada had increased dramatically, rising to almost 150,000 from 50,000 in 1901. Most immigrants came from the United Kingdom, but many also came from other European countries as well as the United States. The population of Canada that year was just under 6 million.

The Canadian 1905 50-cent piece has the distinction of having the lowest mintage of all coins struck during the reign of Edward VII, with only 40,000 being produced. It is also the key to this series. For comparison, the United States, with a population of 83,822,000, produced 662,727 Barber half dollars in 1905. The United States thus minted 0.0079 50-cent coins per person, while Canada produced 0.0067, remarkably similar numbers.

Both the obverse and reverse of the Edwardian 50-cent coin were designed by G.W. DeSaulles, an engraver at the Royal Mint. He passed away in 1903, but his design lived on through the end of the Edwardian era in 1910, except for one minor aspect. When Canada began striking these coins in 1908 at the Ottawa Mint, a problem developed. This can be seen in the enlargements of three 50-cent coins below: 1905, 1908, and 1910. On the 1905 coin, which was struck by the Royal Mint before the Ottawa Mint opened in 1908, the leaves come right up against the denticles at the far right. When these coins were struck in Ottawa beginning in 1908, they had almost no rim, as can be seen in the middle example. The Royal Mint then modified the dies in 1910, making the rim larger and redesigning the leaves so they were further away from the rim. The latter variety is called the "Edwardian Leaves," while the original design is termed "Victorian Leaves." The rightmost coin below is an example of an Edwardian Leaves variety. This variety is much scarcer than the Victorian Leaves variety for the 1910-dated coin, with only four MS examples at PCGS (MS-64+ is the highest), compared with 25 Victoria Leaves in Uncirculated condition, with three MS-66 examples leading the way.

There is always excitement whenever a high-grade 1905 Edwardian half dollar appears at auction. An almost-Uncirculated example will likely bring around US$2,000. The highest-graded coins are MS-64 (two of these exist in the PCGS population report), and while none have appeared at auction recently, a very attractive MS-63 example reached US$42,000 in very active bidding at a 2019 Heritage auction.

Three different reverse designs for Edwardian 50-cent coins. On the left is a 1905 example struck in London. Note that the leaves are right up against the denticles. In the middle is a 1908 example struck in Canada, with the rim almost entirely gone. The example on the right is a 1910 coin struck in Ottawa, but with a redesign of the leaves so they no longer reach the denticles. The rim is now well defined.

NO. 55 1906 25 CENTS, LARGE AND SMALL CROWN ON REVERSE

Standards—**Weight:** 5.81 grams. **Composition:** 0.925 silver, 0.075 copper. **Diameter:** 23.62 millimeters. **Edge:** Reeded. **Designers:** G.W. DeSaulles ("DES" can be seen below the bust in the image below), obverse; reverse largely adapted from the Victorian coins designed by Leonard C. Wyon. **Rarity:** Large Crown variety (left), not particularly scarce; Small Crown variety (right), a major Canadian rarity.

King Edward VII was crowned in 1902, the year after his accession to the throne following Queen Victoria's death. His reign was moderately short, lasting only until 1910. Of course, the obverse of coins for his reign had to be redesigned with a different monarchial portrait. The chief engraver at the Royal Mint, G.W. DeSaulles, carried out this work and his initials appear below Edward's bust on the obverse of the coins.

The obverse of a 1906 25-cent coin. Just below the bust are the letters DES to signify the designer of the coin, G.W. DeSaulles.

DeSaulles died in July 1903 at only 41 years of age, so this may have been his last major commission. The reverse of the coin was largely the same as that of the 25-cent coins of Victoria, designed by Leonard Wyon, but with two significant changes. CANADA had appeared on the obverse of all the coins of Canada during the Victoria era. For the Edwardian and subsequent monarchs' coinage, it was moved to the reverse of all circulating coins. This became necessary for the Edwardian coinage after it was decided to make a longer legend on the obverse by adding IMPERATOR. Additionally, the design of the crown on the reverse replaced the St. Edward's Crown (left below), the centerpiece of the Crown Jewels of the United Kingdom, with the Imperial State Crown (right below), which symbolizes the sovereignty of the British monarch.

Left: The St. Edward's Crown, seen at the top of the reverse of Victorian silver coins. Right: The Imperial State Crown, which first appeared on Canadian coins in 1902. The version seen here is the original one before the crown was slightly enlarged.

In 1906 there was a further redesign of the Edwardian silver coins. The major change involved replacing the rather small rendition of the Imperial State Crown (shown to the right just above) with a somewhat larger version to more adequately fill the space. In addition, the design of the wreath of leaves was modified to improve their appearance. Supposedly all 1906-dated 25-cent pieces were struck from dies with these characteristics. This version is shown to the left at the beginning of this essay. No other version of a 1906 Canadian 25-cent coin should exist.

The Small Crown coin does exist, however! It is a 1906-dated 25-cent coin with a small crown and no improvement to the appearance of the leaves. Clearly, therefore, some

25-cent coins were produced with the older reverse dies and a 1906 date. How many is not known, but it is clear that this variety is a major Canadian rarity. In Mint State, there are 31 Large Crown examples in the PCGS registry, with the highest being graded MS-66+, while only a single Uncirculated example is recorded for the Small Crown variety. Recent auction price comparisons clearly illustrate the rarity of this coin. The MS-64 Large Crown coin, at left on the previous page, recently sold at auction for US$2,400, while the Small Crown variety shown garnered a winning bid of US$38,400 in a 2019 Heritage auction even though its grade was only MS-62. It is the highest-graded coin of this variety.

Edward VII.

NO. 100 1890-H AND 1907-H CENT

Standards (1890-H)—**Weight:** 5.67 grams. **Composition:** 0.95 copper, 0.04 tin, 0.01 zinc. **Diameter:** 25.4 millimeters. **Edge:** Plain. **Designer:** Leonard C. Wyon. **Rarity:** Not rare.

Standards (1907-H)—**Weight:** 5.67 grams. **Composition:** 0.95 copper, 0.04 tin, 0.01 zinc. **Diameter:** 25.4 millimeters. **Edge:** Plain. **Designer:** G.W. DeSaulles ("DES" below bust, same reverse design as on Victorian 1-cent coins except smaller leaves). **Rarity:** Not rare.

were struck. The 1915 25-cent piece is the rarest and most expensive coin in the Canadian George V 25-cent series.

In 1915 there was little interest in collecting the coins of Canada by date. Since a type coin was considered satisfactory, many truly rare coins were generally underappreciated and choice examples were not "put away." The 1915 25-cent coin clearly falls into this group. As a date, it has the smallest population of examples that have been graded in gem condition by PCGS (MS-65 or higher), with only four recorded in MS-65 and none higher. By contrast, the 1918 coin has 38 examples in grades of MS-65 or higher, with five recorded in MS-67. The example shown on the previous page is one of the four 1915 coins in MS-65 grade, and it sold at auction for US$16,800 in 2019. The lowest graded one I was able to trace was a Good (G-6) example that sold for CAD$20.25.

No. 43 1920 Large and Small Cent

Standards (large cent)—**Weight:** 5.67 grams. **Composition:** 0.950 copper, 0.040 tin, 0.010 zinc. **Diameter:** 25.4 millimeters. **Edge:** Plain. **Designers:** Sir E.B. Mackennal, obverse; W.H.J. Blakemore, reverse. **Rarity:** Not rare, except in superb grades.

Standards (small cent)—**Weight:** 3.24 grams. **Composition:** 0.955 copper, 0.030 tin, 0.015 zinc. **Diameter:** 19.05 millimeters. **Edge:** Plain. **Designers:** Sir E.B. Mackennal, obverse; Fred Lewis, reverse. **Rarity:** Not rare, even in superb grades.

Large cents were first struck for the Province of Canada in 1858 and 1859. They were not produced again until 1876 (this time for the Dominion of Canada), as the first two mintages were so large (together totaling 10 million pieces) that a significant residual was not depleted for another 18 years after the first emission. The large cent of Canada is indeed a *large* cent. The diameter of 25.4 millimeters is exactly 1 inch and remained unchanged from 1858 to 1920, while the original weight of 4.54 grams in 1858 grew to 5.67 grams by the time George V ascended the throne, so these later coins were thicker. Oddly, in 1920 both a large and a small cent were struck.

Between 1921 and 1922 the Canadian 5-cent piece was completely redesigned and the composition went from largely silver to nickel. The small silver coin was minted in 1921 and the larger nickel coin in 1922. The two coins were not both minted in the same year, as with all the circulating coinage of Canada at least until 1968, when the circulating dollar and half dollar changed in size and composition due to the rapid increase in the price of silver. The 25-cent piece did not change significantly in size over the years, and the 10-cent coin has remained exactly the same size from the first Victorian pieces to the most recent Queen Elizabeth pieces. Hence, 1920 was really a very unusual year for Canadian coinage, as two very different cent coins were struck in that year, of almost the same composition (mostly copper) but differing in size by 25 percent. What was the reason for this?

Almost from the time the first Canadian coins were produced, there had been a consensus among officials that the coinage should be similar to that of the United States. When the value of the Canadian dollar was first established in 1857, it was made equal to that of the U.S. dollar. Canada's early coinage matched that of the United States closely in both size and composition. Some differences did exist. Canada kept its silver 5-cent coin until 1920, while the United States minted its last half dime in 1873. The United States manufactured 20-cent pieces between 1875 and 1878, long after Canada had ceased to do so in 1858. This, however, was largely due to pressure from the Nevada-based silver mining industry, coupled with a scarcity of silver coinage circulating in the western United States. Canada did not mint circulating gold coins until 1912 (and these did not circulate much), whereas the United States minted gold coins as early as 1795. The last U.S. large cent had been minted in 1857, after which it was replaced by the smaller Flying Eagle cent for two years and then by the Indian Head and Lincoln pennies. Thus, even as Canada was minting its first large cents, the United States was already replacing its own with a smaller coin.

By 1920 the Canadian large cent had become an expensive coin to produce. The price of copper almost doubled during the war years and by 1917 was more than twice as expensive as in 1911. Combined with a mintage of large cents that had more than doubled from the early years of George V's reign to the latter years of the war, it was clear that something had to be done to bring the costs under control. There was also a general desire to bring the cent coin in line with its American cousin, which by this time was the small (19.05 millimeters) Lincoln penny. In size and weight, the existing Canadian large cent was based on the British half penny, and it was now time to comply with the U.S. standard. The obvious solution was to reduce the size of the coin, which occurred in 1920. But why did Canada produce coins of both sizes that year? The answer is not clear. It is possible that since a new reverse design was used for the small cent, the dies were not ready on time and large cents were produced until the new dies were available. It is worth noting that the small cent was the first Canadian coin designed with no rim denticles or dots. This may also have complicated the transition to the smaller cent, necessitating the minting of large cents early in the year.

Neither of the 1920-dated cent coins is particularly rare. The large cent had a mintage of 6,762,247, about the average number of those struck during the previous decade, while the small cent had the second-highest mintage among the George V small cents (15,483,923). In MS-65 Red, the large cent will command around US$1,500 at auction, while its smaller sibling can be acquired for US$500. A 2012 Heritage auction presented a beautiful MS-66 large cent that required a winning bid of US$2,300.

No. 13 1921 5 Cents

Standards—**Weight:** 1.17 grams. **Composition:** 0.800 silver, 0.200 copper. **Diameter:** 15.50 millimeters. **Edge:** Reeded. **Designers:** Sir E.B. Mackennal, obverse; W.H.J. Blakemore, reverse. **Rarity:** Most melted in 1921; around 400 thought to exist today.

Canada began striking small, primarily silver 5-cent coins in 1858, almost ten years before Confederation. These were minted more or less continuously until 1921, with very little change in either composition or size. In the United States in 1920–1921, the circulating 5-cent coin was the "Buffalo nickel," an immensely popular copper-nickel coin that was 5 grams in weight, 21 millimeters in diameter, and with a plain edge (no reeding). During this time, Canada planned to replace its circulating 5-cent coin (a small, mostly silver coin with 20 percent copper mixed in) with a coin of pure nickel and of the exact same size as the U.S. piece. The small size of the Canadian 5-cent coin then in circulation made it difficult to keep track of and clumsy to use. Since nickel was widely mined in Canada, it was thought that a larger, pure nickel coin would be preferred.

In May 1921 the bill to replace the silver coinage was enacted by Parliament. By this time, most of the mintage of the 1921 silver 5-cent coins had already been completed. The government decided to melt the entire 1921 mintage of these coins, producing a major rarity in the Canadian series. In total, more than 3 million 5-cent coins were destroyed. This number exceeds the mintage of 1921 silver 5 cents (thought to be just over 2.5 million), so it is presumed that some 1920-dated coins that had not yet been distributed were also destroyed. About 400 1921 coins escaped the melting pot. Some of these were obtained by visitors to the Canadian Mint earlier in the year. A few more surviving examples came from specially prepared Specimen coins that had been distributed to dignitaries as part of complete 1921 sets of Canadian coins. Five Specimen examples have been graded by PCGS.

The 1921 5-cent coin is thus very scarce and is prized by collectors. An example (MS-65) recently sold for US$50,400 at Heritage Auctions' Cook Sale in 2019, while the highest-graded example (MS-67) sold for US$115,000 at public auction in January 2010. Even a VG-10 example commands a price of US$3,600 (Heritage, 2018). The PCGS population report lists 27 in various grades of Mint State, out of a total of 139 in all grades encapsulated by that service.

No. 4 1921 50 Cents

Standards—**Weight:** 11.66 grams. **Composition:** 0.800 silver, 0.200 copper. **Diameter:** 29.72 millimeters. **Edge:** Reeded. **Designers:** Sir E.B. Mackennal, obverse; W.H.J. Blakemore, reverse. **Rarity:** About 75 believed to exist. While not the rarest Canadian coin, it is certainly one of the most sought-after and expensive.

The mintage of this classic Canadian rarity was not particularly small. A total of 206,398 pieces was coined, very roughly average for the George V 50-cent series. Two dates have significantly smaller production numbers: 1932 with 19,213, and 1936 with 38,550 coins. During the reign of George V, Canada produced this large coin with 92.5 percent silver every year between 1911 and 1919. Between 1920 and 1936 (specifically in 1920, 1921, 1929, 1931, 1932, 1934, and 1936, as 50-cent coins were not struck every year during this period) the silver content was reduced to 80 percent. Together with the mintage of 1921 50-cent pieces, the government had produced a very large mintage of 1,113,429 coins dated 1919 and another 584,429 coins in 1920.

The demand for such a large silver coin in Canada in the 1920s was not particularly high. The large and heavy coin of relatively high value was a burden to carry. If high-denomination cash was required, paper money was a more practical solution. Because of this, the government melted almost 150,000 50-cent pieces in 1920. It is believed that these consisted solely of coins dated 1919, whose original mintage was so high that the coins were likely languishing in government vaults. In 1929 more than 480,000 additional 50-cent coins were melted, all of them dated 1920 or 1921. Almost the entire mintage of 1921 coins is believed to have been eliminated in this way, with only about 75 examples escaping the melting pot, which accounts for the rarity of this coin.

This is by no means one of Canada's rarest coins, however. There are several coins with only a single example known and many with two to ten pieces extant, but most of these do not command the price of a 1921 50-cent piece. A mystique has grown around this coin and any auction appearance is met with raised hands all around the auction room. This is similar to the situation with the classic U.S. rarities, such as the 1804 dollar or 1913 5-cent coin, the main difference being the price for the 1921 50-cent piece is about one-tenth the price for these U.S. coins.

A lowly VG-8 example realized US$32,900 several years ago (Heritage, April 7, 2017), and very recently two spectacular examples appeared in the same auction at the American Numismatic Association World's Fair of Money, in the 2019 Heritage Auctions George Hans Cook Collection Sale. A beautiful MS-63 example (very conservatively graded, in my opinion) realized US$120,000, while an unimprovable MS-66 example, formerly in the Norweb Collection and the finest known (illustrated on the previous page), climbed to an impressive US$240,000 in very spirited bidding.

No. 89 1923 Cent

Standards—**Weight:** 3.24 grams. **Composition:** 0.955 copper, 0.030 tin, 0.015 zinc. **Diameter:** 19.05 millimeters. **Edge:** Plain. **Designers:** Sir E.B. Mackennal, obverse; Fred Lewis, reverse. **Rarity:** Except the 1936 Dot cent coin, this is the scarcest small-cent coin of George V.

In 1923 William Lyon Mackenzie King was prime minister of Canada. He was the most important political figure in Canada from about 1920 until his death in 1950. He led Canada through the Second World War, mobilizing the country to help support Britain. His more than 21 years as head of government make him the longest-serving prime minister in Canadian history.

The year 1923 also saw a law passed making marijuana illegal, the formation of the Canadian National Railway from a merger of four other railways, and the Nobel Prize in Medicine being awarded on October 25 to Frederick Banting and John Macleod for the discovery of insulin. Canada would not win another Nobel Prize in Medicine until 1983, when David Hubel won it for mapping the visual cortex. The population of Canada was about 9 million people in 1923.

Three years earlier, the country had switched from minting large copper cents to a coin more aligned with that of the United States: a small cent with a diameter of 19.05 millimeters, compared with the 25.4-millimeter large cent minted up until 1920 (see the earlier essay, "Canada 1920 Large and

Small Cent," on page 88). In 1923 Canada minted approximately a single cent coin for every nine people in the country. By comparison, the United States minted 83 million Lincoln cents that year, when its population was about 112 million people—or one coin for every 0.74 inhabitants, about seven times the rate of Canada.

Of all the George V small cents (1920–1936), the 1923 is the scarcest and most costly except, of course, for the prohibitively rare and expensive 1936 Dot coin, which sells for over US$300,000. The PCGS population report lists no 1923s in MS-65 and only four in MS-64RD (Red). In 2019 the coin illustrated on the previous page sold for US$4,560 in Heritage Auctions' George Hans Cook Collection of Canadian Coins sale at the American Numismatic Association World's Fair of Money. The 1925 cent has about the same mintage as the 1923 but typically sells for about half the price. Two examples of this date, both of them graded MS-65RB (Red-Brown), sold for US$2,540 in the Cook Sale. The 1925 coin has a PCGS population in Mint State (RD or RB) almost 50 percent higher than that of the 1923 coin.

No. 75 1926 5 Cents, Near 6 and Far 6

Standards—**Weight:** 4.54 grams. **Composition:** 100 percent nickel. **Diameter:** 21.21 millimeters. **Edge:** Plain. **Designers:** Sir E.B. Mackennal, obverse; W.H.J. Blakemore, reverse. **Rarity:** Both varieties are the rarest for this series (1922–1936) except the 1925 coin. The Near 6 variety is shown at top. The main diagnostic is the closeness of the tip of the "6" to the maple leaf.

To fully appreciate the importance of these two varieties of the 1926 5-cent coin, it is important to understand how coins are manufactured. The process begins with the production of a master matrix from the artist's (designer's) original sketches. This matrix, if for the obverse of the coin, will usually have just the portrait of the monarch, with the lettering added while the metal is still soft. The matrix is incuse, or a mirror image of how the coin is to appear. This master matrix is then hardened and used to produce a master punch (which is not incuse), from which working dies (incuse) are manufactured. The dies are later used to strike the coins.

Most world mints are in the business of mass-producing coins for their countries, so cost efficiency is paramount in their manufacturing processes. For this reason, in Canada and especially at the Royal Mint, reverse punches often contained only the first three digits of a date (e.g., "192" for coins to be struck between 1920 and 1929). The fourth digit would be inserted by hand into the working die with a simple tool. The inevitable result of this was that the final digit would move around slightly since the position of the insertion was subject to human estimation, which is never perfect. Usually, such variations were minuscule and hence indiscernible, but in 1926 the final digit in the date of the 5-cent coins was punched too close to the leaves on the reverse in one of the punches (the Near 6 variety). When the original punch was retired from use due to excess wear, a second variety of this date was introduced (the Far 6 variety) where the date was farther from the leaves.

As a date, 1926 is the second rarest (after 1925) in the series of George V 5-cent nickel coins, and the 1926 Far 6 coin is somewhat scarcer than the Near 6 variety. The PCGS population report lists 79 Near 6 examples in all Mint State grades, with a single MS-66 example being the highest. The Far 6 variety has 35 in Mint State, with four examples in MS-65 leading the way. In addition, there are five Specimen examples in the PCGS inventory, all of them of the Near 6 variety (the highest are three examples in SP-67).

In April 2012 a very choice MS-65 Far 6 coin attracted a strong winning bid of US$16,675 in a Heritage auction. In January 2020 an MS-65 example of a Near 6 coin sold for US$4,320, also in a Heritage auction.

NO. 81 1932 50 CENTS

Standards—**Weight:** 11.66 grams. **Composition:** 0.800 silver, 0.200 copper. **Diameter:** 29.72 millimeters. **Edge:** Reeded. **Designers:** Sir E.B. Mackennal, obverse; W.H.J. Blakemore, reverse. **Rarity:** Rare, with the smallest mintage of any George V 50-cent piece (the 1921-dated coin is rarer due to its having been heavily melted).

The Edward VII 25- and 50-cent coins of Canada (issued between 1902 and 1910) included on the obverse the rather extensive legend EDWARDVS VII DEI GRATIA REX IMPERATOR (Edward 7th by the Grace of God King Emperor). This was somewhat abbreviated on the smaller-sized silver coins to EDWARDVS VII D.G. REX IMPERATOR. This legend occupied so much space that CANADA, which had appeared below Queen Victoria's bust on all her Canadian 50-cent coins, had to be moved to the reverse on the Edwardian coins. Even so, the obverse of these pieces remained cluttered and was not artistically appealing. With the change of monarch from Edward VII to George V (coins issued 1911–1936), the mint attempted to improve the aesthetics by dropping DEI GRATIA ("by the grace of God"), and replacing IMPERATOR with ET IND:IMP ("and Emperor of India"). The phrase DEI GRATIA (or some variant of it) had appeared on British coins for over a century and on all Canadian coins up to that time, so its removal did not sit well with the Canadian public. The government responded by adding DEI GRA to all coins in 1912.

This was preserved until well into Queen Elizabeth II's reign. It is interesting to note that Canada's first silver dollar, dated 1935, was also "Godless," permitting mention of the fact that it was the 25th year of George V's reign (ANNO REGNI XXV). This can be seen in the image of a 1935 $1 coin in the next essay.

The 50-cent coin of George V went through a number of other changes. It began life as a 0.925 silver coin (0.346 ounces pure silver) with a "Godless Obverse" (1911); displayed DEI GRA: on its obverse from 1912 until the end of the George V's reign; had its composition debased somewhat to 0.800 silver (0.300 ounces pure silver) in 1920; and came to an end in 1936 as war began to threaten in Europe.

The mintages of the George V 50-cent coins were always modest, particularly from 1931 to 1936. Of course, one of the greatest Canadian coins, the 1921 50-cent piece, is from this monarch's reign. The 1921 routinely sells for US$100,000 or more depending on condition. One of the finest known examples (MS-66) sold at auction for US$240,000 in 2019. The 1921 50 cents is rare since most were melted, but the 1932 is a genuine low-mintage rarity, with the smallest mintage (19,213) of any George V 50-cent piece. The single finest known 1932 50-cent coin is graded by PCGS as MS-66+; there are two in MS-66 and four in MS-65. The highest known price at auction was US$25,850 for an MS-65 example in a January 2013 Heritage auction. By contrast, an NGC grade G-6 coin garnered only US$79 in a 2015 Heritage auction.

No. 32 1935 $1

Standards—**Weight:** 23.33 grams. **Composition:** 0.800 silver, 0.200 copper. **Diameter:** 36.00 millimeters. **Edge:** Reeded. **Designers:** Percy Metcalfe, obverse; Emanuel Hahn, reverse. **Rarity:** Not a great rarity, but of great numismatic importance to Canada.

The 1935 silver dollar was the first circulating $1 coin struck for Canada. The 1911 dollar was never struck for circulation, with only one lead and two silver examples ever produced. The year 1935 marked the 25th anniversary of King George V's reign, providing a good reason for striking a silver dollar. It took Canada a very long time to actually produce this large silver coin. It had contemplated striking a crown-sized silver coin in 1911, when two trial coins were produced. In the holder for the Specimen sets of that year (shown on the following page), a hole had been left for a dollar-sized coin, but no coin occupied it. The holder includes spaces (right to left) for cent, 5-cent, 10-cent, 25-cent, 50-cent, and $1 coins. Most known cases have only five openings, with none for the dollar. It is not obvious why Canada waited 24 years to produce its first circulating dollar coin.

The 1935 dollar coin features an obverse design of the king that had been used previously on Australian and New Zealand issues. The Latin legend surrounding the monarch's effigy is somewhat unusual and translates as "George the Fifth King Emperor in the Twenty-fifth Year of Reign," so that Canada's first silver dollar is actually a commemorative coin. The reverse, by Emanuel Hahn, is one of the most beloved in the entire Canadian series. It features a canoe paddled by a voyageur (generally French Canadians working to transport furs) in the stern with an Indigenous Canadian in the bow. The canoe is passing a small island with two jack pines swept

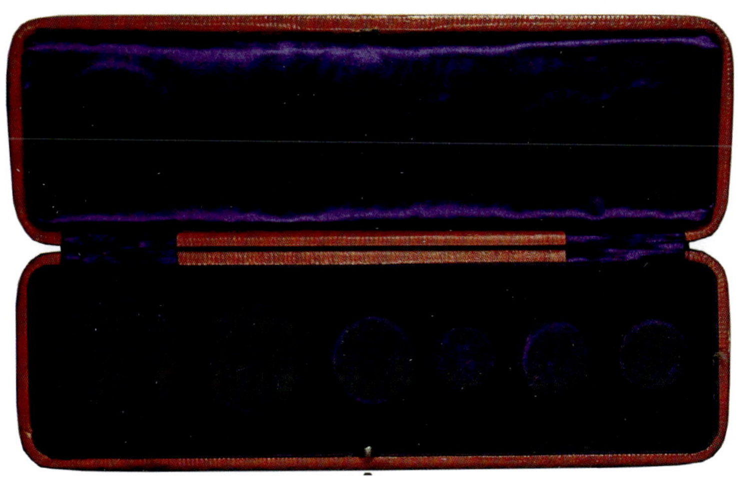

A case made by the Royal Mint to hold the 1911 Specimen coins of Canada. Note that it contains six spaces, including a slot for the $1 coin. Even this case is a rarity, realizing US$1,265 in a May 31, 2007, Heritage auction.

by the wind. In the canoe are several beaver pelts. The bundle on the right has HB stamped on it, signifying the Hudson's Bay Company. The vertical lines stretching across the entire reverse represent the Northern Lights, easily seen from most northern locations in Canada. This is likely the most iconic design of any coin produced for Canada, and no other better captures the early spirit of Canada.

The voyageur reverse design persisted for more than 50 years, until 1987, except for several interruptions for special commemorative coins. The current design on the reverse of the circulating dollar coin portrays a loon.

A specially struck Specimen coin grading SP-67, one of the finest known, last sold for US$8,400 at a 2019 auction. For casual collectors who want a single Canadian coin in their collection, I would suggest an example of this dollar. An MS-66 example from the George Hans Cook Collection sold for only US$528 at a Heritage auction in 2019. With the PCGS population report listing 2,176 in all grades of Uncirculated, there are many opportunities to acquire a very nice example for only a modest cost.

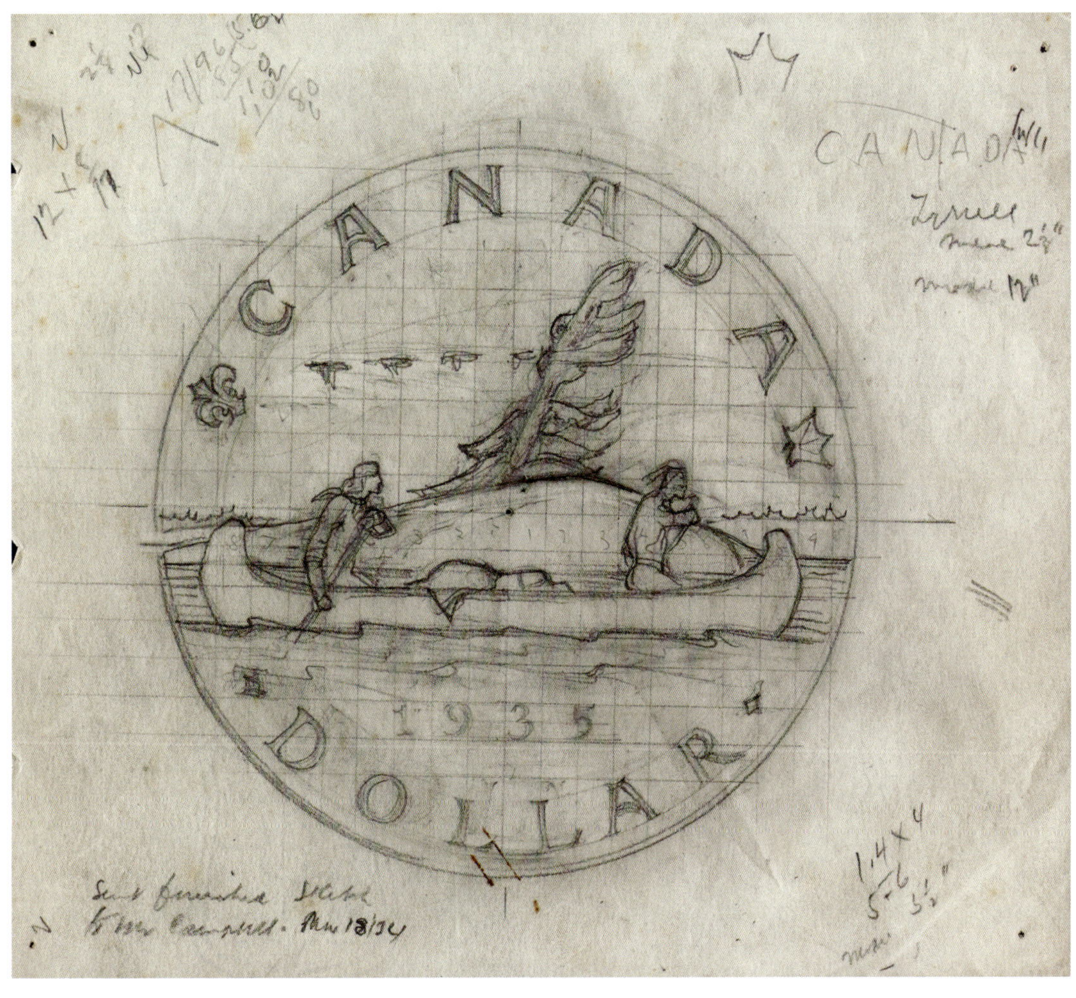

An early sketch by Emanuel Hahn of his proposed design for the reverse of the 1935 Canadian silver dollar. Note that it is almost exactly the final adopted design, except for the fleur-de-lis and maple leaf at the left and right edges, and the geese in flight. The final adopted design also included a second, smaller jack pine.

No. 28 $1, J.O.P. Counterstamp

Standards—**Weight:** 23.3 grams. **Composition:** 0.800 silver, 0.200 copper. **Diameter:** 36.00 millimeters. Edge: Reeded. **Designer:** Emanuel Hahn. **Rarity:** Moderately rare; in great demand by collectors.

Counterstamped coins are often considered to be defaced and are likely to sell for little over face value. Of course, this is not always the case; some coins increase in value if they have historically important counterstamps. Included in this category are the U.S. 1815 and 1825 Capped Bust 25-cent pieces with an "E" or "L" counterstamp (US$1,500), thought to be associated with the death of William DuBois, the assayer of the Philadelphia Mint and curator of the U.S. Mint collection, and the 1925 U.S. Stone Mountain commemorative half dollar with a letter or number counterstamp ($500). The same can be said for early Canadian silver dollars dated from 1935 to the 1950s that have a J.O.P. counterstamp, the origin of which remained a mystery for many years.

In the 1920s a method was developed in British Columbia to refine silver at a significantly lower cost than with other technologies at the time. One of the financial backers of the plan was Joseph Oliva Patenaude, a jeweler residing in the city of Nelson in the southern interior of British Columbia, on the west side of Kootenay Lake. Located roughly equidistant from Vancouver, Calgary, and Spokane, Washington, Nelson today attracts tourists from these large metropolitan areas and has a vibrant restaurant scene boasting more eating establishments per capita than San Francisco. The city came of age in 1986, when Steve Martin chose it as the locale of the movie *Roxanne*, his hugely popular adaptation of Edmond Rostand's *Cyrano de Bergerac*. However, Patenaude's Nelson of the 1920s and 1930s was a quiet mining town whose major employer was the Silver King Mine, located on Toad Mountain just 7 kilometers south of the city. The famous Sullivan Mine was located in nearby Kimberly. Once the largest silver producer in Canada, it is now closed.

When Canada minted its first circulating silver dollar in 1935, Patenaude secured 1,000 examples, on which he stamped his initials (J.O.P.) on the reverse between the canoe and the date. This was particularly well executed. In general, the procedure would cause damage to the opposite side of the coin, but Patenaude was able to counterstamp his initials with no disruption to the obverse. It is against the law to deface coinage, but Patenaude was likely unaware of this, and while ignorance is not a valid defense in such matters, he was never called upon to defend his actions in court. He distributed these coins to friends and customers and gave them as change for purchases as a form of protest against the strong mining interests, which refused to adopt the apparently more efficient silver refining method in which he had invested. This dispute ended in litigation, which Patenaude and his group lost, along with most of his bank account. The counterstamping was both a way for Patenaude to continue the protest and an experiment to see how far away from Nelson the coins would travel. And they traveled quite a way! J.O.P. dollars were eventually found in circulation in nearby Spokane and as far east as the Maritime provinces.

Not only were 1935 silver dollars counterstamped by Patenaude but virtually every date up to 1954 can be found with a J.O.P. stamp. There are even examples known for some rare dates, including the low-mintage and key date 1948. There are at least three distinct types of counterstamps. One has all three initials in a common stamp, while another has the appearance of letters punched in individually. Likely the rarest one, the third type has Patenaude's full last name stamped above the date. Patenaude passed away in 1958, and there are few examples of his counterstamps dated after 1950.

Although collectors actively pursue J.O.P. silver dollars, prices are strong but not excessive. An MS-66 example of a 1935 counterstamped silver dollar garnered US$2,640 in a recent Heritage auction. A similarly graded coin without the counterstamp was auctioned for US$528 in 2019. The J.O.P. dollars dated 1935 are by far the most common. A counterstamped MS-62 example dated 1936, likely the next most common year, was auctioned for US$1,116 in 2014. A similarly graded coin without the counterstamp would sell for under US$100. A 1939 MS-63 example with J.O.P. counterstamp yielded US$2,333 in a 2014 auction, whereas one without the counterstamp would likely sell for about US$50. The 1946 dollars are moderately scarce, with typical MS-63 examples without the counterstamp selling for US$500, whereas a J.O.P. counterstamped example sold at auction for US$3,055 in 2014.

The J.O.P. counterstamp on Canadian silver dollars is clearly an example of a counterstamp on a coin increasing as opposed to decreasing the coin's value. The history of these coins and the gregarious and flashy Joseph Patenaude have made these issues a favorite with collectors.

J.O. Patenaude Jewellers, 300 Block, Baker Street, Nelson, B.C., circa 1910. Patenaude is standing on the far right in this image.

No. 3 1936 Dot Coins

Standards (cent)—**Weight:** 3.24 grams. **Composition:** 0.955 copper, 0.030 tin, 0.015 zinc. **Diameter:** 19.05 millimeters. **Edge:** Plain. **Designers:** Sir E.B. Mackennal, obverse; Fred Lewis, reverse. **Rarity:** These coins, particularly the 1- and 10-cent pieces, are among Canada's rarest and most sought-after coins.

Standards (10 cents)—**Weight:** 2.32 grams. **Composition:** 0.925 silver, 0.075 copper. **Diameter:** 18.03 millimeters. **Edge:** Reeded. **Designers:** Sir E.B. Mackennal, obverse; W.H.J. Blakemore, reverse. **Rarity:** One of Canada's rarest and most expensive coins.

Standards (25 cents)—**Weight:** 5.83 grams. **Composition:** 0.925 silver, 0.075 copper. **Diameter:** 23.62 millimeters. **Edge:** Reeded. **Designers:** Sir E.B. Mackennal, obverse; W.H.J. Blakemore, reverse. **Rarity:** Not as rare as the Dot 1-cent and 10-cent coins, but still an actively sought-after Canadian rarity.

The history behind the striking of the Canadian cent and 10-cent Dot coinage of 1936 has been chronicled in every catalog on Canadian coins and in numerous television, radio, and newspaper stories. It is important to separate, however, the narrative behind the two lower-denominated coins and the 25-cent piece.

King George V passed away on January 20, 1936. He was 82 years old and the cause of death was likely lung disease brought on by his heavy smoking. He was the grandson of Queen Victoria, who had died in 1901, and the grandfather of Queen Elizabeth II. His death was not unexpected, as he had been ill for some time. George V was succeeded by his eldest son, Prince Edward Albert (born in June 1894), who became King Edward VIII.

Edward VIII's reign did not go well. He was disdainful of established protocol. Several months into his reign, he made known his intention to marry Wallis Simpson, a twice-divorced American socialite whom the Church of England considered unacceptable. The marriage was also opposed by the prime ministers of Britain and the self-governing Dominions of the British Empire. Finally, on December 11, 1936, Edward VIII abdicated the throne and his brother, the Duke of York, became King George VI.

The coinage backstory to these events is almost as interesting. With the transition from George V to Edward VIII, the Royal Mint began preparing dies for the coinage of the new monarch. The dies were more or less complete by the time Edward VIII abdicated, but now the Mint was in a quandary: it had no dies available for George VI. It could not strike coins with the portrait of Edward VIII on the obverse because he was no longer king. In this era the dies for new Canadian coins still came from the Royal Mint in England, so the Canadian Mint suffered from a lack of dies for a 1937 coinage of George VI. Quantities of all the denominations were required except for the 5-cent and 50-cent coins, for which there was little demand. The Canadian Mint's solution was to use the 1936-dated dies for George V and punch a small dot on the reverse, near the bottom of the coin. The location was below the date on the cent and below the wreath on the two silver coins. This dot can be easily seen in the examples illustrated on the previous page, and it was meant to signify that the coin had been struck in 1937 and was not to be confused with a 1936 issue.

Mystery and intrigue ensued and produced what many consider the rarest and most desirable coins in the entire Canadian series. For some undocumented reason, these "Dot" coins were never released from the Canadian Mint, whose records indicate that 678,823 Dot cent pieces were struck, together with almost 200,000 10-cent coins. The mint claimed that they were all melted, but four examples of the 10-cent coin are known, all of them Specimens that were specially struck for dignitaries. A single circulation-strike cent also survives, together with three Specimens. From 1961 until his death in 1996, John J. Pittman owned all the Specimen cents, having acquired them from an employee at the Canadian Mint. All the images of the coins shown here are of Specimen strikes. Over the years numerous circulated pieces have surfaced, but none have been authenticated. Most experts believe that no genuine 1936 Dot cents ever circulated. Apparently, this did not deter Pittman from assembling as many rolls of Uncirculated 1936 cent coins as he was able to locate, in the hope of finding another example. In the sale of his collection, no fewer than seven rolls of these coins were auctioned, all of which he had obtained at face value.

The 25-cent coin has a history similar to that of the smaller denominations, with one major exception: the entire mintage of this coinage was actually released into circulation. With 153,000 struck, it is not a major rarity, but it shares some of the mystique of its smaller siblings.

Auction records are very impressive for all three of these coins. The highest price paid for a Specimen cent was US$402,000, sold at a Heritage auction in 2010 and graded SP-66. Pittman had paid US$250 for this coin in 1950. The 10-cent Specimen illustrated in this essay (SP-68) sold for US$184,000, also in 2010. And while a nice Dot 25-cent (MS-65) coin can be had for around US$7,000, the absolutely superb SP-68 example shown here realized US$80,500 in the same 2010 auction.

Edward VIII.

George VI.

CHAPTER 6

DEVELOPMENT OF CANADIAN GOLD COINS

This relatively short chapter surveys the history of Canada's gold coinage. Plans were much more ambitious than what was actually accomplished. Starting in 1908, Canada was burdened with the task of minting sovereigns, coins that were hardly wanted and saw very little circulation. This was because the new mint in Ottawa was effectively a branch of the Royal Mint and was required to strike sovereigns. Some experts argue that these coins were not really Canadian but British, while others suggest that they were true Canadian coins. They were legal tender in Canada but were mostly used for export purposes. The real desire of the Ottawa Mint was to produce gold coins similar to U.S. denominations. This was actually planned and design sketches were produced, but only $5 and $10 gold coins were actually minted for circulation from 1912 through 1914. The distribution of these coins was hampered by the war. To help fund the war effort, the Government of Canada recovered the majority of gold coins that had already been released into circulation and withheld those that remained in its vaults. The net effect was that only small quantities were released, and these saw little use. During and after the war, Canada had restrictions on the convertibility of paper money into gold. When these were finally lifted, there were plans to reintroduce a gold coinage and patterns were even struck in 1928. Things moved too slowly, however, and in 1931 Canada went off the gold standard entirely, ending the possibility of any circulating Canadian gold coinage.

NO. 26 1908 GOLD SOVEREIGN

Standards—**Weight:** 7.99 grams. **Composition:** 0.917 gold, 0.083 copper. **Diameter:** 22.05 millimeters. **Edge:** Reeded. **Designer:** G.W. DeSaulles ("DES" below bust), obverse; Benedetto Pistrucci ("B.P." below ground at right), reverse. **Rarity:** Relatively rare, with only 636 struck, all in Specimen condition.

In 1908 Canada finally opened its own mint, the Ottawa Mint. Since it was considered a branch of the Royal Mint, it was obligated to mint British gold sovereigns, as had occurred earlier in Australia and would occur later in South Africa and India. The coins were identical to those minted in Britain except for a small letter "C" on the reverse, above the second and third digits in the date, on the ground below the dragon (shown in the enlargement below).

A small section of the reverse of a 1908 Canadian sovereign illustrating the "C" mintmark, signifying that the coin was struck in Canada. The letter "C" can be found just above the 9 and the 0 of the date.

To celebrate the opening of the Ottawa Mint, 1908 sovereigns were struck, apparently all in one day, as Specimens only—that is, special care was taken to produce as high quality a coin as possible, but without full Proof characteristics. The gold for these coins had been mined in Canada, some in British Columbia and some from Northern Ontario. The sovereign series was never popular in Canada and the coins did not circulate very widely. They were legal tender in Canada, but this was not a great distinction since U.S. gold coins were also legal tender at the time. The 1908 sovereign does, however, have the distinction of being the first gold coin struck for Canada. The very small number (636) minted in 1908 was mainly for the purpose of establishing the series, but there was so little demand that the coin did not sell out. Later emissions were more robust, with the largest mintage consisting of just over 250,000 coins in 1911. The smallest number minted after 1908 was a paltry 3,715 in 1913.

High-grade 1908 sovereigns command hefty prices at auction. In August 2015 a spectacular SP-67 example from the Heritage Eric Beckman Sale garnered US$28,200. This was the same coin that had realized US$4,620 in the 1996 Bowers and Merena Norweb Sale. A circulated example of a 1908 sovereign is actually rarer than a pristine one, as the coins were made as Specimens only and presumably provided to dignitaries or sold by the Mint to those who wanted an example of Canada's first gold coin. Even so, not all were sold and at the end of 1908 the remaining coins were simply placed into circulation. This accounts for the odd circulated coin showing up at auction. An unusual circulated Specimen (EF-45) attracted a winning bid of US$3,525 in a 2015 Heritage auction.

There are 95 examples of this coin in the PCGS population report, with two in SP-67 and a further six in SP-66. Fifty-eight examples exist in SP-64 or lower grade, so virtually anyone desiring an example of this coin should be able to locate one, but the price is never cheap. In 2021 several SP-62 examples came to market with an average auction price of about US$8,000.

NO. 52 1909 GOLD PATTERN $2.5 AND $10

Standards—There are no specifications for these coins, as they were never struck and exist only as sketches. Had they been produced, their standards would have been identical to those of the U.S. coins of the same denomination, as follows:

$2.5 coin: Weight: 4.18 grams. **Composition:** 0.900 gold, 0.100 copper. **Diameter:** 18.00 millimeters.

$10 coin: Weight: 16.718 grams. **Composition:** 0.900 gold, 0.100 copper. **Diameter:** 27.00 millimeters.

These coins were never minted, so why do I include them in a compilation of the greatest coins of Canada? There are several reasons. The design shown on the previous page is one of the earliest known designs for a Canadian gold coinage in dollar denominations; it was similar, although not identical, to those eventually produced for circulation from 1912 to 1914; it highlights the early thinking on Canada's gold coins; and the $2.5 coin was canceled with no great thought as to its efficacy as a circulating coin.

In 1910 Canada passed a Currency Act that provided for a gold coinage in denominations of $2.5, $5, $10, and $20. All these coins were to be 0.900 gold and 0.100 copper, in line with U.S. standards. A $2.5 gold coin would weigh 4.18 grams and a $10 coin four times as much. In his article "The Lost Half George" in the May 2007 issue of the *CN Journal*, Daniel Gosling presents the correspondence between Canada (mostly from Minister of Finance W.S. Fielding) and Deputy Master of the Royal Mint William Ellison-Macartney. In the first letter, dated August 11, 1908, Fielding stated that Canada had determined that gold coins in denominations of $10, $5, and $2.5 were desired. He asked the Royal Mint to supply suitable designs for these coins, as there was no one in Canada capable of executing them. As early as the date on this letter, the idea of a $20 coin seems to have gone by the wayside (but see the 1910 correspondence at right, where the $20 gold coin seems still very much in play). Fielding also requested that the Coat of Arms of Canada be present on all the coins, with the Imperial State Crown above it. In addition, he wanted the king's head on the obverse, with CANADA below it. All the coins were to have the same physical specifications as the U.S. coins of the same denomination. Ellison-Macartney replied that he thought it would be impossible to have both the crown and the Coat of Arms of Canada on the reverse.

In October 1908 Ellison-Macartney provided sketches for a 1909-dated mintage of these coins. During more back and forth extending over an entire year, the crown on the reverse was removed since it already appeared on the obverse, wreathes of maple (seen on the $10 sketch) replaced the leaves surrounding the shield (seen on the $2.5 sketch), and the date was positioned as an extension of the denomination on the reverse. On January 15, 1910, Ellison-Macartney wrote that while it would be possible to inscribe in letters the denominations of the $5 and $10 coins as requested by Fielding, it would not be possible to do so for the smaller $2.5 coin. That was as far as the discussion went; the topic never appeared again in any correspondence. Hence, largely because of an unsatisfactory design, Canada was denied a small-denomination gold coin that likely would have facilitated commerce, as a $2.50 coin (the quarter eagle) was popular and circulated widely in the United States.

Apparently, things were still not settled even as late as November 1910, when James Bonar, the deputy master of the Ottawa Mint at the time, wrote Ellison-Macartney requesting minting tools for sovereigns, $2.5 through $20 gold coins, a silver $1 coin, and minor coins (see letter shown below). Three pairs of sovereign dies were provided in early February 1911, followed by matrices and punches for the $5 and $10 gold coins only (no $2.5 or $20 coins) in October 1911. The sovereign dies almost certainly were used to strike the large emission of 1911-C sovereigns (256,946 minted), while the matrices and punches were presumably used to produce the first emission of Canadian $5 and $10 gold coins dated 1912. (See, however, the discussion of the 1911 $5 and $10 gold coins on page 104).

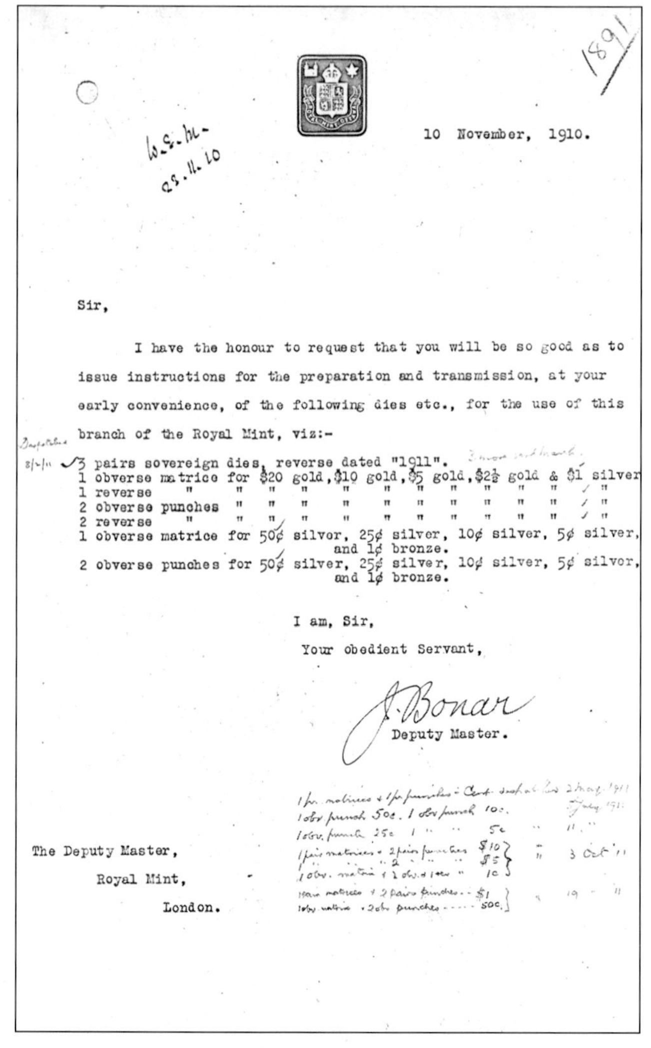

10 November, 1910.

Sir,

I have the honour to request that you will be so good as to issue instructions for the preparation and transmission, at your early convenience, of the following dies etc., for the use of this branch of the Royal Mint, viz:-

3 pairs sovereign dies, reverse dated "1911".
1 obverse matrice for $20 gold, $10 gold, $5 gold, $2½ gold & $1 silver
1 reverse " " " " " " " " " " " " "
2 obverse punches " " " " " " " " " " " "
2 reverse " " " " " " " " " " " " "
1 obverse matrice for 50¢ silvor, 25¢ silver, 10¢ silver, 5¢ silver, and 1¢ bronze.
2 obverse punches for 50¢ silver, 25¢ silver, 10¢ silver, 5¢ silvor, and 1¢ bronze.

I am, Sir,

Your obedient Servant,

J. Bonar

Deputy Master.

The Deputy Master,

Royal Mint,

London.

Letter dated November 10, 1910, from the Deputy Master of the Ottawa Mint, James Bonar, to the Deputy Master of the Royal Mint in London, William Ellison-Macartney (whose name is not included on the letter), requesting minting tools for, among other things, a gold coinage in denominations of $2.5, $5, $10, and $20.

NO. 50 1910 GOLD UNIFACE PATTERN $5

Standards—**Weight:** 8.36 grams. **Composition:** 0.900 gold, 0.100 copper. **Diameter:** 21.59 millimeters. **Designer:** G.W. DeSaulles. **Rarity:** Only one example known of each.

The 1910 uniface Edwardian $5 gold patterns shown above are not listed in either Fred Bowman's *Canadian Patterns* or the *Charlton Standard Catalogue, Canadian Coins.* These pieces are so rare that they are largely unknown to the Canadian collecting community, and it literally takes a visit to the Royal Mint Museum in Llantrisant, Wales, to see them—and then only if you can gain access to the collection in the back rooms.

In 1908 the Canadian government began striking gold sovereigns with a design identical to that of the British sovereigns, except for the addition of a small "C" on the reverse that identified them as Canadian coins. With a newly opened mint, Canada wanted to produce its own clearly identifiable gold coins. In August 1908, as discussed in the previous essay on page 102, Minister of Finance W.S. Fielding wrote William Ellison-Macartney, deputy master of the Royal Mint, that Canada desired to have gold coins in denominations of $10, $5, and $2.5 similar to those in the United States. He suggested a design that would clearly differentiate these coins from the sovereigns, with the Coat of Arms of Canada on the reverse together with the denomination, date, and the Imperial State Crown. The obverse would display the king's head with CANADA below it. Fielding specified that in all aspects (size, weight, and fineness) these coins should be identical to those of the United States.

A sketch of a possible reverse for a Canadian gold coinage in 1910. If a $5 gold coin had been struck for Canada in that year, it likely would have incorporated the obverse seen in the bottom image at the beginning of this essay and the reverse seen here.

In an early design (see the reverse designs of the 1909 patterns on page 101), the crown was felt to be too large, so it was reduced and the denomination was spelled out fully. A later rendition removed the crown from the reverse entirely (as it was already on the obverse), redesigned the crossed boughs of maple leaves, repositioned the date, and fully developed the Coat of Arms of Canada. If a 1910 gold coinage for Canada in dollar denominations had come to fruition, the coin would almost certainly have looked like the obverse on the right at the beginning of this essay, and the reverse in the sketch above.

The full suite of gold coins (a $20 coin had also been contemplated) did not materialize, and in 1912 Canada minted $5 and $10 coins from dies provided by the Royal Mint that were distinct from the sovereigns. All that remains of the Mint's initial efforts are a few sketches (see also the following essay) and these uniface $5 patterns of Edward VII, one of which is dated 1910 (cataloged in the Royal Mint Museum as Model A) whereas the other is an undated pattern (cataloged as Model B). The bust of Edward VII is smaller on Model A in order to accommodate the date.

We know these obverse patterns were designed by G.W. DeSaulles because the letters DES appear on both gold obverses below the bust. DeSaulles never had the official title, as Leonard Wyon did, of chief engraver of the Royal Mint. He was officially known only as "Engraver to the Mint" during his tenure from 1893, following the death of Wyon in 1891, until his own passing in 1903. DeSaulles's obverse design, without the date, had been used on all the other Edward VII coins of Canada struck from 1902 to 1910. There would be no opportunity for him to create new dies for the $5 coin, however, as by 1910 he had already been dead for seven years.

Although there is no direct information on the composition of these patterns, they are likely 0.900 gold and 0.100 copper, in line with the U.S. standard that Canada was attempting to emulate. No provenance for these trial pieces is listed in the archives of the Royal Mint Museum in Llantrisant, Wales.

No. 33 1911 Gold Pattern $5 and $10

Standards ($5)—**Weight:** 8.36 grams. **Composition:** 0.900 gold, 0.100 copper. **Diameter:** 21.59 millimeters. **Edge:** Reeded. **Designer:** Sir E.B. Mackennal, obverse; W.H.J. Blakemore, reverse. **Rarity:** Only one example known. Bowman 41.

Standards ($10)—**Weight:** 16.72 grams. **Composition:** 0.900 gold, 0.100 copper. **Diameter:** 26.92 millimeters. **Edge:** Reeded. **Designer:** Sir E.B. Mackennal, obverse; W.H.J. Blakemore, reverse. **Rarity:** Only one example known of this pattern coin. Bowman 42.

The designs for a mintage of Canadian gold coins in dollar denominations were finalized in 1911. Starting in 1908, Canada had struck sovereigns with a small "C" mintmark. These hardly circulated in Canada, where they were viewed by some as British coins and not Canadian ones. The Canadian government had always planned to mint gold coins with design elements that were recognizably Canadian, and by 1911 the plan was close to being realized.

The obverse of the 1911 $5 and $10 pattern coins was designed by Sir E.B. Mackennal and the reverse by W.H.J. Blakemore. These are the same designs used for the gold coins struck for circulation and dated 1912 through 1914. There is one curiosity regarding these 1911 pattern coins, however. All the other denominations for that year did not have the legend DEI GRA ("by the grace of God"). The engravers at the Royal Mint had been under enormous pressure to get the new dies completed for the new monarch, George V, and the legend had been inadvertently omitted. There was an uproar over these "Godless" coins in Canada, and the legend was restored for the 1912 coins and remained on all subsequent issues of this and future monarchs until some recent Queen Elizabeth II emissions (for example, the 25-cent commemorative issues for the Vancouver 2010 Olympic Winter Games). The presence of the legend on these patterns suggests that they were likely produced late in 1911, following the uproar over the legend's omission from the minor coins of that year.

Although there is no detailed documentation concerning the origin of these patterns, we can surmise that their history is similar to that of the silver 1911 Canadian dollar—namely, there was a plan to mint $5 and $10 coins and these 1911 patterns were likely struck to test the dies before the coins were produced for circulation. The major difference, of course, is that the gold coins were struck for general usage in 1912–1914, whereas no Canadian silver dollars were struck for circulation in Canada until 1935. The gold coins struck from 1912 to 1914 saw little use in Canada due to the onset of the First World War, and they languished in vaults for many years. Tragically, almost a quarter million $5 and $10 coins were melted by the Canadian government in 2015 after lying untouched in a government vault for over a century.

Sir E.B. Mackennal.

Many collectors of Canadian coins have never heard of, let alone seen, these unique 1911 patterns, even though they are listed with images in the *Charlton Standard Catalogue, Canadian Coins*—such is their rarity. The Accession Book of the Royal Mint lists "provenance unknown" for the origin of these pieces.

No. 45 1912 Gold $5 and $10

Standards ($5)—**Weight:** 8.36 grams. **Composition:** 0.900 gold, 0.100 copper. **Diameter:** 21.59 millimeters. **Edge:** Reeded. **Designer:** Sir E.B. Mackennal, obverse; W.H.J. Blakemore, reverse. **Rarity:** Readily available to collectors in all grades of Uncirculated up to MS-66, particularly after June 2015, when thousands were released by the Canadian government for sale to collectors.

Standards ($10)—**Weight:** 16.72 grams. **Composition:** 0.900 gold, 0.100 copper. **Diameter:** 26.92 millimeters. **Edge:** Reeded. **Designer:** Sir E.B. Mackennal, obverse; W.H.J. Blakemore, reverse. **Rarity:** Readily available to collectors in all grades of Uncirculated up to MS-66, particularly after June 2015, when thousands were released by the Canadian government for sale to collectors.

After the Ottawa Mint opened in 1908, Canada rapidly developed plans to produce its own uniquely Canadian gold coinage. The Currency Act of 1910 contained a provision for this, and the original plan was to follow the U.S. lead and mint $2.5, $5, $10, and $20 coins with the same fineness as the U.S. coins, namely, 0.900 gold and 0.100 copper. Although sketches were made for an early version of the $2.5 coin (see the essay "Canada 1909 Gold Pattern $2.5 and $10" on page 101), only $5 and $10 coins were eventually minted. No designs or official mint correspondence could be found for the suggested $20 coin.

The obverse of both the $5 and $10 coins is similar to all other George V designs (except for the 1911 coinage, which omitted DEI GRA), but the reverse is entirely distinct, consisting of the Coat of Arms of Canada (as it was at the time) resting on crossed boughs of oak leaves. These coins were first minted in 1912 but production ceased only two years later, with the onset of war in 1914, when Canada adopted wartime measures to restrict the circulation of gold coins. By then, many coins dated 1912 were already circulating and only relatively small numbers remained in government vaults. By contrast, a large fraction of the mintage of 1913 and 1914 $5 and $10 coins were still in storage, so only a small fraction was in circulation. After the war, Canada did not mint any further gold coins except for sovereigns. There was a half-hearted attempt to reintroduce gold coins about a decade after the war, when new patterns were produced for a possible circulating gold coinage (see the essay "1928 Bronze Pattern $5 and $10" on page 108), but this never came to fruition.

The $5 and $10 gold coins that were not released for circulation remained in government vaults for over 100 years, a fact not well known to most Canadian numismatists. In June 2015 the Canadian government melted all but 30,000 of these coins, which were sold to collectors. Approximately 215,000, or one-third of the entire mintage, were melted. The government realized a windfall in the process, as the melt value of the coins amounted to over US$110 million.

Even with the release of so many coins in Uncirculated condition, these pieces remain very desirable collectibles. Prior to the government release, the finest known MS-66+ 1912 $10 coin realized US$21,850 in an April 2012 Heritage auction. The post-release sale of a similarly graded example garnered only US$8,812.50 in a 2017 sale by the same auction company. Superb Specimen examples (SP-68), like the one illustrated on the previous page, still attract aggressively high hammer prices at auction. A trio of these appeared at Heritage auctions between 2015 and 2019, averaging a solid US$23,267. The $5 coin sells at auction for somewhat lower prices. On January 7, 2018, an MS-66 1912 example sold for US$7,200 at a Heritage auction, while a superb SP-67 example reached US$15,862.50 in April 2017.

The 1868 Coat of Arms of Canada, showing the quartered arms of the four founding provinces.

The population reports for circulation-strike 1912 $5 and $10 coins reflect the government release. Before 2015, the population in grades above and including MS-65 was very small. Currently, however, PCGS lists 967 $5 coins in various Mint State grades, with five examples in MS-66 topping the list and another 26 in MS-65. For the $10 coin, the total population comprises 612 examples in various MS grades, including five in MS-66 and seven in MS-65.

These $5 and $10 gold coins are of paramount importance in the history of Canadian coinage. Virtually every aspect of these coins was Canadian, from the gold used in their manufacture to their design elements, although the designers were still British. In 1912 the gold came from the Klondike in the Canadian Yukon, and for the 1913 and 1914 issues it came from the Northern Ontario Porcupine Mine. The reverse of the coin featured for the first time the Coat of Arms of Canada adopted in 1868, with the symbols of the four provinces that had come together in Confederation in 1867. Ontario was represented by St. George's Cross, Quebec by a pair of fleurs-de-lis, Nova Scotia by a salmon between Scottish thistles, and New Brunswick by the British lion and a sailing ship.

No. 6 1916-C Sovereign

Standards—**Weight:** 7.99 grams. **Composition:** 0.917 gold, 0.083 copper. **Diameter:** 22.05 millimeters. **Edge:** Reeded. **Designer:** Sir E.B. Mackennal ("B.M." on truncation), obverse; Benedetto Pistrucci ("B.P." below ground at right), reverse. **Rarity:** Very rare; only about 50 extant.

CHAPTER 7
NO. 72

CANADIAN COINS OF CONSUMMATE BEAUTY AND CONDITIONAL RARITIES

CANADIAN COINS OF CONSUMMATE BEAUTY IN THE BRITISH MUSEUM

The pieces in the first part of this essay are from the British Museum collection, where the coins have remained in more or less pristine condition, giving the viewer the rare opportunity to examine fully the genius of the designer, the engraver, and the Royal Mint.

Over the course of more than a century and a half since these coins were produced, they have been examined periodically by collectors and curators, handled by visitors, and, in some extreme cases, even switched by unscrupulous individuals for more common examples of the same type. I first examined the British Museum collection of Canadian coins in 1977 and wrote a brief article about it for the Canadian Numismatic Association's journal in 1979, in which I pointed out that the extremely rare 1889 Canadian 10-cent coin had been switched for a circulated 1858 piece. Security has been improved since then! There are very few coins available in the marketplace of comparable quality to those illustrated here. All the coins displayed here are specially produced Specimen examples with mirrored fields and all design details fully struck up, representing the finest achievements in the areas of design, manufacture, and preservation. After looking through the entire Canadian and Provincial collection in the British Museum, it was my opinion that the coins illustrated here were absolutely the finest present in the collection for their particular denomination. These are personal choices, of course; other collectors would likely choose different examples to highlight.

Newfoundland Cent, 1873

Standards—**Weight:** 5.45 grams. **Composition:** 0.95 copper, 0.04 tin, 0.01 zinc. **Diameter:** 25.5 millimeters. **Edge:** Plain. **Rarity:** Only a few examples known in Specimen.

Newfoundland 5 Cents, 1873

Standards—**Weight:** 1.40 grams. **Composition:** 0.925 silver, 0.075 copper. **Diameter:** 15.5 millimeters. **Edge:** Reeded. **Rarity:** Extremely rare in Specimen.

Newfoundland 10 Cents, 1870

Standards—**Weight:** 2.39 grams. **Composition:** 0.925 silver, 0.075 copper. **Diameter:** 17.98 millimeters. **Edge:** Reeded. **Rarity:** Extremely rare in Specimen.

Newfoundland 20 Cents, 1865

Standards—**Weight:** 4.71 grams. **Composition:** 0.925 silver, 0.075 copper. **Diameter:** 23.19 millimeters. **Edge:** Reeded. **Rarity:** Rare in Specimen.

Canada 25 Cents, 1870

Standards—**Weight:** 5.81 grams. **Composition:** 0.925 silver, 0.075 copper. **Diameter:** 23.62 millimeters. **Edge:** Reeded. **Rarity:** Rare Specimen issue.

Canada 50 Cents, 1870

Standards—**Weight:** 11.62 grams. **Composition:** 0.925 silver, 0.075 copper. **Diameter:** 29.72 millimeters. **Edge:** Reeded. **Rarity:** Rare Specimen issue, with unknown but modest mintage.

Conditional Rarities

"Conditional rarities" are coins that are at least moderately rare and difficult to acquire in any reasonably high grade, but the condition of a specific example is such that it is at least one full grade (more is better) higher than any others of that date, and it is not exceeded in grade by any other date of that series. They must be spectacularly preserved and possess outstanding eye appeal. Coins like these rarely find their way to auction, but when they do the prices can be almost incomprehensible as collectors vie for the best of the best. Below I illustrate and briefly discuss five conditional rarities in the Canadian series.

1871-H 50 Cents, MS-67

Standards—**Weight:** 11.62 grams. **Composition:** 0.925 silver, 0.075 copper. **Diameter:** 29.72 millimeters. **Edge:** Reeded. **Designer and engraver:** Leonard C. Wyon. **Rarity:** Moderately rare in the Victorian 50-cent series.

Only 45,000 1871-H 50-cent coins were struck at the Heaton Mint for Canada in that year. This makes it the third-smallest mintage in this entire series and distinguishes it as a moderately rare coin. The outstandingly scarce coins among the Victorian 50-cent series are the 1890-H, 1894, and 1898, which has a slightly larger mintage than the 1871-H. In lower grades the 1871-H is not a particular rarity, and heavily circulated examples can sell for less than US$100. A solid MS-60 coin is worth around US$6,000, while the absolutely spectacular coin illustrated above (MS-67) sold for a whopping US$120,750 in a January 2010 Heritage auction. By comparison, the rarest coin in the Victorian 50-cent series, the 1890-H, which was graded three points lower (MS-64), attracted a bid of US$149,500 in the same 2010 auction.

1903-H 50 Cents, MS-67

Standards—**Weight:** 11.62 grams. **Composition:** 0.925 silver, 0.075 copper. **Diameter:** 29.72 millimeters. **Edge:** Reeded. **Designers and engravers:** G.W. DeSaulles, obverse; Leonard C. Wyon, reverse. **Rarity:** About average rarity in the Edwardian 50-cent series.

Among Edwardian 50-cent pieces, which were minted between 1902 and 1910, the 1903 is undistinguished in its rarity (falling roughly in the middle in terms of mintage) and stands out mainly for being the only emission from the Heaton Mint for this series. The mintmark "H" can be seen below the ribbon on the reverse. In the lower grades of almost Uncirculated (AU-50 to AU-53), an example can be purchased for less than US$500. Attractive AU-58 examples have sold for up to US$2,000. A not particularly attractive MS-65 example recently sold at auction for US$11,400, while the coin shown here, when it was in a PCGS MS-66 holder (note that it is currently graded MS-67), sold for US$32,200 at a Heritage auction in 2010. This coin is tied with one dated 1908 as the highest-graded Edwardian 50-cent piece of any year.

1904 25 Cents, MS-68

Standards—**Weight:** 5.81 grams. **Composition:** 0.925 silver, 0.075 copper. **Diameter:** 23.62 millimeters. **Edge:** Reeded. **Designer and engraver:** G.W. DeSaulles. **Rarity:** The second-lowest mintage of any Edwardian 25-cent coin.

Except for the Small Crown variety dated 1906, the 1904 25-cent piece is the rarest coin in this short Edwardian series. The illustrated example is the only MS-68-graded example in the entire series, so it definitely qualifies as a conditional rarity. As far as can be traced, it has not sold recently at auction. A brilliant MS-65 piece sold for US$8,400 in June 2020, while an exceptional MS-66 example reached US$14,900 in a 2010 Heritage auction. This coin would attract bids of multiples of that amount if it were auctioned today.

1907 10 Cents, MS-68

Standards—**Weight:** 2.32 grams. **Composition:** 0.925 silver, 0.075 copper. **Diameter:** 18.03 millimeters. **Edge:** Reeded. **Designer:** G.W. DeSaulles. **Rarity:** Second-highest mintage of any 10-cent coin in this series.

The 1907 10-cent Edwardian coin has the second-highest mintage in the series. Even so, there is little price difference among most Edward VII 10-cent pieces in Uncirculated grade, so this coin will sell at about the same level as other 10-cent examples from this monarch. MS-65 examples without exceptional eye appeal typically sell at auction for slightly over US$1,000. The illustrated example sold for US$8,050 in a 2010 Heritage auction. At that time it was in a PCGS MS-67 holder, whereas it now resides in an MS-68 holder from the same grading service. Does that change its value? There have not been any auction appearances since it was upgraded, so we will have to wait until the current owner makes this coin available to the collecting public once again.

1931 50 Cents, MS-68

Standards—**Weight:** 11.66 grams. **Composition:** 0.800 silver, 0.200 copper. **Diameter:** 29.72 millimeters. **Edge:** Reeded. **Designer:** Sir E.B. Mackennal, obverse; Leonard C. Wyon, W.H.J. Blakemore, reverse. **Rarity:** All George V 50-cent coins are scarce in high grade.

In the George V 50-cent series, all the mintages are small; only for a single date (1919) did the mintage exceed one million coins. In the early 1920s there was so little demand for these large silver coins that the Ottawa Mint melted much of the 1921 issue (206,398 struck), together with about half of those struck in 1920 (mintage 584,429). This produced one of Canada's great rarities, the 1921 50-cent piece, which currently sells for well over US$100,000 in Uncirculated condition. The 1931 50-cent piece had a paltry mintage of only 57,581 coins, but even that small number is only the fourth smallest in this very highly collected series. Coins grading MS-64 sell for somewhat in excess of US$2,000, while an MS-67 example reached US$17,250 at a recent auction. Specimens also exist of this coin, several examples in SP-67 having sold for in excess of US$16,000. The illustrated MS-68 coin does not appear to have sold at auction recently. It is the only MS-68 coin in the entire series and would likely command a price well in excess of US$30,000 if it appeared at auction today.

Chapter 8

Canadian Coins from the Reign of King George VI

This chapter focuses on the coinage of King George VI, whose reign covered the years 1936–1952. Breaking with the tradition of changing direction with every new monarch, the king's portrait faces left on all his coinage, just as his father's had done. Also, for the first time in the history of Canadian coinage, the monarch's portrait was uncrowned. George VI's daughter, Queen Elizabeth II, would continue this uncrowned tradition for the first dozen years of her reign. The most popular, as well as the most interesting, series during this period was the silver dollars. They were struck for this monarch between 1937 and 1939, omitted during the war years, and resumed in 1945. A number of great rarities appear in the dollar and 50-cent series during this era. With the exception of the $1 piece, all Canadian coinage exhibited new reverse designs beginning with George VI, as the government strove to modernize the appearance of Canadian coinage. To enjoy these new designs in one fell swoop, the reader is invited to examine the coins illustrated in the first essay.

No. 24 1937 New Coinage Designs

Standards (cent)—**Weight:** 3.24 grams. **Composition:** 0.955 copper, 0.030 tin, 0.150 zinc. **Diameter:** 19.05 millimeters. **Edge:** Plain. **Designers:** T. Humphrey Paget, obverse; George E. Kruger Gray, reverse. **Rarity:** Not a rare coin.

Standards (5 cents)—**Weight:** 4.54 grams. **Composition:** 1.000 nickel. **Diameter:** 21.21 millimeters. **Edge:** Plain. **Designers:** T. Humphrey Paget, obverse; George E. Kruger Gray, reverse. **Rarity:** A common coin, easily obtained.

Standards (10 cents)—**Weight:** 2.33 grams. **Composition:** 0.800 silver, 0.200 copper. **Diameter:** 18.03 millimeters. **Edge:** Reeded. **Designers:** T. Humphrey Paget, obverse; Emanuel Hahn, reverse. **Rarity:** A common coin.

Standards (25 cents)—**Weight:** 5.83 grams. **Composition:** 0.800 silver, 0.200 copper. **Diameter:** 23.62 millimeters. **Edge:** Reeded. **Designers:** T. Humphrey Paget, obverse; Emanuel Hahn, reverse. **Rarity:** An easily obtained coin.

Standards (50 cents) **Weight:** 11.66 grams. **Composition:** 0.800 silver, 0.200 copper. **Diameter:** 29.72 mm. **Edge:** Reeded. **Designers:** T. Humphrey Paget, obverse; George E. Kruger Gray, reverse. **Rarity:** Not a rare coin.

In 1935 Canada took the first step in modernizing its coinage with the introduction of a circulating $1 coin with a distinctly Canadian reverse: the Voyageur dollar. It took the accession of a new monarch in 1937 for the redesign to be completed, with new reverse images appearing on all the remaining coins. The obverse design for King George VI, together with the new reverses on all the circulating coins, are illustrated above. The $1 reverse is excluded here because it is the same as that on the 1935 coin discussed on page 94.

As mentioned in the introduction to this chapter, the monarch's portrait is unusual as he is uncrowned and facing left. The portrait is youthful and radiates a sense of strength and confidence, qualities that were soon needed during the horrendous conflagration that engulfed the world. Anyone who has seen the movie *The King's Speech* is aware, however, that George VI was initially anything but highly confident and self-assured.

Shortly after the death of King George V, the master of the Royal Canadian Mint, J.H. Campbell, suggested to the government that new designs for the reverses on all Canadian coins except the dollar be created, pointing out that the change in the monarch's portrait was an opportune time to carry out this redesign. In the best of Canadian traditions, a committee was formed consisting of directors of art galleries, numismatists, and archivists, and chaired by Campbell. Design proposals were solicited and 77 were received from the artistic community. The committee made a selection, but the government rejected all of them. The committee then commissioned six of the original respondents to provide plaster casts and asked the Royal Mint to solicit designs from British artists experienced in coinage design. In the end, two plaster casts produced by Emanuel Hahn of Toronto and three sketches from George Kruger Gray were submitted to and accepted by the Canadian government. Hahn had earlier designed the reverse of the 1935 silver dollar—the famous Voyageur reverse—while Kruger Gray was an important designer for the Royal Mint who had provided sketches for coins for several parts of the Commonwealth, including Australia, New Zealand, and South Africa, and produced designs for numerous issues of the coinage of Great Britain.

The reverse of the 1937 Canadian cent coin features a twig of maple leaves. The simple and uncrowded design captures the beauty of Canada on a rather small coin. Kruger Gray's initials appear prominently on the reverse right edge. This design was originally submitted for the 5-cent reverse, but the government chose it for the cent instead. The 5-cent piece features a beaver sitting on a mound of rock and earth rising out of the water. For some unknown reason, the date is followed by a dot, which was removed for subsequent issues. The initials K.G. again appear, this time to the left of the mound. This design was originally intended for the 10-cent piece but was chosen for the 5-cent coin.

The reverse of the new 5-cent coin may owe its origins to a rare token issued by the North West Company in 1820 that featured a beaver resting on a grassy rocky mound. This token, of which perhaps less than 20 exist, was issued for use in and around Hudson Bay, although it apparently was first employed in the United States. The token was good for one beaver skin.

Standards—**Composition:** Brass. **Edge:** Plain. **Rarity:** Very rare—the token pictured here, the finest known of the type, sold for US$42,000 in a recent Heritage Auction. Breton 925.

Gaining much approval from the public was the appearance on the 10-cent coin of the schooner *Bluenose*, although it was not officially recognized as this particular vessel until generations later, in 2002. Designed by Emanuel Hahn, it was originally submitted for the 25-cent piece but was chosen for the 10-cent coin. A small "H" (for Hahn) appears just above the waterline to the left of the schooner. A caribou head, also designed by Hahn, appears on the 25-cent coin. His initial "H" can be seen just below the chest of the caribou at the bottom of the coin. The design was originally submitted for the 5-cent piece but was chosen for the quarter dollar instead. The original drawings included the Big Dipper (the seven principal stars in the constellation of Ursa Major—the Great Bear—seen year-round from much of Canada), but only three of the stars made it to the final coin design. Finally, the new reverse of the 50-cent piece featured a wonderful design centered on the Canadian coat of arms. Kruger Gray also designed this coin, and his initials, somewhat grandly, appear on either side of the crown atop the shield.

Specimen sets of these six 1937 coins appear reasonably frequently at auction, both as matte and as mirror examples, with the latter being decidedly scarcer. Superb sets are moderately scarce, and one of the finest went for US$6,325 in a June 2010 Heritage auction. This was the ex-Pittman set, and the coins averaged almost SP-67. Many sets are sold with their original holders, 150 of which were made. Perhaps the most outstanding example of a 1937 set was the "Double Set" auctioned by Heritage in August 2015. This consisted of two of each coin in mirror Specimen condition, together with an original mint case. The lot sold for US$11,750. An average set with grade range SP-64–SP-65 can often be had for not much more than US$1,500, a beautiful and rather inexpensive acquisition for such a numismatically important set.

No. 80 1938 50 Cents

Standards—**Weight:** 11.66 grams. **Composition:** 0.800 silver, 0.200 copper. **Diameter:** 29.72 millimeters. **Edge:** Reeded. **Designers:** T. Humphrey Paget, obverse; George E. Kruger Gray, reverse.

The year 1938 was an important one for Canada. The winds of war were blowing and the Canadian government was not particularly enthusiastic about making preparations for the upcoming conflict. There was serious debate in Canada whether to stand again with Britain only 20 years after the end of the First World War. Canada's military preparedness was almost non-existent, and Prime Minister William Lyon Mackenzie King was keen to keep the country on the path of neutrality. His reasons were both political—parts of the country were not enthusiastic about helping Britain in another war—and practical, as Canada had a very small standing army, few aircraft, and a minuscule navy. In a desperate move to appease Adolf Hitler, King actually traveled to Berlin to see the dictator. The two met on June 29, 1937, and King was absolutely mesmerized by Hitler, who professed that he was a man of peace.

King also had a close relationship with Franklin Roosevelt. The American president was very fond of Canada and even had a summer cottage in New Brunswick. In August 1938 Roosevelt visited Ottawa, the first American president to do so, and gave a speech before the Parliament Buildings affirming the solidity of U.S.-Canadian relations. The speech had the effect Roosevelt desired, as King feared that if Canada were invaded by a foreign country (likely Germany or Japan), it would most probably mean the presence of U.S. troops on Canadian soil. King subsequently ordered increased funding for the Canadian military.

The mintage of 50-cent pieces during the years leading up to the war was sparse, with 1937 and 1938 having the smallest emissions of the entire series (192,000 each) except for the rare 1948 coin, which had a tiny mintage of only 37,784 examples. Even so, the 1938 coin sells for considerably more than its 1948 cousin, typically by a factor of two to three. In Specimen strike, 1938 is the rarest and most expensive coin in the entire 50-cent series of George VI. During the Second World War and shortly thereafter, the mintages in this series climbed up to the range of 2 to 3 million pieces.

**Prime Minister
William Lyon Mackenzie King.**

The finest known Mint State 1938 50-cent coin (MS-66) sold for US$10,350 at a Heritage auction in January 2010, while an ex-Belzberg example in SP-67 reached US$17,250 in a 2006 auction. By contrast, the more famous 1948 50-cent coin in SP-67 (finest known, ex Pittman, Belzberg) sold for only US$6,900 in the same 2006 sale, while a high-grade Mint State example (MS-66) can be had for about US$1,500 today.

No. 61 1939 $1

Standards—**Weight:** 23.3 grams. **Composition:** 0.800 silver, 0.200 copper. **Diameter:** 36.06 millimeters. **Edge:** Reeded. **Designers:** T. Humphrey Paget, obverse; Emanuel Hahn, reverse. **Rarity:** Not rare, with more than 1,000 examples in Mint State among the various population reports.

Queen Victoria never visited Canada. She limited her travel to Scotland, Ireland, and a few European countries such as Germany and Italy. That may be forgiven considering the difficulty of travel during her reign. Neither did her son Edward VII ever make it to Canada as king, although he did visit in July 1860 when he was Prince of Wales. King George V also never set foot on Canadian soil. The first reigning monarch to visit the country was King George VI, who with Queen Elizabeth, his consort, toured Canada from coast to coast in 1939. To commemorate this royal visit, Canada struck a specially designed silver dollar coin with the same physical specifications and obverse as the dollars from 1937 and 1938. The reverse was entirely new, however, and was designed and engraved by Emanuel Hahn, an experienced designer who had created the very popular Voyageur design for the reverse of the 1935 dollar.

This new reverse depicted the Parliament Buildings in Ottawa with the 92-meter-high Peace Tower in the center. This tower had been designed by architect John Andrews Pearson and reconstructed after the earlier, somewhat smaller one burned down in 1916. The Latin inscription on the reverse of the coin, FIDE SUORUM REGNAT, translates to "He reigns by the faith of his people." The effects of the Great Depression were still hanging over the country, so while almost 1.4 million coins were produced, more than 10 percent remained unsold at the end of the royal tour and were returned to the Ottawa Mint to be melted.

The 1939 dollar was also produced in matte or mirror Specimen coins, which are considerably more expensive than normal circulation-strike examples. A spectacular SP-68 (matte) example sold for US$3,995 in a 2017 Heritage auction. Two SP-67 examples sold through Heritage in 2014 realized US$4,700 (mirror) and US$4,112.50 (matte). An exceptional circulation-strike MS-66+ example garnered US$4,312.50 in a January 2011 Heritage auction. A nice MS-63 circulation-strike example is much less expensive and can be obtained for only about US$100. The population report confirms that this coin is relatively common, with 904 circulation-strike examples in Mint State at PCGS and a further 88 in Specimen, about a quarter of which are the rarer mirror type.

King George VI and Queen Elizabeth in Toronto during their 1939 royal tour of Canada.

No. 38 1942–1945 Tombac and Steel 5 Cents

Standards—**Weight:** 4.54 grams. **Composition:** Tombac (0.88 copper, 0.12 zinc); steel with plating of nickel and chromium. **Diameter:** 12-sided; 21.3 millimeters opposite corners, 20.0 millimeters opposite sides. **Edge:** Plain. **Designers:** T. Humphrey Paget, obverse; George E. Kruger Gray, 1942 reverse; Thomas Shingles, 1943–1945 reverse. **Rarity:** Not particularly rare, but of historical importance.

In 1922 Canada moved from a small (15.5 millimeters) silver 5-cent coin to a more substantial nickel piece (21.2 millimeters). This was largely in response to two points of pressure: the increasing price of silver and the desire of the Royal Canadian Mint (as the Ottawa Mint was renamed in 1931) to make Canadian coins more similar to those in the United States. The new Canadian 5-cent piece was almost the same diameter as the Buffalo nickel, the circulating U.S. 5-cent piece at the time. Nickel was chosen for the composition of the new coins because Canada possessed enormous deposits of the metal and was the world's largest producer at the time. (It has currently slipped to sixth place, behind such countries as Indonesia and Russia.)

Pure nickel was the sole component of the Canadian 5-cent coins from 1922 to 1942, even though the metal is quite hard and difficult to work with. In the early years of production many of the 5-cent coins were poorly struck because of this. With Canada's entry into the Second World War in 1939, careful management of materials required for the war effort was instituted. In 1942 the government suspended the mintage of coins in nickel because the metal was useful for hardening steel used in the manufacture of tanks and anti-aircraft guns. Experiments with other metals led to the choice of tombac as the metal for striking the 5-cent coins. Tombac is an alloy consisting largely of copper with a 5–20 percent zinc component. Other metals, including arsenic, lead, or tin, were added largely to obtain a particular coloration. Tombac is relatively cheap and quite malleable, making it ideal for coinage purposes.

The first coins produced in tombac were dated 1942 (top images) and had exactly the same design as the George VI 5-cent pieces that had been minted beginning in 1937. The only substantial differences were that the coins now had a brownish tint and were 12-sided instead of round. Even though tombac does not tarnish easily, there was some concern that if it did, it could be confused with the copper cent, which was only 1 millimeter in diameter smaller, so the 5-cent piece was made 12-sided.

In 1943 a new design for the 5-cent coin was introduced (middle coin on the previous page). It was meant to be patriotic, with a large V for victory on the reverse and Morse code messaging along the inside of the reverse rim. The coded message reads: "We Win When We Work Willingly." The only 5-cent pieces struck were in tombac that year, but by 1944 copper and zinc were becoming important war metals so the composition was changed again, this time to steel plated with nickel and chromium (bottom images). All the 5-cent coins dated 1944 and 1945 had this composition.

None of the coins pictured are particularly scarce or expensive. Any of them can be obtained in gem condition (MS-65) for a few hundred dollars—with one exception. In 1944 the composition switched from tombac to plated steel, so there should be no 1944 tombac 5-cent coins in existence; all should be of plated steel. However, the mint report lists 8,000 tombac pieces as having been struck in 1943 but dated 1944. Only a single example has been recorded, and the CoinsandCanada.com website lists a price for this coin of US$88,500. In 1999 likely the only known example sold for US$35,075 in a Heritage auction. Recently, on the Heritage Auctions website (August 5, 2021) there was a "Make Offer to Owner" green sticker—you can own the 1944 tombac coin for not less than US$777,778!

No. 90 1944 Specimen Set

Standards (cent)—**Weight:** 3.24 grams. **Composition:** 0.955 copper, 0.030 tin, 0.150 zinc. **Diameter:** 19.05 millimeters. **Edge:** Plain. **Designers:** T. Humphrey Paget, obverse; George E. Kruger Gray, reverse. **Rarity:** Very rare in Specimen and the rarest in the set; perhaps as few as four available.

Standards (5 cents)—**Weight:** 4.54 grams. **Composition:** Steel with 0.013 mm nickel plating and 0.0003 chromium plating. **Diameter:** 21.3 millimeters (corner to corner), 20.9 mm (opposite sides). **Edge:** Plain. **Designers:** T. Humphrey Paget, obverse; Thomas Shingles, reverse. **Rarity:** The most readily available of the 1944 Specimen coins; about 26 known.

Standards (10 cents)—**Weight:** 2.33 grams. **Composition:** 0.800 silver, 0.200 copper. **Diameter:** 18.03 millimeters. **Edge:** Reeded. **Designers:** T. Humphrey Paget, obverse; Emanuel Hahn, reverse. **Rarity:** Very rare; only about six known.

Standards (25 cents)—**Weight:** 5.83 grams. **Composition:** 0.800 silver, 0.200 copper. **Diameter:** 23.62 millimeters. **Edge:** Reeded. **Designers:** T. Humphrey Paget, obverse; Emanuel Hahn, reverse. **Rarity:** Rare; about ten known.

Standards (50 cents)—**Weight:** 11.66 grams. **Composition:** 0.800 silver, 0.200 copper. **Diameter:** 29.72 millimeters. **Edge:** Reeded. **Designers:** T. Humphrey Paget, obverse; George E. Kruger Gray, reverse. **Rarity:** Very rare; about seven known in Specimen.

Full disclosure: 1944 was the year of my birth, and for the past several years I have been attempting to put together a Specimen set of Canadian coins from that year. The set is expensive, but not prohibitively so since no $1 coins were minted in that year, so only five coins constitute the entire set (the cent, 5 cents, 10 cents, 25 cents, and 50 cents); nevertheless, the coins are very difficult to locate in nice condition. In 2019 I had actually been offered 60 percent of the complete set in one fell swoop, from the Cornerstone Collection. The three coins were all very nice—the 5-cent piece in SP-67 (with a choice of two examples) and the 10- and 25-cent examples were both in SP-65—and would have made a fine addition to my collection. Very unwisely, however, I passed on this offer, thinking that I might find the 1944 coins elsewhere for less money. Instead, I spent my coin budget on other items that, in the end, turned out to be of less significance to me. This was a terrible mistake, one that I rue to this day. As of March 2022, I have been able to acquire three of the most readily available pieces from this set: a 5-cent coin (by far the commonest of the five coins), and a 25-cent and 50-cent coin. The cent and 10-cent coins still elude me.

But I have gotten ahead of myself here. We need to go back to 1939 to understand this set and its significance and rarity.

Canada officially entered the Second World War on September 10, 1939. By 1944 it was a full five years since Canada had begun committing a major proportion of its resources to the war effort. From a coinage perspective, mintages of coins for circulation did not decrease during these years; if anything, they increased. However, the mintage of Specimen coins was very sparse. These are specially struck coins on polished planchets, generally made for collectors or for distribution to dignitaries. No Specimen sets were minted from 1940 to 1943, and there were only four complete sets minted for 1944, although population reports list higher numbers for most denominations in Specimen (four cent coins, twenty-six 5-cent coins, six 10-cent coins, ten 25-cent coins, and seven 50-cent coins, just at PCGS). These small numbers were unquestionably related to the government's lack of interest in minting coins specially for collectors during wartime. Whether there are four or perhaps somewhat more complete sets available, the bottom line is that a complete set is very rare and difficult to assemble. Sandy Campbell, Canada's premier rare-coin dealer, writes in the Cornerstone catalog that he has owned only a single original set.

Population reports help establish the rarity of these coins. Using the PCGS report, we can get an estimate of the number of each of these Specimens available, together with a recent indication of their value:

- Cent: Coin illustrated, SP-65 Brown; four available in all grades, SP-63–SP-65; recent sale US$4,830 SP-64, Heritage Belzberg Sale, 2003

- 5 cents: Coin illustrated, SP-67; 26 available in all grades, SP-63–SP-67+; recent sale US$2,585 SP-67, Heritage Beckman Sale, 2015 (resold for US$3,500)

- 10 cents: Coin illustrated, SP-65; six in all grades, SP-63–SP-65; recent sale CAD$5,000 SP-65, Cornerstone Collection (ex Norweb)

- 25 cents: Coin illustrated, SP-65; ten in all grades, SP-63–SP-66; recent sale CAD$5,500 SP-65, Cornerstone Collection

- 50 cents: Coin illustrated, SP-64+; seven in all grades, SP-64–SP-67; recent sale CAD$6,169 SP-66, Heritage Beckman Sale, 2015

Two complete sets were sold in the 1989 Bowers and Merena sale of the Kissel and Victoria Collections. The first set, somewhat superior in quality, realized US$22,000, while a somewhat lower-quality set attracted a final bid of US$9,350. At the end of the description of the first set, the auctioneer wrote: "We have not discovered a similar offering of a 1944 Specimen set in a United States auction sale, and the appearance of this example marks the present offering as one of the most outstanding in memory."

NO. 73 1947 MAPLE LEAF SILVER DOLLAR

Standards—**Weight:** 23.3 grams. **Composition:** 0.800 silver, 0.200 copper. **Diameter:** 36.00 millimeters. **Edge:** Reeded. **Designers:** T. Humphrey Paget, obverse; Emanuel Hahn, reverse. **Rarity:** Scarce; the mintage was one of the smallest of any date in the series.

On August 15, 1947, the Indian Independence Act passed by the U.K. Parliament came into effect. It created the nations of India and Pakistan out of the South Asian section of the former Mongol Empire. The march towards independence took place much more quickly than expected, as Britain was concerned that it might have to referee a civil war in the area if events did not move ahead as expeditiously as possible. The young Lord Louis Mountbatten was appointed as Britain's last viceroy of India, with a mandate to hand over power to India and leave the region as quickly as possible. In the end he convinced India and Pakistan to agree to a partition into two independent countries. Such was his haste that he moved up the date of Partition a full ten months earlier than expected. The British judge charged with drawing the boundaries of the two countries had just over a month to complete the task, finishing a few days after the partition agreement was signed by the two parties!

This haste caused real problems in the mints of the Commonwealth countries. In the middle of the year, all of a sudden, the obverse of the coins they had been producing was no longer correct or legal. The illustrated Canadian 1947 dollar demonstrates the problem. Up until mid-1947, King George VI had been the Emperor of India (ET IND: IMP:) as well as the British monarch. That all changed after India became independent. The obverse of the George VI coins had to be changed as soon as possible to remove the reference to India. Since the dies for this transition still came from London and were not yet available in Canada, and since silver dollars were in high demand by the public, the Canadian Mint settled on a neat and simple solution. Using the dies for 1947, the mint added a small maple leaf to the right of the date on the reverse. The obverse of the coin was unchanged from the 1947 striking and thus still bore the legend ET IND: IMP:. The maple leaf signified that that the coin had been struck in 1948, even though it was dated 1947.

The 1947 Maple Leaf silver dollar is a rarity, since only 21,135 pieces were produced. Exceptional MS-64 examples, such as the gorgeous one illustrated here, can reach over

US$3,000 at auction, with this particular example realizing US$3,450 in a 2008 Heritage auction. The finest known, a superb MS-67 coin from the Belzberg Collection, realized an astounding US$46,000 in a 2006 Heritage auction. In the same sale two MS-66 examples sold for US$10,350 and US$7,475. Specially struck Specimen examples of these Maple Leaf varieties typically sell for strong prices. One of the finest known, an SP-66 example, sold for US$11,162.50 in a 2014 Heritage auction.

Every so often an odd variety of silver dollar shows up, and the example illustrated at right is certainly one of these. The coin has been stamped with the initials J.O.P. for Joseph Oliva Patenaude. The full story of this interesting counterstamp can be found in the chapter on the coins of King George V, on pages 96–97. This is a very rare stamp on a 1947 $1 coin and it attracted a winning bid of US$3,055 in a 2014 auction.

A 1947 maple leaf silver dollar that has been counterstamped "J.O.P." just above the date.

No. 37 1947 50 Cents, Maple Leaf, Curved Right 7

Standards—**Weight:** 11.66 grams. **Composition:** 0.800 silver, 0.200 copper. **Diameter:** 29.72 millimeters. **Edge:** Reeded. Designers and engravers: T. Humphrey Paget, obverse; George E. Kruger Gray, reverse. **Rarity:** A rarity in the George VI 50-cent series.

There are a bewildering number of varieties of the Canadian 1947 50-cent piece. Four have been officially recognized: 1947 Curved Left 7; 1947 Curved Right 7; 1947 Maple Leaf, Curved Left 7; and 1947 Maple Leaf, Curved Right 7. Examples of all these varieties are shown on the next page. The top images are the no–Maple Leaf varieties, with the leftmost one being the Curved Left 7 (the "7" in the date curves slightly leftward). The bottom two images are the same, except that there is a small Maple Leaf to the right of the 7 in the date.

As mentioned in the case of the 1947 dollar on page 125, the mint issued a number of 50-cent pieces in 1948 in which the obverse of the coin was identical to that for 1947. By 1948 India had become independent and the legend ET IND: IMP: was now obsolete. The dies reflecting this change were not ready early in 1948, so the mint added a small maple leaf to the right of the 7 in the date, producing the two major varieties—Maple Leaf and No Maple Leaf—in order to distinguish the 1947-dated coins that were actually struck in 1948. Additionally, there were two different styles of the 7 in the date. These have various names, but "Curved Right" and "Curved Left" will suffice.

Among the 1937–1947 half dollars (before Indian independence), all 1947s are on the scarce side, with every variety commanding at least several hundred dollars at auction. The Maple Leaf, Curved Right 7, is the jewel among these coins. The no–Maple Leaf coins have a total mintage of 424,885, with no breakdown available for Curved 7, left or right. The Curved Right 7 is slightly scarcer and commands a higher price at auction. A pair of these coins in MS-65 sold in a January 2010 Heritage auction for US$1,725 (Curved Left) and US$2,300 (Curved Right). The Maple Leaf variety has a much smaller mintage of only 38,433 examples, again with no breakdown available for the two varieties. There are only three 1947 Maple Leaf Curved Right examples in the PCGS population report in all grades of Uncirculated: MS-61, MS-62, and MS-63. Only the MS-61 coin has appeared at auction recently, and it realized US$13,800 in a 2010 Heritage auction. By contrast, the Maple Leaf, Curved Left, is much more available and typically sells at auction for just a few hundred dollars in the lower Uncirculated grades.

No Maple Leaf, Curved Left 7

No Maple Leaf, Curved Right 7

With Maple Leaf, Curved Left 7

With Maple Leaf, Curved Right 7

No. 9 1948 $1

Standards—**Weight:** 23.3 grams. **Composition:** 0.800 silver, 0.200 copper. **Diameter:** 36.00 millimeters. **Edge:** Reeded. **Designers:** T. Humphrey Paget, obverse; Emanuel Hahn, reverse. **Rarity:** Scarce; the mintage was the smallest of any date in the series.

Due to the change in the status of India, the legend ET IND: IMP: had to be removed from all Canadian coinage for 1948. But the dies were not ready, so a maple leaf placed on the coins indicated that they had been struck in 1948 even though dated a year earlier (this is discussed in the essay on the 1947 Maple Leaf dollar, on page 125). In the end, the design change actually resulted in more pleasing coins because the obverse was less cluttered. This can be seen by comparing the coin illustrated here with the 1947 Maple Leaf silver dollar shown on page 125.

The production of the 1948 Canadian dollar at the Royal Canadian Mint did not begin until the middle of the year, when it bore the new obverse inscription GEORGIVS VI DEI GRATIA REX. This delay severely impacted overall mintage numbers so that only 18,780 examples were struck, including a small number of Specimen strikes produced expressly for collectors. The small number made the 1948 silver dollar the lowest mintage of the entire series and subsequently the most expensive coin. Additionally, aside from the late start to the production run, there was less demand for dollars in 1948 than normal because extra silver dollars were produced and dated 1947.

The lovely example illustrated here is graded MS-65 and would sell for an amount in excess of US$10,000 if offered today. The Belzberg coin, an amazing MS-66, the single highest graded, attracted active bidding when it sold for US$21,850 in 2003. The 1948 dollar was also produced in Specimen, specially struck coins of high reflectivity but not quite up to full Proof specifications. These are somewhat more common than the circulation-strike examples. An SP-66 example, surpassed only by four examples in SP-67, sold for US$14,100 in 2014.

Even well-circulated examples of the 1948 dollar are highly prized today. Coins grading F-12 often surpass US$700, and pieces in the AU-50 range often require bids of US$1,000 or more. Remarkably, the PCGS population report indicates that the 1948 dollar has the second-largest number of King George VI Mint State certified examples, 825, surpassed only by the 1949 (to be discussed in the next essay, below) with 1,431. Here, I think, the population does not properly reflect the rarity of the coin. With the small mintage of the 1948, collectors are more likely to send an example for professional grading than for a date with a larger mintage. In spite of this generous population, the 1948 dollar always attracts serious attention at any auction.

No. 63 1949 $1

Standards—**Weight:** 23.3 grams. **Composition:** 0.800 silver, 0.200 copper. **Diameter:** 36.00 millimeters. **Edge:** Reeded. **Designers:** T. Humphrey Paget, obverse; Ernest Maunder and Thomas Shingles, reverse. **Rarity:** Not rare, even in lofty Uncirculated grades, but extremely popular.

Many history books trace the "discovery" of Newfoundland to John Cabot's visit in 1497. Cabot, though Italian, sailed under the British flag at the time. But, of course, the island had been visited many times earlier, by the Vikings around A.D. 1000 and much earlier by the Maritime Archaic Natives, peoples who left no skeletal remains, only some tools and weapons. The Viking settlements can still be seen at L'Anse aux Meadows on the northern tip of Newfoundland, now a UNESCO World Heritage Site. Evidence of a much earlier Indigenous presence comes from a burial site in Southern Labrador, L'Anse Amour, proving that Newfoundland had Indigenous settlements as early as around 9,000 years ago. These people likely came originally from Siberia, crossing over to North America from what is now Russia near the end of the last glaciation period, while the ice bridge across the Bering Sea was still intact.

In 1497 Cabot claimed the "New found Isle lands," as Newfoundland was known to the English, for King Henry VII. It is not clear that he had any right to do so, since Portugal had earlier claimed it in 1494 in the Treaty of Tordesillas. However, since Newfoundland possessed nothing to compare with the riches that the Portuguese and Spanish had found in South America and elsewhere, it was of no great value to the former and they did not dispute the English claim. Even Henry VII was unimpressed, granting the very modest reward of £10 "To Hym that found the New Isle."

During the run-up to Canadian Confederation in 1867, Newfoundland considered becoming part of the new country, sending observers to the 1864 Quebec Conference that was convened to discuss unification. Nothing came of this, however, and for 82 years after the establishment of the Dominion of Canada, Newfoundland remained a British colony of sorts. It did become a Dominion of the British Empire in 1907, with its own government, but most matters were still decided in London. Finally, after two hotly contested referenda, Newfoundland voted to join the Dominion of Canada and became its tenth province on March 31, 1949.

To celebrate this historic event, Canada struck a special circulating silver dollar in 1949 with a new reverse that recognized Cabot's visit to Newfoundland. The design of the coin shows a rendering of the *Matthew*, which was almost certainly named after Cabot's wife, Matea, and thought to be the ship that Cabot sailed to Newfoundland. Below the ship is the Latin phrase FLOREAT TERRA NOVA ("May the New Found Land Flourish"). The design of the reverse is extremely detailed and was very carefully produced. Thomas Shingles, chief engraver of the Royal Canadian Mint at that time, engraved the coin completely by hand and directly in steel. Generally, a large plaster model would have been produced, then reduced in size with an engraving machine.

The mint decided to produce these coins until the demand for them waned, so 613,500 were struck in 1949 and an additional 40,718 in 1950. Except for the 1939 silver dollar, which commemorated the visit of King George VI and Queen Elizabeth to Canada, this was the highest mintage of any Canadian dollar coin during the reigns of George V and George VI. This large mintage means that these coins are not rare. Further, since they were also carefully packaged by the mint in coin tubes for protection, many are preserved in high grades. The PCGS Mint State population is 1,431 examples, second only to the first Canadian silver dollar, struck in 1935, for which there are 2,229 Mint State coins. There are two MS-68 examples and a single MS-68+ entry in the August 2021 population report for 1949 dollars. The MS-68+ example sold for US$6,325 in a 2011 Heritage auction. By contrast, a beautiful MS-67 example can be acquired for under US$500.

No. 78 1950–1952 and 1955 $1, Arnprior

Standards—**Weight:** 23.3 grams. **Composition:** 0.800 silver, 0.200 copper. **Diameter:** 36.06 millimeters. **Edge:** Reeded. **Designers:** T. Humphrey Paget, obverse; Emanuel Hahn, reverse. **Rarity:** Modestly rare; an interesting variety that always attracts interest at auction.

Small variations on some coins can lead to huge differences in value. Take, for example, the presence of an absolutely tiny dot on the reverse of a 1936 Canadian cent or 10-cent coin (see pages 98–99). The price difference between a coin with a dot and one without is a factor of around 1,000! A similar but much less dramatic situation occurred with the Canadian dollars dated 1950–1952 and 1955.

In 1949 Newfoundland voted (just barely) to join Canada, becoming its tenth province. To commemorate this event the reverse of the 1949 Canadian dollar was redesigned, with the Voyageur canoe being replaced by the *Matthew*, John Cabot's ship. The 1949 Newfoundland dollar was so popular that production of the coin continued until well into 1950.

In 1950 the Voyageur reverse design was once again employed for the silver dollar, but the design had undergone some subtle differences that did not go unnoticed by the collecting public. It was observed on some coins dated between 1950 and 1952 that the number of water lines visible to the right of the canoe varied from rather few (1-1/2) to perhaps 3 or 4. These differences can be seen in the images that follow:

the one on the left has 4 full lines, whereas the one on the right has barely 1-1/2. This was likely caused by overzealous polishing of some reverse dies, which had the effect of removing these subtle features from the struck coin.

The coins with fewer waterlines came to be called "Arnprior dollars." This name comes from a small town in Eastern Ontario where a factory that manufactured women's underwear was located. As a small gift to its employees at Christmas in 1955, the company ordered 2,000 silver dollars from the mint. The coins it received had been struck from over-polished dies, resulting in fewer, short water lines to the right of the canoe. Naturally, these came to be called Arnprior dollars, and the name was used retroactively for all coins with similar die characteristics going back to 1950.

These coins are very popular with collectors and command serious prices when choice ones are auctioned. A superb SP-67 1950 Arnprior dollar reached US$9,400 in a January 2014 Heritage auction, while an MS-66 example of a 1951-dated coin commanded US$5,750 in a 2011 sale by the same auctioneer. A 1950 or 1951 silver dollar in MS-66 with the normal four water lines can generally be acquired for less than US$500.

Left: 1951 normal reverse, with 4 full water lines to the right of the canoe.

Right: 1951 Arnprior reverse, with 1-1/2 water lines to the right of the canoe.

No. 88 1951 5 Cents, High Relief

Top—obverse and reverse of high-relief 1951 Canada 5 cents. Bottom—left: obverse of low-relief 1951 Canada 5 cents; right: reverse of 1951 Canada commemorative 5 cents.

Standards—**Weight:** 4.54 grams. **Composition:** Commemorative, 1.00 nickel; high and low relief, steel core with 0.0127-millimeter plating of nickel and 0.0003-millimeter plating of chromium. **Diameter:** 12-sided; 21.3 millimeters opposite corners, 20.9 millimeters opposite sides. **Edge:** Plain. **Designers:** T. Humphrey Paget and Thomas Shingles, obverse; George E. Kruger Gray and Thomas Shingles, high- and low-relief reverse; Stephan Trenka, commemorative reverse. **Rarity:** High relief is scarce, particularly as a circulation strike; less scarce as a Specimen. Low relief and commemoratives are very common.

In the early seventeenth century copper miners in Germany discovered a previously unknown reddish rock. Thinking it was another type of copper ore, the miners unsuccessfully attempted to extract the copper from the rocks. The miners blamed the mischievous German mythological demon, Nickel, for trying to fool them, and began calling the ore "kupfernickel," which can be translated as "copper demon." In 1751 the Swedish chemist Axel Fredrik Cronstedt isolated a new chemical element from kupfernickel that eventually came to be known as nickel.

The element itself has a silvery color and is even harder than iron. In mineral deposits it is usually found together with iron or in deposits thought to be of extraterrestrial origin—that is, from meteoritic impacts. This is likely the reason why Canada has such substantial deposits in the area around Sudbury, Ontario, where large nickel mines are located. The region is thought to contain the third-largest impact crater (130 kilometers wide) on the surface of the Earth (after South Africa's Vredefort impact crater and the Chicxulub crater in Mexico), the site of an immense bolide impact from around 1.8 billion years ago. Canada is one of the world's largest nickel producers today. Other major suppliers include Australia, Japan, and Russia.

The year 1951 marked the 200th anniversary of Cronstedt's discovery of nickel, and Canada planned to mint a commemorative coin to celebrate the event. The 5-cent coin was chosen for this because it was the only Canadian coin then being struck in nickel. The Royal Canadian Mint held an open competition, and the winning design featured a nickel refinery with a large smokestack in the center. The obverse was to remain unchanged. The Korean War was at its peak in 1951, however, and as nickel was an important war material, production was halted after just over 8 million pieces were struck, of an intended run of around 13 million.

The mint then reverted to the beaver reverse design, which dated back to 1937, with a composition of steel plated with a very thin layer of nickel (0.0127 millimeters) and chromium (0.0003 millimeters). Just over 4.3 million examples were produced with this composition. Steel is a harder material than nickel, however, so the details in the reverse design did not come out as well as they had with the pure nickel composition. The mint prepared lower-relief designs for both the obverse and reverse of the coin, but an error occurred at the mint, and a small number of steel 1951 5-cent coins were struck from the high-relief obverse dies. There is no record of exactly how many were produced from this die/composition combination. It is not a trivial matter to decide whether a 1951 5-cent coin is high or low relief from just a cursory examination, but a simple diagnostic can be used. On the high-relief coins, the second A in GRATIA has its apex pointing directly at a denticle, whereas on the low-relief example the apex of the A points between two denticles. These characteristics can be easily seen in the images on the previous page.

The world's largest coin—the "Big Nickel," a thirty-foot replica of the 1951 Canadian five-cent piece—is at the Dynamic Earth science museum in Greater Sudbury, Ontario.

The 1951 low-relief 5-cent coin is very common, and a gem Uncirculated example can be purchased for around US$200. The commemorative coin of the same date is also common and attracts a similar price at auction. There are, however, a small number of superb Specimens known that have sold for over US$700. There are also a very few commemorative coins known in plated steel—coins that should not exist! An MS-63 example sold for US$4,025 in a 2006 Heritage auction. The high-relief coin sells for a much greater price, with the highest-graded gems reaching US$8,050 (at a 2010 Heritage auction).

CHAPTER 9

CANADIAN COINS FROM THE REIGN OF QUEEN ELIZABETH II

This final chapter discusses the coinage of Queen Elizabeth II, who ascended the throne in 1952 and was crowned in 1953. At the time of writing (spring 2022), she is still the reigning monarch. She has been on the throne several years longer than her great-great-grandmother Queen Victoria. The Canadian coinage from her reign does not contain great rarities similar to those of earlier monarchs but, more in keeping with modern coinage, consists of large numbers of commemorative emissions and specially struck coins made to sell at a premium to the public. No less than nine silver $1 commemoratives were produced between 1953 and 1984, with none of them of any great scarcity. Among the most interesting and popular coins were the 1967 commemorative issues produced for Canada's centennial. In recent decades the Royal Canadian Mint has produced all sorts of unusual and bizarre gold coins not for public consumption, including the 100-kilogram gold coins and a number of special commemorative gold dollars and the unique 2003 gold dollar. All of these coins are discussed in the essays below.

No. 87 1953 $1, Without and With Shoulder Strap

Left: obverse, 1953 $1 Without Shoulder Strap variety (slightly rarer version); right: obverse, 1953 $1 Shoulder Strap variety.

Standards—**Weight:** 23.3 grams. **Composition:** 0.800 silver, 0.200 copper. **Diameter:** 36.00 millimeters. **Edge:** Reeded. **Designers:** Mary Gillick, obverse; Emanuel Hahn, reverse (not shown, but it is the same voyageur design begun in 1935). **Rarity:** The Without Shoulder Strap variety is somewhat scarcer than those exhibiting the shoulder strap.

On February 6, 1952, King George VI died of complications related to heavy smoking. Princess Elizabeth, his eldest daughter and heir presumptive, was in Kenya with her husband Prince Philip, Duke of Edinburgh, at the time. This was the end of an era for the monarchy: George VI had been born during the reign of his great-grandmother Queen Victoria, whereas Elizabeth was born in 1926, thus truly ending direct contact with the Victorian era in Britain. The new queen was crowned at Westminster Abbey on June 2, 1953, at the young age of 27 years.

In keeping with British minting traditions, no coinage with the portrait of the new monarch was required for 1952, the expectation being that the new coins would not appear until 1953. This gave the Royal Mint plenty of time to produce the necessary obverse minting tools for Britain and the rest of the Commonwealth. The crucial first step was to develop the portrait of Her Majesty that would appear on the obverse of the coins. The Royal Mint solicited plaster casts from a variety of artists. None of the artists had access to the queen herself but produced the casts from photographs of her profile. The Royal Mint committee in charge of the process chose the submission of Mary Gillick, who then had in-person sittings with the queen to complete the portrait.

Britain agreed, for the first time, that Canada could produce its own obverse dies directly from an incuse matrix. The matrix included the monarch's portrait but not the associated lettering, which the Royal Canadian Mint inserted. When coins were actually struck, however, the relief on the queen's portrait appeared to be too high, so that details on the highest points of the design were indistinct. This coin is shown on the left on the previous page and is termed the "Without Shoulder Strap variety." The details in the queen's hair and tiara are similarly indistinct, the rim of the coin is not very broad, the denticles are quite small, and the shoulder strap of the queen's dress is missing.

The chief engraver at the Royal Canadian Mint, Thomas Shingles, stepped in and solved most of these problems. It was he who had brilliantly engraved, by hand and directly onto a steel plate, the reverse of the 1949 Canadian dollar featuring the *Matthew*, the ship John Cabot had sailed to Newfoundland (see page 128). Shingles restored the two shoulder folds from the original design, lowered the relief of the coin, sharpened the details in the monarch's hair and laurel wreath, and made the radius of the coin somewhat larger in order to broaden the rim. An example of this effort is seen in the image to the right on the previous page, variously called the Shoulder Strap or Shoulder Fold variety. The minting difficulties were not unique to this denomination. All the new Queen Elizabeth II coins suffered from similar production issues and were corrected over the next several years.

Of the two varieties, the Without Shoulder Strap variety generally sells for somewhat higher prices at auction. The single finest known example, an SP-67+, sold for US$12,925 in a 2014 Heritage auction, while an MS-64 example can be acquired for around US$1,500. The example at right on the previous page, the finest known, Prooflike-67, exhibiting a shoulder strap and residing earlier in the Pittman Collection, sold for US$6,900 in a September 2006 Heritage auction. The PCGS population reports indicate that just under 300 examples have been graded in Mint State for each variety.

Thomas Shingles, chief engraver of the Royal Canadian Mint, 1943 to 1965.

As with all the other denominations for the first year of Queen Elizabeth's reign, the 5-cent dies were similarly modified to improve the appearance of the coin. However, an unmodified obverse die from 1953 appears to have been inadvertently used to mint a small number of 1954-dated coins. This produced a major Canadian rarity, a 1954 No Shoulder Strap 5-cent coin. Apparently, only four examples of this coin are known. The CoinsandCanada.com website lists a price of CAD$7,500 in EF-40, however, a verifiable photograph of this coin could not be found.

A similar but more common minting error seems to have also occurred for the cent coins. The coins dated 1953 exhibit both the Shoulder Strap and Without Shoulder Strap varieties, with the Shoulder Strap examples being much scarcer. The 1954 cent coins should have been all Shoulder Strap examples, but an unknown number exhibit the Without Shoulder Strap variety. These latter examples are much scarcer, typically selling for more than US$1,000 at auction.

No. 76 1966 $1, Small Beads

**Left: 1966 $1 Large Beads obverse;
right: 1966 $1 Small Beads obverse (rarer version).**

Standards—**Weight:** 23.3 grams. **Composition:** 0.800 silver, 0.200 copper. **Diameter:** 36.00 millimeters. **Edge:** Reeded. **Designers:** Arnold Machin, obverse; Emanuel Hahn, reverse. **Rarity:** Scarce and eagerly sought after by collectors.

In 1964 Canada changed the design of the reverse of the $1 coin, forgoing the "canoe with paddlers" design for a commemorative reverse celebrating the 100th anniversary of the meetings held in Charlottetown, Prince Edward Island, and Quebec City that paved the way for Confederation in 1867. Since the introduction of the dollar coin in 1935, the original reverse design (see the essay "1935 $1" on page 94) had remained the same except for the years 1939 (commemorating the visit of King George VI and Queen Elizabeth to Canada), 1949 (welcoming Newfoundland to Canada), and 1958 (commemorating the establishment of British Columbia as a Crown colony and the Cariboo Gold Rush in British Columbia's Fraser Canyon). In 1965 a new obverse portrait of the queen on the dollar coin was introduced, picturing her as somewhat more mature and wearing a tiara instead of the ribbon she had worn in her hair since 1953. It is this redesign of the portrait and other features on the obverse of the dollar that set the stage for the accidental production of the Small Beads rarity.

The new obverse dies produced for the 1965 Canadian silver dollars did not result in an acceptable coin. The fields were very flat, with the result that the queen's features were not well struck up and the die life was unacceptably short. Experimentation at the Royal Canadian Mint showed that if the field was slightly concave (sloping upward towards the edge), the design features would be more prominent and die life improved. This design had "large beads" around the obverse of the coin, just inside the rim. Both Large Bead and Small Bead examples were struck in 1965, with little or no difference in price or rarity between the varieties. In 1966, however, the mint's plan was to produce only the Large Bead variety because it was the more attractive coin. While some claim that it is difficult to tell the two varieties apart, there is a simple diagnostic: on the Large Bead dollar, the apex of the A in REGINA points directly at a bead, while in the Small Bead variety the apex points between two beads.

A branch mint had been established by the Royal Canadian Mint in Hull, Quebec, just across the Ottawa River from the city of Ottawa, in order to help the mint if it was overwhelmed with coinage demands. Such a situation occurred in 1966 when the mint in Ottawa was preparing to provide a special series of coins for the 1967 Canadian centennial (see pages 135–136). The dies for the dollars were shipped to Hull (only a few kilometers away), where a Small Bead obverse die was inadvertently combined with a 1966 reverse die to produce the rare variety. In his *Canadian Coins*, William K. Cross raises the question of whether this was an accident or a clandestine striking. In either case, it was recognized that these dollars had a "prooflike" appearance as soon as they were struck. The entire mintage was sent back to Ottawa for melting, but apparently this did not happen. Some were released into circulation or sold to collectors.

The mintage of 1966 dollars was 9,912,178 coins, with some small but unknown fraction being the Small Bead variety. The Large Bead variety is a very common coin, with MS-66 pieces selling for less than US$100. An MS-68 example sold at auction for US$2,056.25 in 2014. A Small Bead coin sold for US$9,888 in a 2013 Heritage auction.

No. 40 1967 Commemorative Coin Set

Standards (cent)—**Weight:** 3.24 grams. **Composition:** Brass. **Diameter:** 19.05 millimeters. **Year issued:** 1967. **Edge:** Plain. **Designer:** Alex Colville. **Modeler:** Myron Cook. **Issuing authority:** Government of Canada. **Rarity:** The entire set is readily obtainable, but one of the most popular items in the entire Canadian coinage series.

Standards (5 cents)—**Weight:** 4.54 grams. **Composition:** Nickel. **Diameter:** 21.21 millimeters. **Year issued:** 1967. **Edge:** Plain. **Designer:** Alex Colville. **Modeler:** Myron Cook. **Issuing authority:** Government of Canada.

Standards (10 cents)—**Weight:** 2.33 grams. **Composition:** 0.800 silver, 0.200 copper. **Diameter:** 18.03 millimeters. **Year issued:** 1967. **Edge:** Reeded. **Designer:** Alex Colville. **Modeler:** Myron Cook. **Issuing authority:** Government of Canada.

Standards (25 cents)—**Weight:** 5.83 grams. **Composition:** 0.800 silver, 0.200 copper. **Diameter:** 23.88 millimeters. **Year issued:** 1967. **Edge:** Reeded. **Designer:** Alex Colville. **Modeler:** Myron Cook. **Issuing authority:** Government of Canada.

Standards (50 cents)—**Weight:** 11.66 grams. **Composition:** 0.800 silver, 0.200 copper. **Diameter:** 29.72 millimeters. **Year issued:** 1967. **Edge:** Reeded. **Designer:** Alex Colville. **Modeler:** Myron Cook. **Issuing authority:** Government of Canada.

Standards ($1)—**Weight:** 23.3 grams. **Composition:** 0.800 silver, 0.200 copper. **Diameter:** 36.00 millimeters. **Year issued:** 1967. **Edge:** Reeded. **Designer:** Alex Colville. **Modeler:** Myron Cook. **Issuing authority:** Government of Canada.

Standards ($20)—**Weight:** 18.27 grams. **Composition:** 0.900 gold, 0.100 copper. **Diameter:** 27.1 millimeters. **Year issued:** 1967. **Edge:** Reeded. **Designer:** Alex Colville. **Modeler:** Myron Cook. **Issuing authority:** Government of Canada.

On July 1, 1867, the British Province of Canada and the colonies of Nova Scotia and New Brunswick came together to form the Dominion of Canada. Immediately after Confederation, what had been the Province of Canada was divided into the provinces of Ontario and Quebec, so the new Dominion was composed of four provinces. Within four years Manitoba, the Northwest Territories, and British Columbia had joined, extending Canada all the way to the Pacific Ocean. Prince Edward Island became part of Canada in 1873, the Yukon Territory in 1898, Saskatchewan and Alberta in 1905, Newfoundland (somewhat reluctantly) in 1949, and Nunavut in 1999. Canada is now the second-largest country in the world after Russia.

For 1967, Canada's centennial year, the government decided to mint a specially produced collector set of seven coins, including a half-ounce $20 gold piece. The coins were to be in prooflike finish, thus highly reflective and almost of true Proof quality. Except for the 1- and 5-cent coins and the gold piece, all were struck in 0.800 silver. The two smallest denominations were largely copper and nickel, respectively, and the $20 coin was produced in 0.900 gold. Specially designed cases were manufactured to house the sets. The total cost for the set, plus the case, was $40 at the time of issue; they were so inexpensive simply because the price of gold was only US$35.50 per ounce at the time. A total of 337,687 complete sets (including gold) were minted, and they sold out almost immediately. I recall my mother buying three sets, one for each of her children. The cost of the sets even today is still dominated by the price of gold, and nice sets can be had for about US$1,000.

Canadian artists, sculptors, and designers participated in a competition for the reverse designs of the coins, and artist Alex Colville was chosen to produce the designs for all six reverses. The original plan was to give the commissions to a number of artists, but Colville's designs were judged the best for all the coins. Colville had also provided a unified theme for the coin reverses: animals that were not simply examples of Canada's wildlife heritage but also emblematic of the values they represented. Colville described his thinking behind the designs as follows:

- Cent (Dove): spiritual values and peace
- 5 cents (Rabbit): fertility, new life, and promise
- 10 cents (Mackerel): continuity
- 25 cents (Bobcat): independence and decisive action
- 50 cents (Howling Wolf): vastness of Canada
- $1 (Canada Goose): serene and dynamic

The $20 reverse was preselected to be the coat of arms of Canada as it appeared in 1967. In a sense, this was unfortunate—one can only image what Colville would have come up with for the reverse of the gold coin.

The artist Alex Colville was born in Toronto in 1920 and passed away in 2013. He joined the army at age 24 and was sent to Europe as a war artist. He returned to Canada in 1945 and produced a large body of work until his death. The National Gallery of Canada acquired seven of his paintings in the 1950s, making him a Canadian artist of the highest order. His most famous works include *Soldier and Girl at Station 1953*, *Horse and Train 1954*, *To Prince Edward Island 1965*, *Woman with Revolver 1987*, and *Dog and Bridge 1976*, which sold at auction for CAD$2.4 million in 2020.

This set of seven coins remains a cherished part of Canadian numismatics largely for the wonderful reverse designs, which, in the minds of many, embody much of what it means to be Canadian.

NO. 48 1967 $1, DIVING GOOSE AND DOUBLE STRUCK

Standards—**Weight:** 23.3 grams. **Composition:** 0.800 silver, 0.200 copper. **Diameter:** 36.00 millimeters. **Edge:** Reeded. **Designer:** Arnold Machin, obverse; Alex Colville, reverse. **Modeler:** Myron Cook, reverse.

Not only was the 1967 Canadian silver dollar a commemorative coin but it also signaled the end of an era for Canadian coinage. From its first striking in 1935, the $1 coin had been produced largely in silver—0.800 silver, 0.200 copper. The composition had not varied at all throughout the reigns of George V, George VI, and Elizabeth II up to 1967. This, together with the wonderful regal portraits and the reverse designs of the Voyageur, the Parliament Buildings (1939), the Newfoundland commemorative (1949), the Confederation commemorative (1964), and the Flying Goose (1967) coins, had made the dollar coin enormously popular with collectors around the world. Additionally, the coin was almost the same size as a U.S. dollar (36 millimeters versus 38 millimeters) and only slightly lower in silver (0.800 versus 0.900), making it popular with American collectors as well. In 1968 the design reverted to the Voyageur reverse with a 100 percent nickel composition. Never again would Canada strike circulating dollars containing silver.

The 1967 Flying Goose dollar was extremely popular with both collectors and the general public. One unexpected feature—and a real bonus for collectors—was that the coin suffered some minting issues. To appreciate this, we need to explore the orientation of the obverse and reverse of coins. If the obverse of a U.S. coin is right-side up and you turn it over either to the right or to the left, the reverse of the coin will be upside down. This is called "coin alignment," and all U.S. coins are produced in this manner. There is no great logic for this other than to distinguish coins from medals. Medals are generally produced in what, not surprisingly, is termed "medallic alignment," where if the medal is flipped over to the left or right, the design will be right-side up. Among other countries, Canada, Australia, and the United Kingdom use this medallic alignment on their circulating coins.

A small fraction of the 1967 silver dollars was minted with the reverse midway between coin alignment and medallic alignment. The top image on the previous page is an example, with the reverse rotated by about 45 degrees, making the goose appear to be diving to the left when the coin is flipped over. This variety came to be known as the "Diving Goose" variety and is quite scarce, with MS-65 examples valued at around US$1,800. There is even an extreme error known with the reverse rotated by a full 90 degrees. Only around a dozen of these are known. An auction appearance of this variety could not be traced, but current catalogs list it at US$15,000 in MS-65. There have been some suggestions that employees of the Royal Canadian Mint were actively involved in making these mint errors for some Canadian coin dealers in 1967 and profited from their sale.

During the minting process, a coin is held in place by a collar that prevents the metal from spreading beyond the intended diameter of the coin and keeps it steady during the striking process. In some cases, the collar also imparts the reeding along the edge of the coin when struck. If a coin is struck more than once, rotation of the collar between strikes can result in spectacular mint errors that collectors actively pursue. Typical double or even multiply struck Goose dollars are also known in which die rotation took place, an example of which is shown in the lower images on the previous page. These multiply struck Goose dollars command a price of around US$500, 20 times what a normal 1967 dollar might fetch.

The 2021 PCGS population report lists a total of 521 Mint State normal 1967 $1 coins, with only ten of the Diving Goose variety. More Diving Goose coins are known with prooflike strikes, where the numbers are 442 normal and 65 diving, respectively. Only a single example is recorded in coin alignment. PCGS does not provide population statistics for the multiply struck examples.

No. 34 1969 10 Cents, Large Schooner, Large Date

Left: 1969 10 cents Large Date; right: 1969 10 cents Small Date.

Standards—**Weight:** 2.307 grams. **Composition:** 1.00 nickel. **Diameter:** 18.03 millimeters. **Edge:** Reeded. **Designer:** Arnold Machin, obverse; Emanuel Hahn and Myron Cook, reverse. **Rarity:** Very rare; only about 20 currently known.

The "fishing schooner under sail" reverse design for the 10-cent coin, introduced in 1937, came to be one of Canada's most cherished coin designs. Coins with this reverse were minted until 1967. In that year Canada issued coins to commemorate the centennial of Confederation, and the 10-cent commemorative featured a mackerel on the reverse. About half of these were minted in 0.800 silver, which had been the standard since 1920, while the other half were 0.500 silver. The change to 0.500 silver resulted from the rapid increase in the price of silver during the period 1967–1969. The coins remained the same weight, however, and are not distinguishable just by visual inspection.

In 1968 the composition of circulating 10-, 25-, and 50-cent and $1 Canadian coins transitioned to nickel, which is magnetic and tends to be darker in appearance than the 0.500 silver coins minted earlier. In the transition year, however, 10-cent and 25-cent coins were minted in both compositions, with about a third of the mintage being in silver. The Royal Canadian Mint in Ottawa was busy producing other coinage at the time and contracted half of the 10-cent nickel coinage to the Philadelphia Mint in the United States.

Early in 1969, when the striking of the newly dated 10-cent coins began, it was quickly realized at the mint in Ottawa that the designs on the coin had deteriorated significantly. New dies were produced and used for the vast majority of that year's production. The ship was made smaller and had more detail, and the date was also reduced in size (compare the large date shown at left on the previous page with the small date shown at right), giving the name "Small Date" to this variety. Only a very few examples of the Large Date coins were actually released into circulation.

The PCGS population report lists only six examples of the large date, with a single example in Mint State. Because the coin is a modern one and so scarce, it has generated the sense of a treasure hunt in Canada. With circulated examples selling for close to US$15,000 at auction (Heritage, 2019), collectors still search their change for examples of this rarity. While about 20 are known, it is thought that several are still likely to be in circulation, just waiting for a sharp-eyed numismatist or reader of this book to spot it.

No. 69 1973 25 Cents, Large Bust

Top: 1973 25 cents Large Bust variety; bottom: 1973 25 cents Small Bust variety.

Standards—**Weight:** 5.07 grams. **Composition:** 1.00 nickel. **Diameter:** 23.88 millimeters. **Edge:** Reeded. **Designer:** Arnold Machin, obverse; Paul Cedarberg, reverse. **Rarity:** The Large Bust variety is modestly scarce, with about 10,000 believed to have been produced. The Small Bust variety is very common.

The North-West Mounted Police (NWMP), who "always get their man," was Canada's first national police force. It was established in 1873 by Sir John A. Macdonald, the first prime minister of Canada. There was a need to have a policing force in the North-West Territories (as it was then called) because the incursion of settlers into what had been Native territory caused numerous conflicts. The force established good relations with First Nations people while extending Canadian law across the region. It helped in the construction of the Canadian Pacific Railway (1881–1885), which the Canadian government promised British Columbia when it joined Confederation in 1871. In 1920 the Royal Canadian Mounted Police (RCMP) was formed from the merger of the NWMP with the Dominion Police.

During the late 1800s and into the twentieth century, the force had an almost mythical reputation for honesty, bravery, and fair play, and was a proud symbol of Canada. Mounties appeared in films and television and on radio, always representing what was best in police forces. In more recent times this image has become somewhat tarnished with accusations of racism, sexism, and corruption in the RCMP, but an attempt is underway to reform the force.

The Canadian government decided to mark the centennial of the establishment of the NWMP/RCMP by producing a special 25-cent commemorative coin. The new obverse design had a smaller portrait of Her Majesty, together with a reduced number of beads placed further from the edge around the rim. This obverse is shown in the lower of the two examples on the previous page, the Small Bust variety. The reverse of this coin was entirely new (a mounted RCMP constable) and was used only for the single emission in 1973. Almost 136 million pieces were struck, making it a very common coin.

However, as seems to occur more often than by chance in the recent minting of Canadian coins, an obverse die from 1972 was used to strike a small number of coins with the RCMP reverse. The number of such coins has been estimated at around 10,000 examples, making this Large Bust variety a modern-day rarity. In this variant the bust is clearly larger and there are more beads surrounding the monarch's portrait, with the beads also being closer to the edge of the coin. These differences can be easily discerned in the two coins illustrated.

I can readily recall the excitement that the two different obverse designs caused among the public. It was known very soon after minting that this rare variety was in circulation, and everyone searched their change trying to locate an example. A decent coin was worth around US$100, so the time spent looking for an example was well worth it. I remember my own excitement when I actually located one in change.

There are both Prooflike (PL) Large Bust coins and regular circulation-strike examples. Some of the PL examples were contained in special sets distributed in 1973 and seem to be somewhat more common. The price quoted for these coins is typically US$300 for PL-65 examples, while a PL-68, the example illustrated in this essay, sold for US$840 at a 2021 Heritage auction. Circulation-strike examples can attract bids in excess of US$1,000 for MS-67 examples. The PCGS population report actually shows equal numbers of Large and Small Bust 1973 25-cent pieces (17). This should not be construed as providing any information at all on the relative rarity of these coins. If you think you have a Large Bust coin, you may want to send it for certification. The Small Bust coin is so common that certification is hardly worth the cost, so very few of these are submitted.

North-West Territories mounted policeman on horseback, Yukon Territory, 1917.

No. 79 2000-P 25 and 50 Cents

Standards (25 cents)—**Weight:** 4.4 grams. **Composition:** 0.940 steel, 0.038 copper, 0.022 nickel. **Diameter:** 23.88 millimeters. **Edge:** Reeded. **Designer:** Dora de Pedery-Hunt, obverse; Emanuel Hahn, reverse. **Rarity:** Very rare; only about three to five known. Only a single example has been certified by PCGS.

Standards (50 cents)—**Weight:** 6.9 grams. **Composition:** 0.9315 steel, 0.0475 copper, 0.0210 nickel. **Diameter:** 27.13 millimeters. **Edge:** Reeded. **Designer:** Dora de Pedery-Hunt, obverse; Cathy Bursey-Sabourin, reverse. **Rarity:** A modern-day rarity, with only about 200 struck for inclusion in Royal Canadian Mint presentation clocks for employees.

Canada does not normally have mintmarks on its coins. During the era when the Royal Mint in England was producing coins for Canada (roughly 1850–1907), no mintmark appeared on the coins they struck. Coins produced by the Heaton Mint for Canada and Newfoundland, however, had an "H" somewhere on the coin. The sovereigns struck between 1908 and 1919 by the Ottawa Mint had a "C" mintmark to distinguish them from those struck for Britain at the Royal Mint (no mintmark) or those struck for other Commonwealth countries ("S"—Sydney, "M"—Melbourne, "P"—Perth, "I"—India, and "SA"—South Africa). Between 1917 and 1920, and later during the war years (except for a few odd years such as 1940 and 1942 for the cent coin, which was struck at the Ottawa Mint but bears no mintmark), Newfoundland coins were minted in Ottawa and carried the "C" mintmark. The Winnipeg branch of the Royal Canadian Mint opened in 1975. This facility is where virtually all circulating Canadian coins are currently struck. Only on a very few recent coins (all 1998 coins and the Uncirculated and Specimen sets produced in 2000 and 2003) is a "W" mintmark present, as seen on the "Loonie" ($1 coin) on the following page.

Given this background, what do we make of the letter "P" on the obverse of the 2000 50-cent coin illustrated above?

In 1999 the Royal Canadian Mint began experiments with various plated-steel compositions for its 50-cent coinage. Thin layers of nickel, copper, then nickel again were electroplated onto a steel core. A small number of these test coins was struck in all denominations between the cent and 50 cents later that year, with the addition of a "P" mintmark indicating the experimental composition. The coins were struck to give the vending machine industry an opportunity to test these coins in their various devices. Collectors, always with an eye on acquiring a rarity, were able to obtain examples of these test coins, so the mint, to reduce their rarity and perhaps also sell more special sets to collectors at high prices, made special strikes of the coins for the marketplace.

A 2000 Canadian dollar coin (Loonie) from a specially struck set minted at the Winnipeg branch of the Royal Canadian Mint (note the "W" mintmark on the obverse at the lower right). The composition is 0.915 nickel, 0.085 bronze. This is a very common coin that can be acquired for around US$10.

In 2000 the Winnipeg branch of the Royal Canadian Mint began full-scale production of these plated coins. To thank its employees for the hard work involved in developing and implementing this technology, the mint distributed 276 of the 2000-dated 50-cent pieces, mounted in clocks. These coins displayed the "P" mintmark on their obverse. Of the 276 specially made pieces, about 50 have made their way into the marketplace, where they are an extreme modern-day rarity. An MS-67 example of the coin, removed from its clock, sold for US$6,900 at a 2019 Heritage auction, a very high price for such a recently produced coin.

A 2000 Canadian 50-cent coin mounted in a clock. These were gifts to Winnipeg Mint employees. The coin's composition is 0.915 nickel, 0.085 bronze. This is a very rare coin. Apparently, only around 50 made their way into the marketplace.

Another extremely rare 2000-dated "P" coin is the 25-cent piece. A series of 25-cent coins commemorating the millennium were struck by the Royal Canadian Mint in nickel, with a different reverse for each month. Mintages were not modest, averaging about 36 million for each monthly design, and the coins did not have the "P" mintmark. An estimated three to five coins, however, were produced with a "P" mintmark on the obverse and the normal caribou reverse, which had been used off and on since 1937. The composition of these coins was electroplated layers of nickel, copper, and then nickel again on a steel core. Only a single example has been certified by PCGS, and it realized US$26,400 at a Heritage auction in January 2020.

No. 97 2003 $1 Gold

Standards—**Weight:** 25.18 grams. **Composition:** 0.999 gold (0.801 troy ounces). **Diameter:** 36.07 millimeters. **Thickness:** 2.66 millimeters. **Edge:** Reeded. **Designer:** Susanna Blunt, obverse; Emanuel Hahn, reverse. **Rarity:** Unique; only a single example was made.

Queen Elizabeth II was crowned on June 2, 1953. In honor of the 50th anniversary of her coronation, the Royal Canadian Mint produced a special non-circulating silver dollar. It featured a new uncrowned rendition of Her Majesty designed by Canadian portrait artist Susanna Blunt, together with the Emanuel Hahn Voyageur reverse that had been introduced on the Canadian silver dollar of 1935 and used, with several interruptions for special commemorative coins, until its 1987 replacement with the loon reverse. The Royal Canadian Mint made 21,537 of these special silver coins in 2003 for sale to collectors, all in Proof finishes and housed in a black leatherette case. The silver coin is identical to the gold example illustrated here.

Around the same time, the Royal Canadian Mint was producing a wide variety of unusual gold coins that were not for public consumption, including the 100-kilogram gold coins (see page 144) and a number of special commemorative gold dollars and half dollars. For example, at right are images of special pure gold 2002 50-cent and $1 coins, of which only five sets were made. One was sent to the queen as a gift from Canada for her Golden Jubilee, another set was given to the governor general of Canada, Adrienne Clarkson, and two sets were deposited in the National Currency Collection of the Bank of Canada.

In a flush of generosity (or was it an advertising ploy?), and building on its successes in minting special gold coins, the Royal Canadian Mint decided to produce a single, solid gold version of the new non-circulating silver dollar and donate the proceeds from its sale to charity. This was accomplished by inserting a solid gold planchet of the same diameter and weight as the silver commemorative into the coin press, but one that was somewhat thinner at 2.66 millimeters instead of 3.33 millimeters, to strike the sole example.

The mint put the gold commemorative up for sale on eBay, where an American coin dealer, representing a client, paid US$55,100 for it. It is not known, at least to this writer, which charity was the beneficiary of this generous sum. The coin was later sold to a Canadian coin dealer, who then passed it along to Calgary collector George Hans Cook. This unique item next appeared publicly at the Heritage Cook Sale of Canadian coins at the 2019 American Numismatic Association convention in Chicago. It was in a PCGS holder grading Proof-67 and sold for US$103,000, making it the sixth most expensive item in that important Canadian collection, after the 1911 dollar, the 1936 Dot cent, two examples of the 1921 50 cents, and a superb 1916-C sovereign. The 2003 gold dollar sold for US$37,000 more than a very acceptable SP-63+ 1936 Dot 10-cent piece.

Examples of the specially produced commemorative 50-cent and $1 gold coins in honor of Her Majesty's Golden Jubilee. Only five sets were minted.

No. 51 2007 $1 Million Gold Coin

Standards—**Weight:** 100,000 grams (3,215 troy ounces). **Composition:** 0.999 gold. **Diameter:** 530 millimeters. **Thickness:** 28 millimeters. **Edge:** Plain. **Designer:** Susanna Blunt, obverse; Stanley Witten, reverse. **Rarity:** Very rare; only six examples made and perhaps one destroyed.

The Royal Canadian Mint has impressive technical capabilities. Aside from producing circulating coinage for Canada and about a hundred other countries, the mint strikes the extremely popular gold and silver Maple Leaf bullion coins, which are recognized and sold worldwide. It also manufactures a remarkable diversity of technically challenging collector coins. Among these are pieces with holographic birds, odd-shaped high bullion value items, colorized coins featuring almost anything and everything Canadian, and even the "Whispering Maple Leaves" design. As detailed in the previous essay, the mint was also capable and willing to strike odd and curious items almost on a whim. In 2007 it embarked on its most challenging and bizarre endeavor yet, producing the world's first million-dollar coin, a gargantuan 100-kilogram pure gold coin.

The reverse of this coin was designed by the Royal Canadian Mint's senior engraver, Stan Witten ("SW" on the lower right reverse) and the obverse by Canadian portrait artist Susanna Blunt ("SB" on the queen's dress at the lower left).

The production of this coin was not done entirely as a lark. The coin was meant to help promote the mint's new line of 0.99999 one-ounce pure Gold Maple Leaf bullion coins. After testing the market for these enormous 100-kilogram collectibles, the mint decided to produce six of them, each weighing in at 3,215 troy ounces. One was retained by the mint and the rest were purchased by investors, not just from Canada but also from around the world. In October 2007 the *Guinness Book of World Records* certified this gold coin to be the world's largest. By spring 2022 its value had exceeded CAD$7.8 million.

One coin was purchased by a private collector in Germany, who loaned it to the Bode Museum in Berlin in 2010. Built between 1898 and 1904, the Bode is located on Museum Island in the historic center of Berlin and is part of a UNESCO World Heritage Site. The museum has one of the most extensive cabinets of coins in the world, extending from the earliest coins minted in the seventh century B.C. up until modern times. They are particularly strong in coins of Greek and Roman origin. Due to this strong numismatic emphasis in their collection, the display of a 100-kilogram gold coin was not entirely out of line with the museum's curating philosophy. In the early dawn hours of March 27, 2017, the $1 Million Gold Coin was stolen from the museum. Four months later the perpetrators were arrested and found to be from a family known by the police to be associated with organized crime. Three of the four defendants were found guilty and sentenced to prison terms of up to four and a half years. The coin itself, often dubbed "The Big Maple Leaf," has never been found. The suspicion is that it was melted, as gold dust was found on the clothes of the perpetrators and in their car.

Of related interest, part of the wildly popular Netflix series on chess, *The Queen's Gambit*, was filmed in and around the Bode Museum. The perpetrators of the crime tried their own gambit to secure the Big Maple Leaf, but in the end they were "checkmated."

APPENDIX: AUCTION RECORDS FOR CANADIAN COINS AND TOKENS

The following table shows the top 100 Canadian coins and tokens prices realized in the last 25 years at public auction. Only the single highest-priced auction result for an individual coin is shown. All values in Canadian dollars have been converted to U.S. dollar value at the time of auction, to ensure accurate ranking. For auctions bid in Canadian dollars, CAD$ prices are listed in parentheses. An asterisk beside the date indicates that the coin/token is discussed in this book.

Rank	Date	Denomination	Grade	Price	Date sold	Firm
1	*1911	Dollar	SP-65	$690,000	Jan 2003	Heritage
2	*1936 Dot	Cent	SP-65	$402,500	Aug 2019	Heritage
3	1862 BC	Gilt Set	SP-63	$262,322 (CAD$348,000)	Jun 2019	TCNC
4	*1890-H	50 Cents	MS-65	$261,000	Jun 2019	TCNC
5	*1921	50 Cents	MS-66	$240,000	Aug 2019	Heritage
6	*1936 Dot	10 Cents	SP-68	$184,400	Jan 2010	Heritage
7	*1916-C	Sovereign	MS-66+	$156,000	Aug 2019	Heritage
8	*1890-H	50 Cents	MS-64	$149,500	Apr 2014	Heritage
9	*1862 BC	Gold $20	SP-61	$143,000	Nov 1996	Bowers-Merena
10	*1670-A	15 Sols	EF-45	$132,000	Jan 2022	Heritage
11	*1921	5 Cents	MS-67	$124,726 (CAD$165,200)	Jun 2016	TCNC
12	1871-H	50 Cents	MS-67	$120,750	Jan 2003	Heritage
13	*2003	Gold $1	PR67	$108,000	Aug 2019	Heritage
14	*1870 No LCW	50 Cents	SP-64	$103,500	Jan 2003	Heritage
15	*1865 NFLD	Pattern $2	SP-63	$102,813	Apr 2014	Heritage
16	*1889	10 Cents	MS-66	$86,250	Jan 2010	Heritage
17	*1892	50 Cents	MS-65	$86,250	Jan 2010	Heritage
18	1872-H	50 Cents	MS-64	$86,250	Jan 2010	Heritage
19	*1670-A	Double	VF	$85,250	Nov 1996	Bowers-Merena
20	*1936 Dot	25 Cents	SP-68	$80,500	Jan 2010	Heritage
21	1898	50 Cents	MS-65	$74,750	Jan 2010	Heritage
22	1902-H	25 Cents	MS-68	$70,500	Apr 2014	Heritage
23	*1875-H	25 Cents	SP-68	$70,500	Aug 2015	Heritage
24	*1880 NFLD	$2	SP-64	$70,400	Nov 1996	Bowers-Merena
25	*1874 NFLD	50 Cents	SP-67	$60,000	Jan 2021	Heritage
26	*1948	$1	MS-66	$59,413 (CAD$67,850)	Jun 2009	TCNC
27	*1914	50 Cents	MS-66	$57,571 (CAD$76,375)	Oct 2019	TCNC
28	*1884	Cent	SP-65	$55,813	Jan 2014	Heritage
29	*1824	Ropery Token	MS	$52,875	Aug 2013	Stacks-Bowers
30	1874-H	25 Cents	MS-67	$51,750	Jan 2010	Heritage
31	1894	50 Cents	MS-65	$51,750	Jan 2010	Heritage
32	1812	2 Sous	PF-65	$50,400	Apr 2018	Heritage
33	1885 NFLD	50 Cents	SP-65	$46,000	Jan 2003	Heritage
34	*1947 Maple Leaf	$1	MS-67	$46,000	Sep 2006	Heritage
35	No date NB	Half Penny	AU-58	$45,600	Apr 2018	Heritage
36	*1820 HBC	Medal	AU-50	$45,600	Apr 2021	Heritage
37	1947	$1	MS-68	$44,063	Jan 2014	Heritage
38	*1837	Half-Penny Token	AU	$44,063	Aug 2013	Stacks-Bowers
39	*1885	$2	SP-66	$44,000	Nov 1996	Bowers-Merena
40	1820 NW Co.	Token	MS-61	$42,000	Apr 2018	Heritage
41	*1905	50 Cents	MS-63+	$42,000	Aug 2019	Heritage
42	c.1844 NFLD	McAuslane Token	EF	$40,413 (CAD$51,600)	May 2015	Geoff Bell
43	*1845	Half Penny Bank of Montreal	Proof	$39,943 (CAD$51,000)	Oct 2015	Geoff Bell
44	1899	50 Cents	MS-63	$38,680 (CAD$50,150)	July 2017	TCNC
45	*1906 Small Crown	25 Cents	MS-62	$38,400	Aug 2019	Heritage
46	1884	5 Cents	MS-65	$36,424 (CAD$47,200)	Oct 2018	TCNC
47	1872 NFLD	$2	SP-65	$35,250	Apr 2017	Heritage
48	*1944	Tombac 5 Cents	VF-35	$35,075	Aug 1999	Heritage
49	1870 NFLD	50 Cents, Plain	SP-66	$34,500	Jan 2003	Heritage
50	*1884	10 Cents	MS-65	$34,500	Jan 2010	Heritage
51	1900	50 Cents	MS-65	$34,500	Jan 2010	Heritage
52	1893	25 Cents	MS-66	$34,500	Jan 2010	Heritage
53	1886/3	25 Cents	SP-65	$34,100	Nov 1996	Bowers-Merena
54	1872-H	25 Cents	SP-67	$32,900	Apr 2014	Heritage
55	1934	25 Cents	SP-65	$32,900	Apr 2014	Heritage
56	1934	50 Cents	SP-68	$32,900	Apr 2014	Heritage
57	1888	50 Cents Obv 2	MS-63	$32,855 (CAD$44,030)	Feb 2020	TCNC
58	*1876	Treaty Medal 6	EF	$32,800 (CAD$41,125)	Jun 2021	TCNC
59	*1908-C	Sovereign	SP-66	$32,400	May 2021	Heritage
60	1903-H	50 Cents	MS-66	$32,200	Jan 2010	Heritage
61	1881-H	50 Cents	MS-64+	$31,967 (CAD$42,840)	Jun 2020	TCNC
62	1904	50 Cents	MS-65	$31,524 (CAD$40,250)	Jul 2015	TCNC
63	1909-C	Sovereign	SP-65	$31,200	May 2020	Heritage
64	*1858	5 Cents	MS-65	$31,200	Aug 2019	Heritage

Rank	Date	Denomination	Grade	Price	Date sold	Firm
65	1872-H	50 Cents, A over V	MS-62	$33,875 (CAD$44,850)	June 2016	TCNC
66	1880-H	25 Cents	SP-68	$30,550	Aug 2015	Heritage
67	1875-H Large Date	5 Cents	MS-64+	$29,936 (CAD$38,812)	Feb 2017	TCNC
68	*1935	$1	MS-68	$29,900	Jan 2010	Heritage
69	1888 NFLD	50 Cents	SP-64	$29,900	May 2003	Heritage
70	*1887	25 Cents	MS-61	$29,900	Sep 2006	Heritage
71	*1859	Brass Cent	VF-20	$28,948 (CAD$36,295)	Feb 2021	TCNC
72	*1870 LCW	50 Cents	MS-65	$28,750	Jan 2010	Heritage
73	*2000 P	25 Cents	MS-65	$26,400	Jan 2020	Heritage
74	1945	$1	MS-66	$26,400	Aug 2019	Heritage
75	*1839	Penny Token	MS	$25,850	Aug 2013	Stacks-Bowers
76	*1912	$10	SP-68	$25,850	Apr 2017	Heritage
77	*1932	50 Cents	MS-65	$25,850	Jan 2013	Heritage
78	1902-H	10 Cents	SP-68	$25,850	Apr 2014	Heritage
79	*1912	$5	SP-67+	$25,850	Aug 2015	Heritage
80	*1862 BC	$20 Silver	SP-61	$25,300	Nov 1996	Bowers-Merena
81	c.1830	Breton 999	VF-30	$24,118 (CAD$31,270)	Feb 2017	TCNC
82	1865 NFLD	Bronze 20 Cents	SP-64	$23,618	Apr 2014	Heritage
83	*1947	$1	SP-68	$23,575	Aug 2001	Heritage
84	1921	25 Cents	SP-67	$23,500	Aug 2015	Heritage
85	1882-H	25 Cents	SP-68	$23,500	Aug 2015	Heritage
86	1911-C	Sovereign	SP-68	$23,500	Jan 2014	Heritage
87	*1875-H	10 Cents	MS-64	$23,000	Jan 2010	Heritage
88	*1913 Broad	10 Cents	MS-64	$23,000	Jan 2010	Heritage
89	1896 NFLD	50 Cents	SP-65	$23,000	Jan 2003	Heritage
90	*1871	Pattern 20 Cents	SP-65	$22,800	Aug 2019	Heritage
91	1875-H Small	5 Cents	MS-65	$22,753 (CAD$29,500)	Feb 2017	TCNC
92	1929	50 Cents	SP-68	$22,325	Apr 2014	Heritage
93	1938	$1	SP-65	$22,325	Jan 2014	Heritage
94	1910 Victorian Leaves	50 Cents	MS-65	$22,000	Nov 1996	Stacks-Bowers
95	1912	50 Cents	MS-66	$21,850	Jan 2010	Heritage
96	1884	5 Cents	SP-65	$21,850	Jan 2003	Heritage
97	*1858	Pattern Cent	SP-66	$21,600	Aug 2019	Heritage
98	1932	5 Cents	SP-67	$21,275	Aug 2001	Heritage
99	1946	$1	MS-66	$19,980 (CAD$26,775)	February 2020	TCNC
100	*1893FT	10 Cents	MS-66+	$18,033(CAD$22,610)	June 2021	TCNC

BIBLIOGRAPHY

"1 Dollar 1967." CoinsandCanada.com, May 9, 2021. https://www.coinsandcanada.com/coins-prices.php?coin=1-dollar-1967&years=1-dollar-1953-1986.

"5 cents 1937 to 1952." CoinsandCanada.com. https://www.coinsandcanada.com/coins-prices.php?canadian_coins=5-cents-1937-1952.

"5 cents 1953 to 1964." CoinsandCanada.com. https://www.coinsandcanada.com/coins-prices.php?canadian_coins=5-cents-1953-1964.

"1935 J.O.P. Discovery More Important Than Originally Thought." Geoffrey Bell Auctions Ltd., September 25, 2017. https://gbellauctions.wordpress.com/2017/09/25/1935-j-o-p-discovery-more-important-than-originally-thought/.

"1956 $1 – 'Patenaude' Counterstamp (Of Jop Counterstamp Fame)." Coin Community Family Coin Forum discussion, August 31–September 1, 2016. https://www.coincommunity.com/forum/topic.asp?TOPIC_ID=268449.

"2007 Canada 1 Million Dollar 100 Kilo Gold Maple Leaf Proof." GovMint.com. https://www.govmint.com/2007-canada-1-million-dollar-100-kilo-gold-maple-leaf-proof.

Berry, Paul S. "The 1936 Dot Set," Bank of Canada Museum, April 18, 2018. https://www.bankofcanadamuseum.ca/2018/04/new-acquisitions-9/.

Bowman, Fred. "Canada's Ten Rarest Coins," *CNA Journal*, 14. 1969.

Bowman, Fred. *Canadian Patterns*. Ottawa: Canadian Numismatic Association, 1957.

Breton, P.N. *Illustrated History of Coins and Tokens Relating to Canada*. Montreal: P.N. Breton and Company, 1893.

Cadigan, Sean T. *Newfoundland and Labrador: A History*. Toronto: University of Toronto Press, 2009.

"Canadian Fifty Cent Obverse Designs." Saskatoon Coin Club. www.saskatooncoinclub.ca/articles/07b_50_cent_obverse.html.

"Coinage Designs of 1967." Canadian Numismatic Publishing Institute, November 2, 2004. http://www.coinscan.com/des/1967d.html.

Cross, W.K. *A Charlton Standard Catalogue, Canadian Coins*, vol. 1. *Numismatic Issues*, 65th edition. Dorval, QC: Charlton Press, 2011.

Cuhaj, George S., and Thomas Michael. *2019 Standard Catalog of World Coins, 1901–2000*. Iola, Wisconsin: Krause Publications, 2019.

Drake, M. *A Charlton Standard Catalogue, Canadian Coins*, vol. 1. *Numismatic Issues*, 74th edition. Toronto: Charlton Press, 2021.

Faulkner, Christopher. *Imperial Designs: Canada's Ships, Colonies & Commerce Tokens*. London: Spink & Son Ltd., 2019.

Faulkner, Christopher. *The Holey Dollars and Dumps of Prince Edward Island*. London: Spink & Son Ltd., 2014.

Forbes, Robert. "Fine Points Revisited." *CN Journal* 64, 3. April–May 2019.

Forbes, Robert. "Fine Points Revisited." *CN Journal* 65, 5. July–August 2020.

Forbes, Robert. "The 1873-H Newfoundland Five-Cent Coin," *CN Journal* 60, 7. October 2015.

Gingras, Larry. *Medals, Tokens and Paper Money of the Hudson's Bay Company*. Canadian Numismatic Research Society, 1975.

Glassford, Patrick. "Coinage Designs of 1937." Canadian Numismatic Publishing Institute. http://www.coinscan.com/des/1937d.html.

"Gold Coins from 1912 to 1914." CoinsandCanada.com. https://www.coinsandcanada.com/coins-prices-gold-1912-1913-1914.php.

Gosling, Daniel. "The Lost Half George," *CN Journal* 52. May 2007.

Haxby, James A. *A Guide Book of Canadian Coins and Tokens*, 1st edition. Atlanta: Whitman Publishing, 2012.

Haxby, James A. *The Royal Canadian Mint and Canadian Coinage: Striking Impressions*, 2nd edition. Ottawa: Royal Canadian Mint, 1986.

"History of HBC." Hudson's Bay Company History Foundation. https://www.hbcheritage.ca/history.

Hodder, Michael. "An American Collector's Guide to the Coins of Nouvelle France." *Proceedings of the Coinage of the Americas Conference*, vol. 8. New York: American Numismatic Society, 1994.

"J.O.P Dollars." *Coinscan*, January 14, 2007. http://www.coinscan.com/silverd/page66.html.

"L'Anse Amour National Historic Site of Canada." Canada's Historic Places. https://www.historicplaces.ca/en/rep-reg/place-lieu.aspx?id=14130.

Laflèche, Anik. "Hudson's Bay Company: 350 Years of Archives," Library and Archives Canada blog, December 21, 2020. https://thediscoverblog.com/2020/12/21/hudsons-bay-company-350-years-of-archives/.

Lees, W.A.D., "Ships Colonies and Commerce Tokens." *The Numismatist* (January 1917).

Levesque, J.C. "The 1885 Over 5 5-Cent Piece," *CN Journal* 24, 4. April 1979.

Library and Archives Canada. "Lower Canada, Montreal British Militia button, one halfpenny token, c. 1830." *CoinsandCanada.com*, March 29, 2004, https://www.coinsandcanada.com/tokens-medals-articles.php?article=lower-canada,-montreal-british-militia-button,-one-halfpenny-token,-c.-1830&id=324.

McLachlan, R.W. *A Descriptive Catalogue of Coins, Tokens and Medals Relating to the Dominion of Canada and Newfoundland*. Montreal: Printed privately for the author, 1886.

McLachlan, R.W. "The Copper Tokens of Upper Canada." *American Journal of Numismatics (1897–1924)*, 49. 1915.

Newman Numismatic Portal. Washington University, St. Louis, MO. https://nnp.wustl.edu/library.

Passmore, Raewyn. "Remembering Alex Colville (1920–2013)." Bank of Canada Museum, July 30, 2013. https://www.bankofcanadamuseum.ca/2013/07/remembering-alex-colville-1920-2013/.

Powell, James. *A History of the Canadian Dollar*. Ottawa: Bank of Canada, 2005.

Pridmore, Fred. *The Coins of the British Commonwealth of Nations: Part 2, Asian Territories*. London: Spink & Son Ltd, 1965.

Richer, Harvey B. "Canadian Coins in the British and Ashmolean Museums." *CN Journal* 23. January 1978.

Richer, Harvey B. "The 1888 Specimen Newfoundland $2 Gold Coins," *CN Journal* 63, 7. October–November 2018.

Richer, Harvey B. *The Gold Coins of Newfoundland*. Portugal Cove–St. Philip's, NL: Boulder Publications, 2017.

Sharples, John. "The Numismatic Collection of the Museum of Victoria," *Journal of the Numismatic Association of Australia* 2. 1986.

Spidle, Katelyn. "Old Nick's Cursed Metal." *CIM Magazine*, December 14, 2015. https://magazine.cim.org/en/in-search/old-nicks-cursed-metal/.

Starck, Jeff. "Royal Romance Leads to Canada's 1936 Dot Cent Rarity." *Coin World*, November 23, 2016. https://www.coinworld.com/news/precious-metals/royal-romance-leads-to-canadas-1936-dot-cent-rarity.html.

Sweeny, James O. *A Numismatic History of the Birmingham Mint*. Birmingham, UK: The Birmingham Mint Ltd., 1981.

"The Million Dollar Coin – A True Milestone in Minting." Royal Canadian Mint. https://www.mint.ca/store/mint/about-the-mint/million-dollar-coin-1600006.

Turner, Rob. *Dies and Diadems: A Die Tracker's Guide to the Victorian Cents of Canada*. 2009.

Turner, Rob. *Past and Nearly Perfect: The Patterns, Trial, Proof, and Specimen Large Cents of Canada*. Markham, ON: Royal Canadian Numismatic Association, 2020.

Waldman, Ben. "The Saga of Canada's Stolen Million-Dollar Coin." *Maclean's*, January 31, 2019. https://www.macleans.ca/economy/money-economy/the-saga-of-canadas-stolen-million-dollar-coin/.

Willey, R.C. "Canadian Decimal Coins and Currencies," *CN Journal* 35, 5. May 1991.

Credits and Acknowledgments

A number of individuals and organizations provided information that was critical in the writing of this book.

As was the case for my previous book, *The Gold Coins of Newfoundland*, my wife, Klara, played a crucial role in the development of this book. As a constant source of inspiration, encouragement, and coffee, no single person contributed more to making possible whatever success this book may enjoy.

Of paramount importance to the overall success of this endeavor was Frank Chow, a wonderful local editor who went through the early versions of the book in detail, checking and correcting numerous details of grammar, phrasing, and fact.

Both Kenneth Bressett and Emily S. Damstra lent their expertise and enjoyment of Canadian coins to the foreword of this book.

Sandy Campbell is always a source of very useful information. He was particularly helpful in discussions on the provenance of the 1911 dollar and the British Columbia gold coins.

David Bergeron, curator of the National Currency Collection of the Bank of Canada, provided critical insight into a number of entries and made available photographs of some objects that are not found online. He also suggested including the Weir & Larminie encased postage stamp in this anthology. As president of the Canadian Numismatic Research Society, he encouraged the group to provide input into the choice of entries for this anthology, several of which found their way into the final selection. Some members of the CNRS also ranked the entries.

Local friends and collectors Warren Long and David Rubin served as sounding boards for various ideas and for coins or tokens to include in the 100 Greatest list.

Christopher Faulkner provided insight into the Prince Edward Island 1804 silver dollar. Michael Joffrey shared his enormous font of knowledge on the 5 and 15 sols pieces of New France. The idea for the Montreal Militia token essay came from Paul Berry, former director of the National Currency Collection of the Bank of Canada. James A. Haxby suggested the Nova Scotia Thistle half-penny token for inclusion in this anthology. Bob Graham first brought the existence of the Newfoundland January 1932 $25 bond to my attention.

Marc Verret at The Canadian Numismatic Company (TCNC) at my request searched through previous auction results and sent important lists of prices realized from auctions by his company. Andrew Lustig provided some first-hand information on the 1670 Double from the Norweb Sale and background on the $20 British Columbia gold coin in the same sale. He also provided personal insight into the provenance of the 2003 gold dollar. Anthony Terranova was the source of some unique insight into the sale and later provenance of the 1670 Double, among other topics. We chatted on the phone for about half an hour, and it was an absolutely delightful experience.

The staff at the American Numismatic Society provided information on the 1670 Double in their collection. They informed me that it was a copy, and not a second genuine example.

The design origin for the 1937 5-cent coin was suggested by Jesse Kraft of the American Numismatic Society, during Long Table Number 78 presented on January 28, 2022.

Image Credits

Images are credited by page number. Where multiple illustrations are found on a given page, they are credited by location, starting with number 1 at upper left and reading left to right, top to bottom. CNC = Canadian Numismatic Company. BOC = Bank of Canada Museum. HA = Heritage Auctions. LOC = Library of Congress. PCGS = Professional Coin Grading Service. RCM = Royal Canadian Mint. RMM = Royal Mint Museum (U.K.). SBG = Stack's Bowers Galleries.

Forewords: Pg v, Kenneth Bressett. Pg vi.1, HA. Pg vi.2, RCM. Pg vi.3, RCM.

Chapter 1: Pg 1.1, public domain, Wikimedia Commons. Pg 1.2, LOC. Pg 2.1–2, SBG. Pg 3.1, Bowers Merena. Pg 4.1, CNC. Pg 4.2, public domain, Wikimedia Commons. Pg 5.1, HA. Pg 6.1, CNC. Pg 6.2, CNC. Pg 7.1, HA. Pg 8.1–3, BOC. Pg 9.1, HA. Pg 10.1, public domain, Wikimedia Commons. Pg 11.1, HA. Pg 11.2, SBG. Pg 12.1, HA. Pg 12.2, SBG. Pg 13.1, BOC. Pg 13.2, McCord Stewart Museum. Pg 14.1, HA. Pg 14.2, BOC. Pg 15.1, BOC. Pg 16.1, HA. Pg 16.2, SBG. Pg 17.1–2, SBG. Pg 18.1, HA. Pg 18.2, public domain, Wikimedia Commons. Pg 19.1, BOC. Pg 19.2, HA. Pg 20.1, SBG. Pg 21.1–3, SBG. Pg 22.1, public domain, Wikimedia Commons. Pg 22.2, SBG. Pg 22.3, HA. Pg 23.1, Library and Archives of Quebec. Pg 24.1–2, HA. Pg 25.1, HA.

Chapter 2: Pg 26.1, HA. Pg 27.1–3, HA. Pg 28.1, Canadian History Museum. Pg 28.2, HA. Pg 29.1–2, PCGS. Pg 30.1–2, PCGS. Pg 31.1, PCGS. Pg 31.2, PCGS. Pg 32.1, PCGS. Pg 33.1–2, PCGS. Pg 34.1, public domain, Wikimedia Commons. Pg 34.2, PCGS. Pg 35.1, PCGS. Pg 36.1, PCGS. Pg 36.2, HA. Pg 36.3, SBG. Pg 36.4, Spink. Pg 37.1–2, BOC. Pg 38.1–2, public domain, Wikimedia Commons. Pg 39.1, PCGS. Pg 39.2, HA. Pg 40.1, PCGS. Pg 40.2, SBG. Pg 41.1–3, BOC. Pg 42.1, Breau / Wikimedia Commons.

Chapter 3: Pg 43.1, PCGS. Pg 43.2, HA. Pg 44.1–2, BOC. Pg 45.1, PCGS. Pg 46.1, public domain, Wikimedia

Commons. Pg 46.2, SBG. Pg 46.3, BOC. Pg 47.1, BOC. Pg 47.2, public domain, Wikimedia Commons. Pg 48.1, BOC. Pg 48.2, Lewis Clarke / Oxford: Ashmolean Museum / Wikimedia Commons. Pg 49.1, PCGS. Pg 50.1, PCGS. Pg 50.2, LOC. Pg 51.1, PCGS. Pg 51.2, public domain, Wikimedia Commons. Pg 52.1–2, HA. Pg 52.3, public domain, Wikimedia Commons. Pg 53.1–3, HA. Pg 54.1–2, HA. Pg 55.1–2, PCGS. Pg 56.1, SBG. Pg 57.1, Harvey Richer. Pg 58.1, Harvey Richer. Pg 58.2, HA. Pg 59.1, PCGS. Pg 59.2, HA. Pg 59.3, Steve Campbell. Pg 60.1, HA.

Chapter 4: Pg 61.1–2, HA. Pg 62.1, PCGS. Pg 63.1, PCGS. Pg 63.2, HA. Pg 64.1, public domain, Wikimedia Commons. Pg 64.2, HA. Pg 65.1, BOC. Pg 66.1, public domain, Wikimedia Commons. Pg 66.2–3, PCGS. Pg 67.1, public domain, Wikimedia Commons. Pg 67.2, HA. Pg 68.1, HA. Pg 68.2, PCGS. Pg 68.3, LOC. Pg 69.1, HA. Pg 69.2, HA. Pg 69.3, SBG. Pg 69.4, HA. Pg 70.1–4, HA. Pg 71.1, PCGS. Pg 71.2, LOC. Pg 72.1, HA. Pg 72.2, LOC. Pg 73.1, PCGS. Pg 73.2, public domain, Wikimedia Commons. Pg 74.1–3, PCGS. Pg 75.1, HA. Pg 76.1–2, PCGS. Pg 77.1–2, SBG. Pg 77.3, public domain, Wikimedia Commons.

Chapter 5: Pg 78.1, HA. Pg 79.1–3, HA. Pg 80.1–5, HA. Pg 81.1, public domain, Wikimedia Commons. Pg 81.2–3, HA. Pg 82.1, University of Montreal / Wikimedia Commons. Pg 83.1, HA. Pg 84.1–2, RMM. Pg 85.1–2, HA. Pg 86.1, PCGS. Pg 87.1, HA. Pg 88.1–2, PCGS. Pg 89.1, HA. Pg 90.1, HA. Pg 91.1, PCGS. Pg 92.1–2, HA. Pg 93.1, HA. Pg 94.1, HA. Pg 95.1, HA. Pg 95.2, BOC. Pg 96.1–2, SBG. Pg 96.3–4, Geoffrey Bell Auctions. Pg 97.1, Touchstones Museum. Pg 98.1–3, HA. Pg 99.1, emka74 / Shutterstock. Pg 99.2, LOC.

Chapter 6: Pg 100.1, SBG. Pg 101.1, SBG. Pg 101.2–3, National Archives of the United Kingdom. Pg 102.1, RMM. Pg 103.1–2, RMM. Pg 104.1, National Archives of the United Kingdom. Pg 104.2, RMM. Pg 104.3, RMM. Pg 105.1, RMM. Pg 105.2, LOC. Pg 106.1–2, HA. Pg 107.1, Fenn-O-manic / Wikimedia Commons. Pg 107.2, HA. Pg 108.1, public domain / Wikimedia Commons. Pg 108.2, RMM. Pg 109.1, RMM. Pg 109.2, PCGS.

Chapter 7: Pg 110.1, Trustees of the British Museum. Pg 111.1–3, Trustees of the British Museum. Pg 112.1–2, Trustees of the British Museum. Pg 113.1, HA. Pg 113.2, PCGS. Pg 114.1–2, PCGS. Pg 115.1, PCGS.

Chapter 8: Pg 116.1–2, HA. Pg 117.1–3, HA. Pg 118.1, HA. Pg 119.1, HA. Pg 119.2, Library and Archives Canada / Wikimedia Commons. Pg 120.1, HA. Pg 120.2, Toronto Public Library Special Collections / Wikimedia Commons. Pg 121.1–3, CNC. Pg 122.1, PCGS. Pg 123.1, HA. Pg 123.2–3, PCGS. Pg 124.1, PCGS. Pg 125.1–2, PCGS. Pg 126.1–3, HA. Pg 127.1–4, HA. Pg 127.5, PCGS. Pg 128.1, SBG. Pg 129.1, HA. Pg 130.1–3, HA. Pg 130.4, PCGS. Pg 131.1, Angela Holmyard / Shutterstock.

Chapter 9: Pg 132.1–2, HA. Pg 133.1, Whitman archives. Pg 134.1–2, HA. Pg 135.1, PCGS. Pg 135.2, HA. Pg 135.3, SBG. Pg 135.4–5, HA. Pg 136.1–2, SBG. Pg 137.1, HA. Pg 137.2, SBG. Pg 138.1–2, HA. Pg 139.1–2, PCGS. Pg 140.1, LOC. Pg 141.1–2, HA. Pg 142.1, Coins Unlimited. Pg 142.2, CNC. Pg 142.3, HA. Pg 143.1–2, BOC. Pg 144.1, Kitco Metals, Inc.

ABOUT THE AUTHOR

Harvey Richer is professor emeritus of astronomy and physics at the University of British Columbia in Vancouver, Canada. He has published over 175 scientific papers in peer-reviewed journals, including *Nature* and *Science*. He was one of Canada's largest users of the Hubble Space Telescope over the past 20 years and has upcoming time on the James Webb Space Telescope, Hubble's successor. Professor Richer was the 2014 recipient of the Carlyle S. Beals Award of the Canadian Astronomical Society, given for lifetime achievement. Recently he was made a Fellow of the Royal Society of Canada, the foremost academic society in the country and of similar stature to membership in the National Academy of Sciences in the United States.

Harvey has been a coin collector since the time (at age 8) he and his brother discovered a large one-cent coin of Queen Victoria under a rock in a vacant lot near his home in Montréal. He lives in Vancouver with his wife, Klara, and has two adult children scattered at opposite sides of the globe.

He has continued the collecting tradition by introducing his two grandchildren to the joys of numismatics through taking them to local shows, buying them vintage Whitman Blue Folders of Canadian Coins, and supplying them with bags of circulated coinage.

Index

1 cent, vi, vii, ix, 23, 26–29, 30, 31–32, 33–34, 35, 39, 42, 43, 44, 49, 58–59, 60, 62, 65–66, 67, 68, 69, 74–75, 81–82, 88–89, 91–92, 94, 98–99, 110, 116–118, 122–125, 129, 133, 135–137, 141, 142, 143, 145
large cents, vii, 28, 59, 60, 74, 82, 88–89, 91
small cents, 59, 60, 82, 88, 89, 91–92
$1 coin, vi, vii, ix, x, 8–9, 11, 28, 33, 35, 40, 45, 51, 60, 62, 75, 83–84, 89, 94–95, 96–97, 102, 104, 105, 116, 117, 118, 120, 124, 125–126, 127–128, 129–130, 132–133, 134, 135–137, 138, 139, 142–143, 145
$2 coin, 44, 45–46, 50, 51–52, 54, 55–56, 57–58, 64, 82, 145
$2.5 coin, ix, 101–102, 103, 106
5 cents, v, ix, 21, 26–29, 41–42, 43, 44, 46, 50, 53–54, 60, 62–63, 70, 86, 88, 89–90, 91, 92–93, 94, 99, 111, 116–118, 121–122, 123–125, 130–131, 133, 135–137, 145
$5 coin, 4, 6, 58, 83, 86, 100, 102, 103–104, 105, 106–107, 108–109
5 sols, 2–3, 5
8 reales, 9, 11
10 cents, ix, 21, 26–29, 36, 41–42, 44–45, 47, 51, 53–54, 61, 62, 63–64, 69, 72, 76–77, 82, 85–86, 89, 94, 98–99, 110, 111, 114, 122–125, 129, 135–137, 138–139, 143, 145
$10 coin, ix, 37–38, 83, 100, 101–102, 103, 104–105, 106–107, 108–109
15 sols, 2–3, 5, 145
20 cents, ix, x, 26–29, 30–31, 40, 41–42, 43, 44–45, 48–49, 53–54, 56, 62, 89, 111
$20 coin, vi, ix, 4, 37–38, 102, 104, 106, 135–137, 145
25 cents, vii, x, 21, 28, 33, 40, 43, 56, 62, 65–66, 71, 80–81, 87–88, 89, 94, 98–99, 105, 112, 114, 116–118, 122–125, 135–137, 139–140, 141–142
50 cents, ix, x, 4, 11–12, 21, 33, 50, 52, 54, 61–62, 73, 75, 78–79, 82, 86–87, 89, 90–91, 93–94, 96, 99, 112, 113, 115, 116–118, 119, 122–125, 126–127, 135–137, 139, 141–142, 143, 145
$50 coin, vi
Alberta, 79, 136
aluminum, 7, 21, 22
American Numismatic Association, 143, 20, 91, 92, 143
American Numismatic Society, 4, 13, 55
animal coins, vi, 9–10, 135–136, 137–138, 142
Arnault, Jean-Marie, 19, 20
Bank of Canada National Currency Collection, vi, viii, 8, 9, 14, 16, 18, 19, 31, 32, 36, 38, 44, 45, 46, 47, 63, 66, 84, 109, 143
"Big Maple Leaf," 144
billon, 3
Birmingham (England), ix, 9, 10, 15, 18, 47, 63
Blakemore, W.H.J., 56, 85, 86, 87, 88, 89, 90, 92, 93, 98, 104, 105, 106, 115
Blunt, Susanna, 142, 143, 144
bonds, ix, 5, 57–58
Boulton and Watt, 18
brass, ix, 13, 14, 20–21, 22, 23, 31–32, 118, 135
Bressett, Kenneth, v–vi
Breton numbers, 10, 12, 18, 19, 20, 47, 118
British Columbia, ix–x, 4, 26, 37–38, 39, 64, 79, 96, 101, 134, 136, 140
bronze, 3, 29, 32, 33, 35, 39, 43, 44, 49, 65, 66, 108–109, 142
Bursey-Sabourin, Cathy, 141
button currency, vii, 1, 13–17
Calgary, 20, 96, 143
Canadian Numismatic Association, v, 40, 48, 83, 110, 145
Canadian Numismatic Research Society, vii, viii, x
Cedarberg, Paul, 140
Charles II (king of England), 20, 24
chromium, 121, 122, 123, 131
City Bank of Montreal token, 18
cleaned coins, 32, 68, 69, 71
Coat of Arms of Canada, 102, 103–104, 106–107, 109, 118, 136
Colville, Alex, vii, 135–137
commemorative coins, ix, x, 94–95, 96, 105, 120, 129, 130–131, 132, 134, 135–136, 137–138, 139, 140, 142, 143
Confederation, vi, ix, x, 1, 12, 17, 26, 28, 34, 35, 39, 40, 42, 43, 56, 59, 60, 62, 65–66, 75, 90, 116, 129, 134, 136, 137, 139, 140
centennial, vi, 132, 134, 136, 139
Cook, Myron, 135–136, 137, 138
copper, ix–x, 3–4, 5, 6–7, 10, 11, 12, 15, 16, 17–18, 19, 23, 25, 26–27, 30, 31, 32, 33, 35, 37, 39, 40, 41, 45, 46, 48, 49, 50, 51, 53–54, 55, 56, 59, 60, 61, 62, 63, 64, 65, 66, 68, 69, 70, 71, 72, 73, 74, 75, 76, 78, 80, 81, 82, 83, 85, 86, 87, 88, 89–90, 91, 93, 94, 96, 98, 100, 101, 103, 104, 105, 106, 107, 110, 111, 112, 113, 114, 115, 166–117, 119, 120, 121, 122–123, 124, 125, 126, 127, 128, 129, 131, 132, 134, 135–136, 137, 141, 142
counterfeits, 5, 8–9, 14–15
counterstamps, ix, 8–9, 96–97, 126
DeSaulles, G.W., 60, 74, 78, 79, 80, 82, 100, 103, 104, 113, 114
Dot coinage, v, ix, x, 69, 82, 85, 87, 91, 92, 98–99, 129, 143, 145
double de L'Amérique Françoise, 2–4
double strikes, 137–138
dumps, 8–9
Edmonton, 20
Edward VII, 56, 78, 79, 80–81, 82, 85, 87, 93, 104, 114, 120
Edward VIII, 78, 99
Elizabeth II, 4, 61, 79, 82, 83, 89, 94, 99, 105, 116, 132–133, 137, 143
Elizabeth (queen consort of George VI), 120, 129, 134
Ellison-Macartney, William Grey, 40, 83, 102, 103
encased postage stamps, viii, ix, 22–23
farthing, 19, 32, 35
Fremantle, Charles W., 30, 52
Gault, John, 22, 23
George III, 10, 25
George IV, 12, 15
George V, 56, 59, 69, 78, 79, 82, 85, 86, 87, 88, 89, 90, 91, 92, 93, 94, 99, 105, 106, 109, 115, 118, 120, 129, 137
George VI, 60, 79, 82, 99, 116, 117, 118, 119, 120, 122, 125, 126, 128, 129, 132, 133, 134, 137
Gillick, Mary, 132–133
"Godless" coins, 39, 83, 94, 105
gold, vii, viii, ix, x, 4, 5, 6, 7, 23, 26, 37–38, 39, 43, 45–46, 50, 51–52, 54, 55–56, 57–58, 62, 64, 78, 82, 83, 86, 89, 100–109, 132, 136, 142–143, 144, 145
gold standard, 58, 100
Hahn, Emanuel, vii, 83, 94–95, 96, 117, 118, 120, 123, 125, 127, 129, 132, 134, 138, 141, 142, 143
half cent, 12, 33, 35
half dime, 89
half dollar, *See* 50 cents
half penny, vi, ix, 6–7, 12–13, 14–15, 16, 17–18, 19–20, 32, 34, 67, 89
Halifax, 18, 35, 69
Heaton Mint, ix, 26, 339, 47, 48, 49, 54, 63–64, 65, 66–67, 69, 73, 74, 75, 82, 113, 141
holey dollars, 8–9
Hong Kong, 36
Hudson's Bay Company, 20–22, 24–25, 95
Indigenous peoples of Canada, ix, 1–2, 3, 7, 10, 16, 20–22, 24–25, 37, 94, 128, 140
Kruger Gray, George, 108–109, 116–118, 119, 121, 122, 124, 126, 131
Küner, Albert, 37–38
Labrador, 16, 128
lead, 83, 94, 122
Lewis, Fred, 89, 91, 98
livre, 5–6
London, ix, 7, 10, 34, 35, 36, 38, 39, 40, 42, 48, 56, 59, 60, 62, 69, 83, 102, 108, 109, 125, 129
"Loonies," x, 96, 141, 142, 143. *See also* $1 coin
louis d'or, 5–6
Louis XIII, 5
Louis XIV, 2–4
Lower Canada, ix, 12, 13–14, 17–18, 19, 22, 23, 28, 75
Machin, Arnold, 134, 137, 138, 140
Mackennal, E.B., 56, 85, 86, 87, 88, 89, 90, 91, 92, 93, 98, 104, 105, 106, 107, 108, 109, 115
made-beavers, 20–22
Magdalen Island, vi, 9–10
Manitoba, x, 24, 39, 136
Maple Leaf (bullion coin), 144
Maunder, Ernest, 128
medals, vii, viii, 24–25, 31, 62, 138
Metcalfe, Percy, 59, 60, 83
million-dollar coin, 144
mintmarks, ix, x, 3, 39, 47, 49, 54, 56, 59, 60, 63, 64, 65, 67, 73, 82, 101, 103, 105, 108, 113, 118, 141–142
Montreal, 3, 13–14, 16, 17–18, 19–20, 22, 23, 24, 50, 63, 72, 82
Montreal Ropery token, 16
Morehen, Horace, 48
New Brunswick, x, 10, 11, 16, 26, 30–31, 33, 34, 35, 36, 39, 41–42, 44, 45, 46, 67, 107, 109, 119, 136
New France, vii, 2–4, 5–6
Newfoundland, vii–viii, ix, 10, 12, 16, 36, 53–60, 64, 82, 110–111, 128–129, 133, 134, 136, 137, 141
Newman, Walter J., 59
nickel, 23, 29, 32–33, 60, 89, 90, 92, 93, 116, 121–122, 123, 131, 135, 136, 137, 138–139, 140, 141–142
Nova Scotia, vi, vii, ix, x, 10, 11, 14–15, 26, 33–34, 35, 39, 42, 79, 107, 109, 136
Ontario, ix, x, 1, 39, 42, 101, 107, 109, 130, 131, 136
Ottawa, vi, x, 56, 59, 78, 79, 83, 100, 108, 119, 120, 134, 139, 141
overdates, 31, 52, 70, 71
Paget, T. Humphrey, 116–117, 119, 120, 121, 122–124, 125, 126, 127, 128, 129, 131
Parliament (Canada), 83, 90, 119, 120, 137
Patenaude, Joseph Oliva, 96–97, 126
patterns, xi, x, 26, 29, 30–31, 32, 33–34, 36, 38, 40, 41–42, 43–45, 46, 50, 51, 63, 65–66, 83–84, 87, 100, 101–102, 103–104, 105, 107, 108–109, 145
de Pedery-Hunt, Dora, 141
penny, vi, ix, 9–10, 15, 17–18, 28, 32
Pistrucci, Benedetto, 100, 107
playing card money, vii, viii, ix, 1, 3, 4–6, 22
Ponthon, Noël-Alexandre, 6–7
Prince Edward Island, x, 8–9, 10, 12, 26, 39, 67, 134, 136
Province of Canada, vi, ix, x, 11, 26–28, 29, 30, 31, 32, 35, 39, 40, 42, 56, 62, 65, 66, 67, 69, 74, 75, 88, 136
Quebec, ix, x, 1, 3, 5, 10, 17, 39, 40, 42, 73, 107, 109, 129, 134, 136
Quebec City, 7, 10, 17, 134
restrikes, 7, 84
Royal Canadian Mint, v, vii, 40, 56, 60, 79, 83, 90, 93, 100, 101, 102, 106, 108, 109, 115, 118, 120, 122, 127, 129, 131, 132–133, 134, 138, 139, 141–142, 143, 144
Royal Mint (London), ix, 8, 11, 26, 28, 30, 31, 32, 34, 35, 36, 39, 40, 42, 44–45, 46, 47, 49, 51–52, 54, 56, 69, 60, 62, 63, 64, 65, 66, 67, 68, 69, 70, 73, 74, 76, 77, 78–79, 80, 83–84, 95, 99, 100, 101, 102, 103–104, 105, 109, 110, 118, 133, 141
Saskatchewan, vii, 79, 136
Saskatoon Coin Club, 76
Shepherd, Joseph, 24
Shingles, Thomas, 121, 123, 128, 129, 131, 133
silver, ix, x, 2–3, 5, 7, 8–9, 11, 23, 24–25, 26, 27–28, 29, 30, 35, 36, 38, 39, 40, 41, 42, 47, 48, 49, 50, 53–54, 56, 58, 60, 61–62, 63, 64, 69, 70, 71, 72, 73, 75, 76, 78, 80, 82, 83, 84, 85, 86, 87, 89, 90, 91, 93, 94, 95, 96–97, 98, 99, 102, 105, 111, 112, 113, 114, 115, 116, 117, 118, 119, 120, 122, 123, 124, 125–126, 127–128, 129–130, 132, 134, 135–136, 137–138, 139, 143, 144
Soho Mint, 7, 9, 17
South Wales copper farthing, 19
sovereigns (coins), ix–x, 33, 46, 100–101, 102, 103, 104, 105, 106, 107–108, 141, 143, 145
Specimen coins, 28, 34, 50, 51–52, 53–54, 55–56, 59, 60, 63, 64–65, 67, 68, 69, 76, 84, 87, 90, 92, 94–95, 99, 100–101, 107, 108, 109, 110–112, 115, 118, 119, 120, 122–125, 126, 127–128, 131, 141
sets, 53–54, 94–95, 118, 122–123, 124–125, 141
St. John's (city), 16, 51
stamps, ix, 22–23, 34, 68
steel, 76, 121–122, 123, 129, 131, 141
thistle tokens, vi, 14–15
Thomason, Edward, 10
tin, 26, 32, 33, 35, 39, 59, 66, 68, 74, 81, 82, 88, 91, 98, 110, 116, 122
tokens, v, vi–vii, viii–x, 1, 3, 6–7, 9–10, 11, 12–13, 14–15, 16, 17–18, 19, 20–22, 118, 145
tombac, 121–122
"Toonies," vii. *See also* $2 coin
Toronto, 50, 118, 120, 136
Trenka, Stephan, 131
Upper Canada, ix, 6–7, 17, 28, 67, 75
Vancouver, 38, 96, 105
varieties, ix, 7, 12, 31, 34, 40, 42, 62, 63, 70, 71, 73, 74–75, 76–77, 79, 80–81, 85–86, 92–93, 114, 126–127, 129–130, 132–133, 134, 138, 139–140
Victoria (city in Canada), 38
Victoria (queen of England), 28, 29, 34, 39, 44, 46, 50, 56, 59, 66, 78, 80, 82, 93, 99, 120, 132, 133
Victorian era, 47, 48, 49, 50, 54, 61–77, 80, 82, 133
Victory coins, v, 121–122
Voyageur design, x, 94–95, 117, 118, 120, 129, 132, 137, 143
wampum, viii, ix, 1–2, 3, 11, 22
Warin, Jean, 2–3
Weir & Larminie, 22–23
William IV, 15
Winnipeg, 20
Winnipeg Mint, 141–142
Witten, Stanley, 144
"World's Most Expensive Coin," ix, x, 83–84
Wyon, Alfred Benjamin, 24
Wyon, Charles, 45
Wyon, George W., 31
Wyon, James, 31, 33
Wyon, Leonard C., 26–27, 29, 30, 31, 32, 35, 36, 39, 40–41, 45, 47, 48, 49, 50, 53–54, 61, 62, 63, 64, 65, 66, 67, 68, 69, 70, 71, 72, 73, 74, 75, 76, 80, 81, 104, 113, 115
Wyon, William, 11, 62
Yukon Territory, 107, 136, 140
zinc, 26, 31, 32, 33, 35, 39, 59, 66, 68, 74, 81, 82, 88, 91, 98, 110, 116, 121–122